Frommer's®

Croatia

with your family

From idyllic islands to medieval towns

by Jos Simon

BICENTENNIAL
1807
WILEY
2007
BICENTENNIAL

Wiley Publishing, Inc.

Published by:
Wiley Publishing, Inc.
111 River St.
Hoboken, NJ 07030-5774

ISBN: 978-0-470-05530-4

UK Publisher: Sally Smith
Executive Project Editor: Martin Tribe
Development Editors: Matthew Tanner and Mark Henshall
Content Editor: Hannah Clement (Frommer's UK)
Cartographer: Tim Lohnes
Photo Research: Jill Emeny (Frommer's UK)
Wiley Bicentennial Logo: Richard J. Pacifico
Production by Wiley Indianapolis Composition Services

For information on our other products and services or to obtain technical support, please contact our Customer Care Department within the U.S. at 800/762-2974, outside the U.S. at 317/572-3993 or fax 317/572-4002. Within the UK tel: 01243 779777; fax 01243 775878

Wiley also publishes its books in a variety of electronic formats. Some content that appears in print may not be available in electronic formats.

Printed in Singapore by Markono Print Media Pte Ltd
5 4 3 2 1

Contents

About the author

Born and raised on the Llŷn Peninsula in North Wales, **Jos Simon's** travelling life kicked off with the traditional '60s student-tour-of-Europe-in-a-battered-old-van, progressed through family holidays with tots-to-teens (touring again), to more recent empty-nester forays across the continent. Jos is currently revisiting the whole travelling-with-kids scene, courtesy of his three- and five-year-old grandchildren. Professionally, his thirty-year teaching career elided at the turn of the millennium into a freelance travel writing career.

Acknowledgements

My thanks are due to the army of people without whose help in the hectic preparation of this book it would have sunk without trace:

At John Wiley & Sons, to Sally Smith for the commission, and editor Mark Henshall for his skillful and patient help in gap-filling and polishing a very imperfect manuscript.

In Croatia, to a whole host of regional tourist board staff who sent me information, answered my questions and fixed me up with guides, and to the many tourism professionals who helped out with resources and advice, especially Stefica Curic in Dubrovnik, Zdravko Banovic in Split, Mili Rasovic and Katarina Lilic in Šibenik, Nina Stohera and Gordana Peric in Zadar, and Raniero Radojkovic in Istria.

To several members of the British Guild of Travel Writers, especially Hugh Taylor, Paul Murphy, Mike Gerrard and Tim Locke who not only provided moral support, but selflessly shared their vast experience of writing guide books.

To the staff of the Croatian Tourist Board in London, and their PR company Charisma PR.

Particularly heartfelt thanks are owed to:

Dubravka Mičić of the Zagreb Tourist Board for her unstinting support in a hundred material ways, and to Iva Čaleta, who answered a thousand questions, patiently took me around the capital and its hinterland for three days, and put up with my driving.

My family: to my wife Doulla for her staunch support during one of the busiest times of her own professional life, my son Daniel who filled me in on Croatian football, and my daughter Catherine who provided not only research assistance, but also insight into the trials and tribulations of 21st century travel in Europe with young children.

Dedication

For my life's fellow-travellers: wife Doulla, son Daniel, daughter Catherine and beautiful grandchildren Lazaros and Eliza.

An additional note

Please be advised that travel information is subject to change at any time and this is especially true of prices. We therefore suggest that you write or call ahead for confirmation when making your travel plans. The authors, editors and publisher cannot be held responsible for experiences of readers while travelling. Your safety is important to us, however, so we encourage you to stay alert and be aware of your surroundings.

Star Ratings, Icons & Abbreviations

Hotels, restaurants and attraction listings in this guide have been ranked for quality, value, service, amenities and special features using a star-rating system. Hotels, restaurants, attractions, shopping and nightlife are rated on a scale of zero stars (recommended) to three (exceptional). In addition to the star rating system, we also use 6 feature icons that point you to the great deals, in-the-know advice and unique experiences. Throughout the book, look for:

FIND	Special finds – those places only insiders know about
MOMENT	Special moments – those experiences that memories are made of
VALUE	Great values – where to get the best deals
OVERRATED	Places or experiences not worth your time or money

A Note on Prices

Frommer's provides exact prices in each destination's local currency. As this book went to press, the rate of exchange was 1 Kuna = £0.09. Rates of exchange are constantly in flux; for up-to-the minute information, consult a currency-conversion website such as www.oanda.com/convert/classic. In the Family-Friendly Accommodation section of this book we have used a price category system.

An Invitation to the Reader

In researching this book, we discovered my wonderful places – hotels, restaurants, shops and more. We're sure you'll find others. Please tell us about them, so we can share the information with your fellow travellers in upcoming editions. If you were disappointed with a recommendation, we'd love to know that too. Please write to;

Frommer's Croatia with Your Family, 1st edition
John Wiley & Sons, Ltd
The Atrium
Southern Gate
Chichester
West Sussex, PO19 8SQ

Photo Credits

1 Family Highlights of Croatia

THE BEST OF **CROATIA**

1. Swimming, Dubrovnik.
2. Ferry, Trpanj to Ploče
3. Diocletian's Palace, Split
4. River boat, Skradin
5. Sea Organ, Zadar
6. Amphitheatre, Pula
7. Gagolitic Alley, Roč and Hum
8. The funicular, Zagreb
9. Hill town, Buje
10. Day out, Lokrum
11. Colossal holes, Imotski
12. Seaside town, Cavtat
13. Krka National Park
14. Island-town, Nin
15. Cable car, Mount Medvednica
16. Hills and dales, The Zagorje

Before starting this book, I hadn't visited Croatia since the break-up of the Yugoslav Republic. I'd driven through it many times prior to that: in the 1960s as one of a band of carefree students in a battered old van, then on honeymoon by train after the car broke down in Cologne; in the 1970s with wife and infants aboard a tiny Italian motor caravan; and finally in the 1980s with older children in a dilapidated car and trailer tent combination. Then the 1990s arrived, the smoke of war drifted across the Balkans, and Croatia became an area that wasn't good to visit, especially with children.

Yet here we are in the 'noughties', and the sun has come out again. The Balkans are at peace, Slovenia is already part of the European Union, and in a matter of two or three years, Croatia is not only knocking at the EU door, but also exploiting its stunning natural advantages to climb up the ladder of international tourism. Although it can't be called an undiscovered gem – Croatia is now firmly re-established in the holiday mainstream – it still offers terrific value-for-money.

Make no mistake; Croatia has bagged the most beautiful bits of the former Yugoslavia – the lovely Istria Peninsula, the rural Zagorje up against the border with Slovenia, the breathtaking Dalmation coast and its islands. And in Zagreb it has a vibrant European capital city. But Croatia isn't just a pretty face – there's a lot more to the country than that.

The attraction is a cultural thing – Croatia has such a rich diversity of influences. In parts of Istria, you could be in Italy (in fact, most of Istria once was in Italy). Along Croatia's northern and eastern borders, you're uncannily reminded of Austria and Hungary (and, of course, Croatia was once in the Austro-Hungarian Empire). Along the Dalmatian coast, the feeling is totally Mediterranean – and the Adriatic is, of course, a branch of the Mediterranean Sea.

Croatia must be one of the oddest-shaped countries in the world. Imagine a swallowtail butterfly, with elegant, elongated wings. That's Croatia. The inland wing is made up of Zagreb and its hinterland – pretty and Austrian to the north, flat to the south. The capital itself combines imposing European architecture and a flourishing open-air pavement society. The culture (and weather) of this part of Croatia is continental. The coastal wing, which sweeps south all the way to Dubrovnik and beyond, is Mediterranean, with a culture and climate that rivals that of Greece or Italy. Postcard views include gorgeous pantile-roofed stone-walled towns, little harbours, limpid, wake-scored seas and jewel-like islands.

Along with other Mediterranean countries, Croatia shares an enviably relaxed attitude to the next generation. Children are accepted, indulged, smiled at. Parents are complimented on their children's beauty, brains, and good behaviour. You never seem to be made to feel that your children are a nuisance, even when they are.

Having said that, Croatia is not yet really into positive intervention. Few hotels and restaurants put a lot of thought into what might keep children interested or occupied. Families have to take their chances. Likewise, many tourist attractions don't seem to have put the same thought into making themselves as child-friendly as the best of those in the UK or US have. It'll come, I'm sure. Until then, positive

The Volta

In common with most north Mediterranean countries, Croatians go in for what the Greeks call the 'Volta' – going out as a family in Sunday best, and walking up and down the front, chatting to neighbours and acquaintances, and eating ice-cream. It makes for a lovely atmosphere, and provides a diamond opportunity for youngsters to become better acquainted.

attitudes go a long way. I'd personally trade a ton of institutional balloons and coloured pencils for an ounce of genuine child-friendliness. And that's what you get in Croatia.

If leisure time is precious, leisure time with our children is the most precious of all. This book aims to give you insider knowledge into the best places to visit and the most enjoyable activities to help make the most of your time in Croatia as a family. If you become, as I did, a born-again enthusiast for this beautiful country, you'll eventually become a source, not a recipient, of advice on Croatia's 'must-see' and 'must-do' sights and attractions.

BEST FAMILY EXPERIENCES

Swimming off the rocks in Dubrovnik. There are many places where you can get access to the rocks upon which Dubrovnik is built. In some of these places, steps and platforms have been carved into the rock, so that it's easy to sunbathe on them or swim from them. And if you can't swim well enough, then you can get a similar experience by hiring a kayak or rubber dinghy and paddling around the foundations of the city's walls. See p.66.

Filling your hat with water at Onofrio's Large Fountain, just inside Dubrovnik's Pile Gate, emptying it, then putting it on your head. It feels lovely on a hot day, and it'll keep you cool for hours. You can have a drink as well, or fill your water bottle. See p.68.

Walking Dubrovnik's walls takes in two kilometres of wonderful views, outwards towards sea or mountain, inwards across the orange rooftops of the city. Take your time, stop on the way to grab a drink at one of the cafés, and don't do the whole walk if it's too hot. See p.66.

Swimming at Lapad, Dubrovnik

Balancing on the gargoyle in Dubrovnik Stradun

Balancing on the gargoyle in Dubrovnik: take it in turns, time each member of the family, and see who can stay up there the longest. See p.70.

Smiling at the reliquary containing Jesus's nappy, in Dubrovnik's Cathedral Treasury. See p.73.

Feeling sombre in the Sponza Palace's 'Memorial Room of the Defenders of Dubrovnik'. It brings home that the 300 who died defending the city were not statistics, but people – portrait photographs of each one line the walls of the room. See p.71.

Taking the ferry from Trpanj to Ploče. You get the choice of a hot, sheltered deck area, an air-conditioned saloon that sells drinks and snacks, or a breezy forward gantry. It's a short respite from the car with full-time access to toilets. Sit back, look at the beautiful scenery and allow the youngsters to let off a little steam. See p.83.

Wandering the vaults of Diocletian's Palace in Split – this was just the basement of that 2000-year old Roman building, so just imagine how enormous the whole palace was. And on hot days it's pleasantly cool. See p.106.

Rubbing the big toe of the statue of Grgur Ninsky just outside the Golden Gate in Split, and making a wish. See p.110.

Walkway on the walls, Dubrovnik

Scuttling under the fountain on Marmontova in Split where water arches from a fist high up on a wall into a bronze funnel-shaped receptacle at the edge of the pavement. See p.111.

Listening to traditional Croatian music in front of Split's Cathedral – there are often musicians singing or playing and selling CDs of their music. See p.106.

Chugging up the river by boat from Skradin to the waterfalls of the Krka National Park at Skradinski Buk, then climbing up the shaded paths beside the torrent. See p.147.

Being lulled by the Sea Organ in Zadar exemplifies the Croatians knack for multi-disciplinary projects, and Zadar's sea organ is one of the best and will entrance children. Built by a designer, a sea hydraulics engineer and an organ maker, there's not much to see – just some broad steps leading down to the water, some with holes or slots cut in them. But the organ's easy to find – just look for people sitting reflectively, looking out to sea, and not talking. They're listening to the throaty flutings of the organ, activated by wavelets forcing air through the concealed pipes. It's absolutely beautiful, and utterly unique. See p.139.

Coming across Pula's Amphitheatre after dark its ethereal floodlit walls rearing out of the surrounding trees with unearthly beauty. See p.166.

Sitting next to James Joyce at Uliks in Pula, having a drink and discussing the meaning of Ulysses. You won't get much sense out of him, though. Trying to explain Joyce's novels to children will also test your storytelling skills. See p.165.

Driving down 'Gagolitic Alley', the lovely country road between Roč and Hum, which is lined periodically by various representational statues celebrating Croatian history in Croatia's own (sadly now defunct) Gagolitic script. See p.187.

Riding the funicular in Zagreb arriving in time (noon) to hear the deafening report of the gun fired out of one the top floor windows of the Burglar's Tower, then, with your ears still ringing,

Monument at Gagolitic Alley, Istria

Zagreb funicular railway

climbing the tower for the view. See p.208.

Taking the cable car up to Sljeme, the highest peak on Mount Medvednica. See p.222.

BEST CHILDREN'S PLAYGROUNDS

Bundek (Zagreb) Without a shadow of a doubt, the biggest and best children's playground you'll come across in Croatia. If the children spend 10 minutes on each type of equipment,

you'll be there for hours. If they need refreshing after such endeavours, the swimming lake is 50 metres away. See p.221.

Lapad Beach (Dubrovnik) On the road up from Lapad beach into the centre of town, there are loads of children's rides, bouncy castles and so on – enough to keep them occupied for hours, if you can afford it (and have got change). The beach is two minutes walk away. See p.78.

Trg Valdibora (Rovinj, Istria) This little playground with its colourful climbing frame, nets, rope-ladders and tube-slide, is perfectly placed to allow some family-members to slip into the market while the children play. Nice view of the Old Town, too. See p.174.

Obala Palih Omladinaca (Šibenik, Dalmatia) Bounded by the boats moored to the quay on one side and the Cathedral on the other, this playground has swings, slides, see-saws, climbing frames, rope ladders and those

Bundek's Playground

little animals on springs the children love bouncing around on, all in a nice clean gravelled area with benches for the adults. It's also next to the coolest place for teenagers (see below), so you might be able to keep everybody happy. See p.146.

Buzet (Istria) On the town terrace, this is just a small playground – a slide, a couple of swings, a ride and a bit of climbing frame, all clustered together with benches for the adults under the trees. But the views! And letting them play puts off having to drive back down that hill, for a while at least. See p.185.

Pazin (Istria) The park in the centre of town has a lot of play equipment located in the shade under trees, and there are benches to relax on. It is a good spot if you've opted for a picnic rather than eating in one of the local restaurants. See p.184.

Marmont's Gloriette (Trogir, Dalmatia) Next to the building called Marmont's Gloriette, at the western end of the island on which Trogir sits, there are trampolines where the children can expend any excess energy they have. It could be part of a pleasant walk right around the island. See p.119.

TOP ATTRACTIONS FOR TEENS

Dubrovnik Almost anywhere in the Old Town. Just walk down Stradun and go with the flow. If you're after pizza, the word's out that Mea Culpa's the place to be, and for ice-cream it's Dolce Vita. See p.66.

Split The whole row of cafés and restaurants along the palm-fringed Riva at the front of Diocletian's Palace. There are nice places inside what was once the Palace, but they tend to be more for tourists – for locals it's definitely the Riva. See p.104.

Šibenik At the northern end of the road that runs along the dockside of the River Krka Obala Palih Omladinaca, there's a string of tables between the water and the road. It's just one table deep, but that's where Šibenik's teenagers take it easy. See p.141.

Zadar You can't do better than sit in the central square Narodni trg. The southern waterfront – along Obala kralja Petra Krešimira IV – is increasingly finding favour with a teenage fan club. See p.132.

Pula Although Pula's small enough for almost every part of the town to have its fans, by far the most popular places to be seen are along Giardini down to the Arch of the Sergians, and in the area around the market. See p.161.

Rovinj No question – the harbour-side Trg Maršala Tita is the place to be. And being bounded on one side by the sea, it's cool as well as '*cool*'! See p.171.

Trg Bana Jelačića

Poreč The best places are along the harbour, and at the town side of Trg Slobode. See p.176.

Zagreb The capital is big enough to boast a number of the 'in' places to hang out. There's

Clubbing In Croatia

Although clubbing is unlikely to form a major part of a family holiday, it may be that older teenagers might want to visit a club. The favourite areas for clubbing are Zagreb and the strip of coastal Dalmatia between Split and Zadar, with Šibenik being particularly well-provided for.

Some of the best bets for clubbers are: Latino Club Fuego (*www.fuego-dubrovnik.com*) near the Pile Gate in Dubrovnik, Aurora (*www.auroraclub.hr*) near Primošten on the Split coast and Hacienda (*www.hacienda.hr*) at Vodice, near Šibenik (thought by some to be Croatia's best club). The Garden (*www.thegardenzadar.com*) in Zadar is owned by *UB40* drummer James Brown and has a spectacular setting, high on the fortifications of the city. In Istria, Club Uljanik in Pula (*www.clubuljanik.hr*) and the Monvi Entertainment Centre in Rovinj (*www.monvicenter.com*) are both pretty well thought of. Also, on the east coast, the Rabac Summer Festival, a week-long DJ festival on the beach, is worth a look (*www.rabacfestival.com*). Pick of the island venues are Carpe Diem on Hvar (*www.carpe-diem-hvar.com*) and the Faces Club on Brač (☏ *021-635-410*), a 2,000 capacity outdoor mainstream club near Bol. Top of the tree in Zagreb has, since independence, been Aquarius (*www.aquarius.hr*), which is on the lakeside at Jarun, but it is under challenge from Gallery (☏ *091-113-32-21*), also out at Jarun, which has star DJs, tight ticket control and a strict dress code.

Technology Museum, Zagreb

the central square Trg Bana Jelačića, which the convergence of tram routes makes easily accessible. North of it, pedestrianised Tkalčićeva is very popular, while the whole area south and west of the square (Gajeva, Bogovićeva and Preradovićeva trg) is a mass of cafés, bars and restaurants, and very lively from early evening. In the summer, Jarun is also worth a visit – local discos and the scene in general moves out there to get away from the heat of the city centre. See p.191.

BEST MUSEUMS

The Treasury of Dubrovnik Cathedral
Children can't fail to be impressed by all those body parts, and all that gold and silver. See p.73.

Bunari Museum (Šibenik)
Interactive, multimedia, multilingual, and designed for children, this museum is situated in the town's 15th century underground water vaults, and has a good café. See p.144.

Technical Museum (Zagreb)
This one will warm the cockles of many children's hearts. It includes

House of Batana, Rovinj

a mock-up of a coal mine, a planetarium, and several exhibits relating to the Croatian scientist Nikola Tesla. See p.218.

Town Museum (Labin) This museum also has a reconstructed coal mine (the town was the heart of Croatia's coal-mining area). It's not as ambitious as Zagreb's Technical Museum, but nevertheless is well worth a visit. See p.188.

School Museum (Zagreb) A little fusty, but guaranteed to get youngsters talking and assessing their own educational experiences. See p.217.

The House of the Batana (Rovinj) Although a lot of the exhibits are labelled only in Croatian, there's an excellent short English language guide, and the museum itself – devoted to the local flat-bottomed boat called the Batana – is modern, interactive and very interesting. See p.173.

The Outdoor Museum, Kumrovec

Natural History Museum (Zagreb) Another of Zagreb's old fashioned yet interesting museums. Lots of exhibits, and some, though not all, have English translations. See p.212.

Antun Augustinčić Gallery, Klanjec (Zagorje) More of an art gallery than a museum, but lots of impressive statues (the sculptor and his wife are buried under one of them) in a beautiful setting. See p.224.

Kumrovec (Zagorje) An excellent outdoor museum of the region's buildings and lifestyle. Includes the house in which Tito, the former Yugoslavian leader, was born and brought up. See p.225.

Natural History Museum, Zagreb

Dubrovnik

BEST COASTAL TOWNS

Being surrounded, or almost surrounded, by water was originally a good thing for defensive reasons, but it has also limited the development sprawl of many Croatian coastal towns and preserved a lot of original buildings and features. There's a feel of living history appealing to children looking for stories and myths.

Dubrovnik Yes, Dubrovnik was once an island – Stradun, the main street, follows the channel that, until it was filled in, separated the old city of Ragusa from the mainland. If you look down on the town from the top of the hill on the way to Cavtat, you can see that the Old City was once an island. See p.55.

Trogir is not only still an island, but also attached by bridges to

the mainland and to another island. Looking at Trogir, you can begin to see how Venice must have started. The channel between Trogir and the mainland is only three or so rowing-boat widths, and is crossed by the road bridge and a snazzy footbridge. See p.116.

Nin The town of Nin is built on a tiny, flat little island in the middle of a bay. It's attached to the opposite headlands of the bay by bridges, and has salt extraction pans and medicinal mud baths at various parts of its perimeter. See p.149.

Rovinj has spread well beyond its original island, but the position of the channel that once separated it from the mainland is marked with a sign. Modern development has been kept to what was once the mainland, so the Old Town itself is totally unspoiled – it's not only lovely from a distance (and much loved by photographers and the Croatian Tourist Board, who make much use of the Old Town in promotional material), but is also delightful to walk around. See p.171.

Poreč Another once-but-no-longer-an-island, Poreč is, despite its huge holiday industry, remarkably untouched in the Old Town, and has retained its Roman plan as well as some bits and pieces of Roman masonry. See p.176.

BEST HILL TOWNS

Just as the sea has limited development of island towns, hill towns, again built where they are for defensive reasons, are similarly limited by the size of their hilltop. So whereas water surrounds Croatia's island towns and cities (to delightful effect), farmland, olive groves and vineyards surround its equally delightful hill towns (mostly in Istria). In both cases, the effect is often stunning.

Imotski Right up in the mountains near the border with Bosnia-Herzegovina, Imotski draws in visitors because of its two spectacular geological features – the Blue and the Red Lakes. But the town is actually very pleasant in its own right – a cool mountain settlement of parallel, contour-hugging streets, pleasant cafés and restaurants, and a sense that people are just getting on with their own lives. See p.124.

Renovation

In Croatia you'll soon become aware that, all over the country, renovation projects are underway. There are several interrelated reasons for this. Although Croatia in its present manifestation only dates from the early 1990s, its history goes back more than a thousand years. Pride in this history is widespread and therefore, all over the land, efforts are being made to repair and preserve the country's heritage. This is especially so because, during the period before independence, the Communist government was keen to play down nationalist feeling, so no attempt was made to celebrate Croatia's national heritage – indeed, it was discouraged. The country is only slowly getting back on its feet economically after the war. Although a huge amount has already been done, it's a long job. So renovation projects have to compete for resources with other equally important initiatives. The result is that, in many places, you'll find churches swathed in scaffolding, or squares closed to the public because of archaeological finds. Be patient – it's all in a good cause and there's much to celebrate.

Buje Differing from most hill towns in being crowned by two churches instead of one, Buje's strength is that it is totally untouristy. So you get a feel for what Istria's other hill towns must have been like before tourism, and local government's admirable attempts to replace departing locals with artists and agri-tourists, started to change the character and atmosphere. See p.181.

Motovun A little commercial, Motovun is nevertheless still a wonderful little town, with not only terrific views in all directions, but also a paved and fenced walk along what were once its ramparts. The chestnut-tree-shaded square in front of the hotel is a delight, and there are lots of arts and crafts shops. See p.182.

Buzet Ignore the modern town, and drive up into the quiet Old Town on the hill. Not for nervous drivers, but worth grinding your teeth for, and you might find hardly anybody else up there. See p.185.

Labin You might find it hard to understand why a coal-mining town is being included in this section. But Labin is like no pit village you've ever seen before. For a start, the pits are now closed, and even when they were open (the head-gear of one is still there), they were at the bottom of the hill upon which Labin stands. So drive up the steep hill, park, and enjoy a

town in transition: its hard times were pretty recent, but you can see that it's fighting back. See p.187.

BEST HOTELS

Hotel Kompas (Dubrovnik) A comfortable modern hotel with everything you need for a stress-free holiday with youngsters, both inside the hotel (connecting rooms, extra beds, cots, high chairs, children's menu, swimming pool with toys) and in the immediate vicinity (a safe beach, a good selection of rides, arcade games, bouncy-castle-type diversions, tennis courts). There are also frequent buses into Dubrovnik's Old Town, and a wide choice of excursions. See p.94.

Solaris Holiday Resort (Šibenik) A complex of five hotels just south of Šibenik, the Solaris Holiday Resort has all you need to keep all members of the family happy – beach, swimming pools, bars and restaurants,

Watersports

a wellness centre, a bowling alley, tennis courts. And though you'd never actually need to leave the hotel complex, it's within a few minutes of the lovely town of Šibenik and the spectacular Krka National Park. See p.145.

Funimation (Zadar) One of a group of hotels in Borik, a suburb of Zadar, the Funimation has all the child-friendly bells and whistles any child could wish for – sport, water activities, games. The problem won't be keeping them amused, but rather winkling them out of the hotel to do other things. Choosing just the right suite for the family should be easy – there's a whole range – and parents will appreciate the professional baby-sitting on offer. See p.140.

Hotel Katarina (Rovinj) On an island just off the beautiful Istrian town of Rovinj, the Hotel Katarina consists of an early 20th century villa with modern annexes both sides. The island boasts a huge range of things for the children to do, and because there's no bridge or causeway, there's no traffic! In both location and facilities, this has got to be one of the most child-friendly hotels in Europe. See p.175.

Westin Zagreb Within walking distance of all the attractions of the city centre, the Westin, whilst having the appearance of a hotel that caters for businessmen, is in fact extremely family-friendly, with a range of facilities designed for families with children. See p.232.

BEST RESTAURANTS

Konavoski Dvori (just outside Gruda, south of Dubrovnik) Lovely food, superb setting with rushing water all around, two water wheels and a tank full of fish awaiting their fate – the children will love it. See p.96.

Café Bar Minčeta (Dubrovnik) A no-nonsense Italian restaurant heavily patronised by the locals (always a good sign), the Café Bar Minčeta has nice views out across Gruž harbour. It's part of a small shopping mall, just around the corner from a large shopping centre, and down the road from a pleasant children's playground. Lots to keep all members of the family happy. See p.98.

Konoba Varos (Split) Another popular local choice, the larger-than-it-looks Varos provides a comfortable setting in which to enjoy its wide menu of Croatian dishes and its even wider wine-list. See p.116.

Pašike (Trogir) Down one of stunning Trogir's narrow alleys, the Pašike offers a complete Dalmatian experience – top-notch Dalmatian food, served by staff in Dalmatian regional costume, often accompanied by live Dalmatian folk music. See p.121.

Scaletta (Pula) Good food in a light and spacious setting, plus a 'children's corner' of toys and games to keep the little ones happy. See p.168.

BEST DAYS OUT

Lokrum (from Dubrovnik) Catch a boat in the Old Port for the 10 minute hop across to the island of Lokrum, explore the Botanical Garden, have a swim in the crystal clear waters, walk the paths and enjoy the superb view across to Dubrovnik. See p.78.

Cavtat (from Dubrovnik) Potter around this delightful seaside town – there's just enough to see to retain interest, and pleasant walks beyond the harbour. See p.84.

Imotski (from Split) The two colossal holes-in-the-ground have to be seen to be believed, and one of them (the Blue Lake) has steps and pathways down to the water, where you can have a swim. The town itself is pleasant and unspoiled. See p.124.

Krka National Park (from Šibenik) Wonderful waterfalls and cascades on the Krka river, accessed via a half hour boat trip up the river from Skradin for the lower falls, or Lozovac for the upper falls. See p.147.

Nin (from Zadar) A peaceful island-town, which was once of major importance in Croatian history. It now offers tranquillity and several nationally important churches. See p.149.

Mount Medvednica (from Zagreb) Accessible by car or tram and cable car, Mount Medvednica is a huge recreational area for the capital city – offering nature, open spaces, hiking trails and ski lifts, all within an hour of the city centre. See p.222.

The Zagorje (from Zagreb) All hills and dales, vineyards and castles, the Zagorje is rich in history and tradition. A circular tour can give you a flavour of the area in a day, although you may find that you want to spend a lot longer there. See p.224.

2 Planning a Family Trip to Croatia

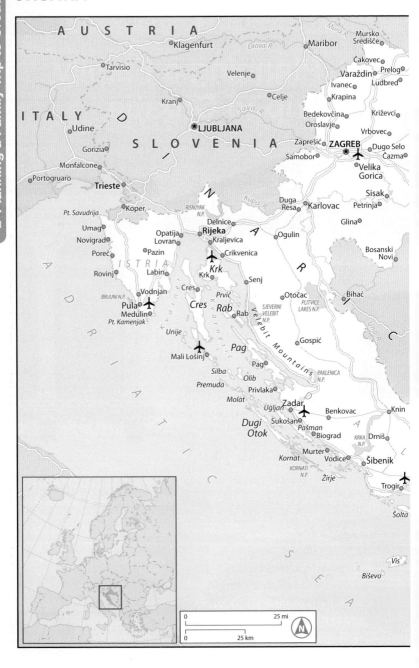

CROATIA

AUSTRIA

Klagenfurt

Maribor

Mursko
Središće

Tarvisio

Velenje

Čakovec

Varaždin Prelog

Ivanec Ludbred

Kranj

Celje

Krapina

ITALY

Udine

LJUBLJANA

Bedekovčina

Oroslavje

Križevci

Gorizia

SLOVENIA

Zaprešić ZAGREB

Vrbovec

Monfalcone

Samobor

Dugo Selo Čazma

Portogruaro

Trieste

Velika
Gorica

Koper

Pt. Savudrija

BISNJYAK
N.P.

Duga
Resa

Karlovac

Sisak

Petrinja

Umag

Delnice

Rijeka

Ogulin

Glina

Novigrad

Opatija

Lovran

Kraljevica

Bosanski
Novi

Poreč

Pazin

ISTRIA

Crikvenica

Rovinj

Labin

Krk

Krk

Senj

Otočac

Bihać

BRIJUNI N.P.

Vodnjan

Cres

Prvić

Cres

Rab

SJEVERNI
VELEBIT
N.P.

PLITVICE
LAKES N.P.

Pula

Medulin

Pt. Kamenjak

Rab

Unije

Gospić

Pag

Mali Lošinj

Pag

PAKLENICA
N.P.

Silba

Olib

Premuda

Privlaka

Molat

Zadar

Benkovac

Knin

Ugljan

Sukošan

Pašman

Biograd

KRKA
N.P.

Drniš

Dugi
Otok

Murter

Vodice

Šibenik

Kornat

KORNATI
N.P.

Žirje

Trogir

Šolta

Vis

Biševo

| 0 | 25 mi |
| 0 | 25 km |

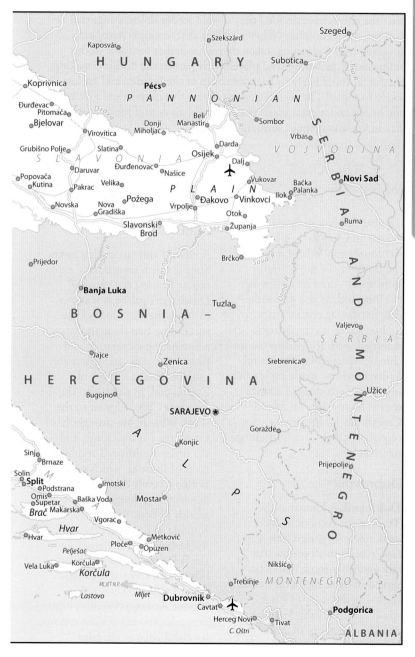

Ideally, the whole family should plan family holidays. There's nothing worse for youngsters than being dragged around to see things that the adults have decided they should see, or doing things they've had no say in choosing. When children and teenagers have been involved in the planning, taken on responsibility for some of the information-gathering, and played their part in the decision-making, they're far more likely to feel ownership of the holiday, and far less likely to moan! The planning starts here – this chapter will give you the bricks and mortar you'll need to build a safe and memorable holiday in Croatia without breaking the bank.

THE REGIONS IN BRIEF

The big division in Croatia, as we saw in Chapter 1, is between the continental inland region – the east wing of the butterfly, so to speak – and its west wing: the long and, as you go south, ever narrowing coastal strip.

Inevitably, it's the Adriatic seaboard, with its Mediterranean climate, spectacularly beautiful Venetian towns, sparkling sea and myriad islands that is Croatia's tourist honey pot. Yet inland Croatia has its attractions – less obvious, perhaps, but intriguing, nevertheless.

Dubrovnik

Dubrovnik is known as the 'Pearl of the Adriatic'. Once seen, never forgotten, this is by far Croatia's most spectacular city and is far more than a pre-served-in-aspic medieval throwback – in the early 1990s it stood up remarkably well to modern weaponry in a six-month bombardment. Bloody but unbowed, its citizens repaired the damage with remarkable alacrity, and it now looks as good as new.

Split

A vibrant and fascinating town, Split is worth several days' exploration. Tracing the ghost of Diocletian's palace as it shows through the accretions of the succeeding two thousand years is a fascinating exercise. Inland from Split, you can explore the tough highland villages of Zagora and, in particular, the Vranjaca Cave, whereas to the south is the pirate stronghold of Omis, the Cetina Gorge, and the other-worldly red and blue lakes of Imotski, which provide brilliant family days out. Other day trips – or longer – to the islands of Brac, Hvar, Vis, Korcula or Lastovo, or south to the lush Makarska Riviera and the Pelijesac Peninsula, make this part of Central Dalmatia a delight to tour. There's also Mount Biokovo (Croatia's highest peak), though scaling it is not for the novice or the faint hearted.

Trogir

Travelling south, you arrive at Trogir (yet another superb island-attached-to-the-mainland Venetian town), pass through the seven villages of the Kastela (each with its own castle), and arrive at the busy port of **Split.**

Central and Northern Dalmatia

The remaining two regions (dealt with in this book as Central and Northern Dalmatia) occupy the same narrowing coastal strip, which is backed by huge, lunaresque mountains. Both regions can boast beautiful fortified towns, which are often on islands attached to the mainland by bridges or causeways, fantastic beaches and some superb inland countryside.

In Northern Dalmatia, Zadar and Šibenik provide substantial touring centres, with lots of historical interest and plentiful accommodation and restaurants, together with port-access to the islands such as Silba and Ugljan and the Kornati Archipelago.

Walking On The Moon: Karst

There can't be many countries in the world where a fact-box on rock would be justified. Not rock *music,* you understand – the mineral substance. But in Croatia, *karst* has such an influence on the landscape that it really is important to understand it.

This limestone rock is light grey in colour and is clearly visible in the huge mountain range that forms the backdrop of most of the Adriatic coast, and on the majority of Croatia's hundreds of islands. Most rock normally stays underground, of course, but thanks to rampant deforestation by the Venetians (who needed lots of wood for their ships), and overgrazing by animals (along with erosion by seasonal winds), the rich mantle of vegetation that once covered the rock has all but vanished. In *karst* areas today, you can stand and see nothing but grey rock, hear nothing but the sighing of the wind – no birdsong, not even the hum of insects. It's like being on the surface of the moon.

You do get pockets of cultivation, though. The collapse of underground caves created by the dissolving of the limestone sometimes leads to surface depressions that, over time, fill with soil that can be cleared and cultivated. These *poljes* are little oases of greenery in a lunar landscape. But under the surface of that skim of soil, the *karst* awaits the next heavy rain to create, for days or weeks, temporary lakes. That's why you'll never see houses built on the *poljes*, but only on the surrounding karst slopes. And that's also why you might see, on the edge of a field and deep in the mountains, miles from the sea and nowhere near a river, a boat!

Inland, a matter of a few kilometres brings you to the spectacular Krka National Park.

Istria

Swinging west, you arrive at the northernmost part of Mediterranean Croatia, Istria. This idyllic peninsula really does feel like (and, of course, was once in) Italy. Most locals speak Italian, and most towns and villages have Italian as well as Croatian names. This is hardly surprising when you consider that Venice is only around 130km away across the gulf.

Istria is a land apart. It juts out into the northern Adriatic, isolated from the rest of Croatia by the Učka Massif. You enter Istria through the spectacular Učka Tunnel, and the landscape spreads out before you like a dream. Istria has everything: stunning coastal towns, a flourishing tourist infrastructure and a peaceful inland heart of vineyards and olive groves. To the east is an ex-coal-mining area that, in its uncanny beauty, puts all other such areas in Europe to shame.

Zagreb

Home to around a fifth of the country's population is a flourishing city combining central European gravitas with Mediterranean swagger. In its civic buildings and flourishing café society, you can sense the enjoyment of its new-found role as the capital of an independent republic, no longer Robin to Belgrade's Batman. It still has plenty of Soviet-style architecture, but why not? Croatia's Yugoslav past is as much a part of its heritage as any other. And Tito (see p.226) was, after all, Croatian.

VISITOR INFORMATION

There is no shortage of help when it comes to finding out about Croatia before you set off. Your first stop should be:

Croatian National Tourist Office, 2, The Lanchesters, 162–164 Fulham Palace Road, London W6 9ER; ☎ 020-8563-7979 (Fax: 020-8563-2616); *www.croatia.hr*. (The website, though disappointing in some respects, does have an excellent series of hyperlinks to 'Upcoming Events'.)

There are a number of other useful websites for information about Croatia, including the following: *www.visit-croatia.co.uk*

Plenty of information for visitors, including details of tour operators and accommodation. *www.visit-croatia.co.uk/whatotherssay*

A useful digest of recent (1998–2006) newspaper articles about Croatia. *www.hr/english*

An authoritative website about all aspects of Croatia. *www.find-croatia.com*

A comprehensive site on all aspects of holidaying in Croatia.

Child Specific Websites

Although Croatia doesn't make it on to all of the family sites, websites can be a great source of general information before setting off.

www.takethefamily.com has useful tips and a discussion board; *www.babygoes2.com* has general guidance including what to take sections; and *www.deabirkett.com* is a handy forum for exchanging tips and views, run by a former *Guardian* family travel specialist. For route planning ahead of a trip, *http://maps.google.com* has zoomable maps of just about anywhere, directions to and from places, and even detailed satellite images.

For more on family travel websites see page 257.

Entry Requirements & Customs

TRAVEL DOCUMENTATION

Visitors to Croatia require a valid passport. No visa is necessary for holidaymakers from EU countries or from North and South America, New Zealand and Australia.

Visitors are permitted to remain in Croatia for up to 90 days. If you initially apply for a longer stay than that, or if your visit is for anything other than tourism or business, then you will need a visa. While in Croatia, you should carry your passport at all times – you must show some form of identification if required. When travelling, keep your passport in an inconspicuous, inaccessible place like a money belt. Be sure to keep a photocopy of the biographical details page (the page to which your photograph is attached) in a safe location, including details of your next of kin. If you lose your passport, visit your nearest consulate or embassy as soon as possible for a replacement.

A list of embassies and consulates can be found on page 50.

Customs Regulations

Croatia customs regulations are in line with those of European Union countries. Foreign currency may be freely brought in and taken out of the country although you must declare amounts above 40,000 Kuna (approximately £ 3,700) (see 'Money' below) in writing. Foreign nationals are exempt from duty on items carried in personal baggage. More expensive professional and technical equipment should be declared at the border, so that you can prove on departure that you didn't buy the items in Croatia.

The duty-free limits on entering Croatia are: 200 cigarettes (or 100 cigarillos/50 cigars/250 grams of tobacco); 1 litre of spirits, 2 litres of wine, 2 litres of liqueur; 50 millilitres of perfume. UK duty-free limits are the same except that the perfume limit is 60 millilitres, gifts are limited to £ 145 worth, and people under 17 cannot use their tobacco and alcohol allowances. For more information, contact

HM Revenue and Customs at ☎ *0845-010-9000* (from outside the UK ☎ *020-8929-0152*), or consult **www.hmce.gov.uk**.

Visitors making purchases in Croatia (apart from petroleum derivatives) that exceed 500 Kuna (approximately £ 46.80) per receipt may reclaim VAT ('PDV'). See 'Fast Facts', Taxes, for further information.

Money

Croatian Currency The currency of Croatia is the Kuna. One Kuna equals 100 lipa. There are 1, 2, 5, 10, 20 and 50 lipa coins, 1, 2, 5 and 25 Kuna coins (though I've never actually come across the latter) and 5, 10, 20, 50, 100, 200, 500 and 1,000 Kuna banknotes. Although Croatia isn't part of the EU (it hopes to be very soon), prices are sometimes given in euros as well as Kunas.

Foreign Currencies Money can be exchanged at banks, exchange offices, post offices and at most tourist agencies, hotels and campsites. Check out the best rates – hotels in particular can sometimes charge exorbitant fees. Banking hours are 7am–7pm Monday to Friday. On Saturdays banks are open until 1pm. In the larger cities some banks are also open on Sundays.

ATM/Cash Machines These are widespread in the coastal areas, but are generally only found in larger towns inland. Don't forget to check your daily withdrawal limit before you leave home, and, if you think there's any chance that you'll need more, get the limit raised.

Traveller's Cheques Now something of an anachronism – most people simply use cash machines – but they are still useful as a secure form of emergency back-up. If you use them, don't forget to keep a record of the serial numbers separate from the cheques themselves.

Available from your bank, Visa, Mastercard, American Express, Thomas Cook and other travel agencies.

Credit Cards All major credit cards (including American Express, Diners Club, Eurocard/Mastercard, Visa, Sport Card International) are accepted in hotels, most restaurants, shops, campsites and marinas. Not only is it safer than carrying too much cash, but using your credit card for everything possible gives you a useful record of your spending while abroad – after the holiday, you can mull over the damage and weep. Credit cards can be used to take cash out of ATMs, though the companies do levy an additional charge.

Rate of Exchange at the Time of Writing £ 1 = 10.93 Kuna (1 Kuna is worth approximately 9 pence); € 1 is worth 7.26 Kuna; £ 1 = $1.90. It is a good idea to exchange at least some money – just enough to cover airport incidentals and transportation to

Keeping Costs Low

There are certain things you can do to keep costs down:

Study hotel tariffs carefully – some charge for cots, for example, others don't, children of certain ages are free in some, but only get a discount in others, and so on. Hotels often put up their tariff by 20% during big local festivals, so avoid staying unless you're actually going to the festival.

Buy bus/tram tickets at kiosks or in hotels – they are often 20% cheaper than paying the driver.

Some museums are free on certain days. Old people and students usually pay the child rate – if in doubt, ask.

Check menu prices before entering a restaurant. There is no need to tip lavishly – it's not expected. Just whatever small change is left is usually enough.

If using taxis, establish a price before setting off – it is sometimes negotiable.

Given a choice, go to Croatia out of season – it's a lot cheaper.

Motorway tolls in Croatia are reasonable, so avoiding the motorway is sometimes a false economy – the extra mileage, wear and tear on the car (and on your nerves) might make it not worth it.

There are sometimes special deals for visitors. In Zagreb, for example, the Zagreb Card, giving free use of all forms of public transport in the city for three days, plus a wide range of substantial discounts in shops, museums, car parks and so on, saves you a fortune (see p.193).

your hotel – before you leave home, so you can avoid queues at airport cash machines.

What to do if your Wallet is Lost or Stolen Report the loss/theft to the police, and cancel all your credit cards (either by phoning the issuing bank, or the following numbers: Visa ☏ +1–410-581-9994 or ☏ +1-410-581-3836 (and reverse charges), MasterCard ☏ 0800-96-4767, American Express ☏ +44 (0)1273–6969

What Things Cost

Croatia is fairly cheap relative to the UK and Ireland, although Dubrovnik is more expensive than the rest of the country. Some typical costs are:

Phoning the UK from a call box 3.5 Kuna (33p) per minute

Draft lager (strong) 10–15 Kuna (95p to £ 1.40) per half litre

Coca Cola 12 Kuna (£ 1)

Public transport 8 to 10 Kuna (75–95p) per trip

Museums 20 Kuna (£ 1.90); children 10 Kuna (95p)

When to Go

As with most things in the country, there is a division between the weather of inland Croatia, which has a continental climate with hot summers and perishing winters, and the coast where the

Temperatures		
	Inland	**Coast**
January	0–2°C	6–11°C
August	19–23°C	21–27°C

Mediterranean climate results in even hotter summers and milder winters.

For hot weather, a fully functioning tourist infrastructure and the majority of the festivals, it has to be July and August. But, in the popular season, expect crowds, queues and top prices.

For pleasant weather and fewer people (but also when festivals are few and far between), go in June or September.

For the great Roman Catholic festivals, go at Easter or 15th August.

For touring or visits to the National Parks, Spring and Autumn are the best bet.

Children's Favourite Croatian Events

Festivals and events are held all over Croatia, and most will have something that should appeal to the children including competitions, performances and colourful processions. The Croatian National Tourist Board website (*www.croatia.hr*) has a useful 'current events/what to see' section, with links to the websites of the individual events. Here is a list of the most popular ones (exact dates are available from the relevant Tourist Office):

January

Old Christmas Orthodox Christians, whose calendar differs from the Roman Catholic one, celebrate Christmas on 7th January.

February

Carnival As in the rest of the world, a carnival is a way of enjoying the good things of life before the deprivations of Lent. It is celebrated all over Croatia, starting any time after mid February, and ending on Shrove Tuesday. One of the best known is in Rijeka and includes theatre, parades and comedy.

Feast of St. Blaise Again, widely celebrated in Roman Catholic areas, but the celebrations are particularly enthusiastic, with lots of eating and drinking, in Dubrovnik – St. Blaise is their patron saint.

March

Easter Week is celebrated throughout Croatia, often with processions. In Korčula (see p.82) there are also mystery plays and singing.

Public Holidays

1st January	New Year's Day
6th January	Epiphany
March/April	Good Friday and Easter Monday
1st May	Labour Day
15th June	Corpus Christi (movable feast)
22nd June	Anti-Fascist Resistance Day
25th June	Croatian National Day
5th August	Victory Day and National Thanksgiving Day
15th August	Assumption
8th October	Independence Day
1st November	All Saints' Day
25–26th December	Christmas Holidays

April

Biennale Zagreb's (see p.229) international festival of contemporary music, held during odd-numbered years. (*www.biennale-zagreb.hr*)

May

International Choir Competition, Zadar Choirs from all over Europe converge on the city towards the end of May.

June

International Children's Festival, Šibenik Festival to highlight young people's theatre and art, at venues across the city in late June and early July.

Opera Festival, Pula Operas are performed in the Amphitheatre all summer (see p.162).

Festival of Croatian Harmony, Omis Traditional folk music.

International Youth Festival of Music, Grosnjan A festival of youth music and art, held from mid-June to mid-September.

Summer Festival, Hvar Music, theatre, dancing and folklore, from the second half of June to the end of September.

July

Festival of Satire, Zagreb First half of July

Film Festival, Motovun Celebrates independent films in this tiny inland Istrian village.

Summer Festival, Split A festival of theatre, concerts, dance and opera in venues across the city, which lasts from mid-July to mid-August.

Summer Festival, Dubrovnik A high-profile event that lasts from early July to late August. It starts with a spectacular firework display, and continues with theatre, concerts, opera and dance performed on open-air stages throughout the city.

International Folklore Festival, Zagreb

A one-week festival in mid-July of folk music, dancing, workshops and exhibitions in the capital.

Rab Festival – Rapska Fjera

A week-long Medieval festival held in the streets of the old part of the town. Includes a knight's parade, crossbow competition and plenty of food and music. Festivities continue well into the night.

Baroque Festival, Zagreb

Evening concerts around the city throughout July. It includes additional events that should appeal to children including costumed parades complete with fire-eaters.

Summer Festival, Krk

From mid-July to end of August.

International Festival of Theatre, Pula

From mid-July to mid-August.

The Moreška, Korcula

The famous sword-dance (similar to English Morris Dancing) re-enacting battles between Christians and Moslems takes place on Mondays and Thursdays at 9pm throughout July and August.

International Tennis Tournament, Umag

End of July.

August

Festival of the Bumbari, Vodnjan

Folk festival and donkey race ('Bumbari' is what the locals call themselves).

Trka na prstenac, Barban

Festival of jousting dating back to the 17th century held on first Sunday in August.

Street Art Festival, Porec

A 10-day festival of music, dance, clowns, jugglers and acrobats, which starts in the second week of August.

International Puppet Festival, Zagreb

Towards the end of the month.

Sinjska Alka, Sinj

Folklore festival with jousting, parades, music and dancing, with local produce on display. The festival commemorates a victory over the Turks.

September

International Doll Festival, Zagreb

Beginning of the month.

Art Programme, Rovinj

Multimedia festival with international artists (second half of the month).

Festival of New Cinema, Dubrovnik

Festival of amateur film-makers, held at end of September/beginning of October.

Grape Festival, Buje

Last Sunday of the month.

October

Bela Nedeja, Kastav Wine festival (first Sunday in October).

Maronada, Lovran Festival of the chestnut held on first Sunday of the month.

November

International Music Festival, Pula Attracts musicians from all over the world. Held during first half of the month.

Martinje A celebration of new wine held on 11th November (St. Martin's Day) in most wine-growing areas. The wine is blessed, and then food and drink are consumed in large quantities. Many Croatian restaurants mark the event with special menus.

December

New Year's Regatta, Hvar Races are held from 28th–31st December.

What to Pack

Even in summer, Croatian evenings can be cool, especially inland or at altitude, so light jumpers or cardigans can be invaluable. If sightseeing is likely to take you into churches or monasteries, take appropriate clothing that keeps shoulders and legs covered. Sunglasses and a sunhat should also be taken if visiting during the summer. If you visit during the winter then a warm coat is essential.

Other general suggestions might be to include some of everyone's clothing in each suitcase (so that if one or more goes missing, you've all at least got the basics), and to separate stuff you need for the journey from stuff you won't need till you get there. So hand luggage should include toiletries, drinks, snacks, and anything else you think you might need in the car, or on the plane/boat/train. In addition, depending on the age of the children, you'll need a survival stock of disposable nappies, bottle and powdered milk, jars of baby food, together with small toys and games, magazines and books, personal stereos, and so on. The secret to successful family travel is a stock of such items, revealed slowly as the journey progresses – a diversion dance of the seven veils.

To get the latest information to restrictions on hand luggage because of terrorism or other security issues check out: *www.dft.gov.uk* and the British Airports Authority: *www.baa.co.uk*

Health, Insurance & Safety

Before you go No special immunisations are needed for Croatia, though it might be wise to get shots against tick-borne encephalitis (TBE) if you're going during the summer months.

Getting treatment There are hospitals and clinics in all of the larger cities. Smaller towns and some villages have first aid clinics and pharmacies where minor complaints can be addressed. Pharmacies have a rota for out-of-hours opening, posted in their windows. In emergencies, go to the nearest hospital or phone for an ambulance (94). For life-threatening situations, there is emergency air (helicopter) and sea (speedboat) transport.

Insurance The UK Foreign and Commonwealth Office strongly recommends that all visitors to Croatia carry full comprehensive travel insurance. Although medical attention is theoretically free for UK and Irish citizens (on production of a valid passport), situations may well arise where what you need isn't available, in which case you'll have to pay. So you still need holiday insurance. Full personal, medical, and (if driving your own car) motor insurance should be taken out before travelling. Having said that, it might pay to check your existing policies – household insurance often covers the loss of property, and many credit cards offer complimentary travel insurance. Once you've listed what's already covered, then you can look for quotes for what's left (and it's sometimes cheaper – and certainly more convenient – to extend one of your existing policies, rather than going for completely new ones).

Safety Croatia is generally safe for visitors, with theft and crimes against the person relatively rare. However, theft from (and of) cars does occur, so you need to be as vigilant as you would be at home, and common sense should be used regarding entering unfamiliar areas after dark. Unaccompanied women might get unwanted male attention, particularly in bars, but this is unlikely to persist if dealt with firmly (see *www.journeywoman.com*).

A significant health risk for those visiting in the summer is the sun. Always use sunscreen and wear a hat.

It is highly unlikely that you'll come across one but a few uncleared mines remain in the country from the recent conflict. As a precaution, stay on well-trodden paths when in the countryside.

Travelling Safely With Children In Croatia

Agree clear procedures with older children for meeting up if you get separated (time and place), and if possible ensure that everybody has their mobile phone for keeping in touch. Make sure everybody has the name, address and phone number of your hotel. Tell younger children to ask somebody in uniform or a shop assistant to help if they get lost.

Hold hands with younger children, especially in busy areas such as markets where they can move faster than you think.

In Croatia, you're likely to find that Croatians are relatively well disposed towards children.

An increasing number of Croatian towns and cities have substantial safe pedestrian-only areas. Croatian towns feel relatively safe as well – you'll see young women out on their own very late at night.

A Word on Cultural Difference

The vast majority of Croatians are polite, helpful and charming. They are proud of their country, and keen to show it in the best possible light. But Croatians can sometimes *seem* rude. This can be for a number of reasons. It may be because of language difficulties – if their English isn't up to the conversation you're having with them (and assuming your Croatian is relatively non-existent), Croatians can sometimes get embarrassed or frustrated. Cultural differences can also be a factor and what seems to be rude to you may not be rude in Croatia. Another factor may be a lack of experience. The Croatian tourist industry is expanding so quickly that some staff in restaurants and hotels may not have been doing the job long. Sometimes misunderstandings take place and what *you* have done/said may have appeared to be rude to a Croatian. Alternatively, if a Croatian seems rude it may actually be because he or she *is* rude.

Specialised Resources

For Single Parents

Single parents might want to link up with friends in the same position for holidays, or book through one of the travel companies that specialise in single parent holidays (such as *www.smallfamilies.co.uk*) or general companies that are starting to cater for this growing sector of the market (e.g. *www.responsibletravel.com*).

There's a useful 'Holidays' page with contact details of useful associations and operators in the UK, see *www.singleparents.org.uk*. The US based *www.singleparenttravel.net* is also good for travel advice. One Parent Families 📞 *0800 018 5026*. *www.oneparentfamilies.org.uk* is a British charity offering info and advice for lone parents; Gingerbread (📞 *0800 018*

4318, *www.gingerbread.org.uk* is similar, with members getting regular emails with discounts and holiday ideas. Members of both get discounts with tour operator Eurocamp (p.37), which has an Arrival Survival service to help lone parents unpack and settle in.

For Families with Special Needs

The following organisations offer advice and information for families travelling with a member with special needs.

Holidaycare: *www.holidaycare.org.uk*

RADAR (Royal Association for Disability and Rehabilitation): *www.radar.org.uk*

Tripscope: *www.tripscope.org.uk*

The 21st Century Traveller

Most towns of any size in the tourist areas have at least one Internet café. Tourist Offices will often allow you to get online, and most high-end hotels also have Internet access. Even relatively modest hotels can sometimes offer the ability to pick up your e-mails. Charges are usually reasonable (anything from 20 to 40 Kuna (£ 1.85 to 3.70 per hour), but it is as well to check before launching yourself into cyberspace. Inland, access to the Internet is likely to be much more limited.

Mobile phone ownership has exploded in Croatia – over half the population are now connected up – so the infrastructure to support mobile technology is in place. Mobile phone networks (GSM 900/1800 standard) cover most of Croatia, though as elsewhere, if you're off the beaten track, a signal can be elusive. You'll need to check with your provider before you leave home as to what, if anything, you need to do to ensure that your mobile works in Croatia. Charges, though, can be ferocious, and remember that you are likely to be charged for incoming as well as outgoing calls.

Taking your laptop to Croatia on the plane shouldn't be a problem – you can pack it into hold luggage, or carry it as hand luggage. If you opt for the latter, you'll be asked by security staff to take it out of its case.

INSIDER TIP

If you think you'll be using your mobile a lot within Croatia, it might be worth considering the purchase of a Croatian VIP or T-Mobile SIM card – it might, at 250–300 Kuna (£ 23.50–28.00), seem expensive, but the charge includes a certain amount of pre-paid credit, and it will certainly be a lot cheaper than paying the current exorbitant roaming charges levied by mobile phone companies on Brits using their phones abroad – cards are available at any mobile phone shop.

Getting There

By Plane The main carriers flying into Croatia are British Airways and Croatia Airlines, flying from Heathrow, Gatwick or Manchester. However, as a result of the recent recovery of Croatia's tourist industry, combined with the growth of Britain's regional airports, new routes are springing up at a remarkable rate and it is now possible to fly from a number of regional airports with carriers such as Ryanair, EasyJet, Wizz Air and Aer Lingus.

In the hunt for the cheapest way of getting there, it might also be worth considering flying to airports in nearby Italy or Slovenia, then going on by bus, train or rental car.

Croatia's three main airports – Zagreb, Split and Dubrovnik – conveniently serve the main regions described in this book. Pula, Rijeka or Zadar increasingly offer alternatives, either direct or via internal Croatia Airlines flights from one of the others. Island airports are accessible only from mainland Croatia.

Summer 2007 – UK flights to Croatia. Scheduled & no-frills flights

British Airways www.ba.com
Gatwick to Split and Dubrovnik. Manchester to Dubrovnik

Croatia Airlines www.croatia airlines.hr London to Zagreb, Rijeka, Split and Dubrovnik

Aer Lingus
www.flyaerlingus.com Dublin to Dubrovnik

Ryanair www.ryanair.com
London (STN) to Pula three times weekly.

Wizz Air www.wizzair.com
London (LTN) to Zagreb four times weekly. London (LTN) to Split three times weekly.

easyJet www.easyjet.com
London (LTN) to Rijeka Krk four times weekly. London (LGW) to Split four times weekly. Bristol to Rijeka Krk three times weekly.

Charter flights to Croatia operated by UK tour operators

Holiday Options www.holiday options.co.uk
Gatwick to Pula, Split and Dubrovnik. Belfast to Pula. Bristol to Split. Birmingham to Split and Dubrovnik. Norwich to Split and Dubrovnik. Manchester to Pula, Split and Dubrovnik.

Thomsonfly
www.thomsonfly.com
Gatwick to Pula, Split and Dubrovnik. Bristol, Birmingham and Glasgow to Pula. Manchester to Pula and Dubrovnik.

Thomas Cook www.thomas cook.com Gatwick to Pula and Split. Bristol to Split. Norwich to Split. Birmingham to Split. Manchester to Pula and Split.

Cosmos
www.cosmosholidays.co.uk
Gatwick, Birmingham and Manchester to Dubrovnik.

Airtours/Mytravel www. airtours.co.uk
Gatwick to Pula and Split. Birmingham to Split. Manchester to Pula and Split.

By Car Croatia shares borders with Slovenia, Hungary, Bosnia-Herzegovina and Serbia and Montenegro, making it easy to drive to and from all over Europe. And the distances, though substantial, are not insurmountable: Zagreb, for example, is just over 1600 km (1000 miles) from London, 1400 km (880 miles) from Paris, 990 km (620 miles) from Berlin, 1325 km (828 miles) from Athens and 970 km (600 miles) from Bern. For the Channel crossing, Dover–Calais or Dover–Dunkirk are the best bet – they've got by far the biggest choice of carriers and sailing times. Driving to Croatia has

Flying With Children

Before you go:

- Check your airlines website for its policies and advice for flying with children.
- If you've got a baby, ask if you can book a bassinet.
- Assemble a survival kit of disposable nappies, bottles, wipes, snacks, drinks, toys, books, stickers, paper and pencils (but check the BAA website (*www.baa.com*) for the frequently changing regulations about what you're allowed to take in your hand luggage).
- Let the children have their own small-wheeled cases – they'll love pulling them, and it reduces the load on you.
- Let the children have their own hand luggage – a back-pack containing their survival kit should do it.

At the airport:

- Make sure you get to the airport in plenty of time.
- Consider using the automatic check-in.
- Reins or a harness for toddlers are essential for waits in the terminal – it only takes a second to lose a child.
- Dress your youngsters in bright clashing colours – then they'll be easy to see!
- Ask if the flight's full. If not, helpful booking clerks might agree to block out the seats next to yours, to give you more room.
- Staff will sometimes allow families with young children to board first. If they don't, board last, when all the other passengers have stowed their luggage and settled down. Always disembark last, when flight staff will be free to help.

During the flight:

- Warn cabin crew if you're going to change a nappy – they may be willing to help by, for example, lowering the changing table for you.
- Scented nappy sacks are useful for all sorts of things – dirty nappies, of course, but also clothes that have been sicked on, used wipes and general rubbish.
- If your children are fussy, bring your own food – airline meals are notoriously patchy in quality.
- Despite pressurised cabins, ears can still be troublesome. Feed babies during take-off and landing. Ear plugs or cotton wool can help older children who haven't learned how to 'pop' their ears.

Useful Websites:

www.TravellingWithChildren.co.uk
www.family-travel.co.uk
www.babyflying.co.uk/travel_tips.htm

many advantages. For a start, you've got your own car. And there's nothing like the smug sense of superiority you feel over other holidaymakers who've done it the easy way and flown.

Then there's the fact that you can take as many of your own possessions as you can fit in – clothes, books, cameras, video-recorders, binoculars, CDs, iPods, laptops, flippers, face-masks, inflatable dinghies. For any other way of going on holi-day – package, for instance, or fly-drive – you're limited to what you can carry. That goes too, in spades, for all the stuff you might want to buy while you're there.

Then there's the trip itself. You can feel the weather getting warmer, see the cultural changes as you travel south, and do all the sightseeing you want. If you just take your time (and with children that's essential), the trav-elling is all part of the holiday.

And that, of course, is one of the downsides – time. If you've only got a week or two, driving to Croatia isn't a realistic option. Don't expect it to be cheaper, either. By the time you've paid for ferries, hotels or campsites, fuel, meals and motorway tolls, you'll find that it's no more eco-nomic than any other method of travel. What you do get is a lot more holiday for your money.

To take your car to Croatia you'll need a valid drivers licence (both bits), vehicle registration document, and vehicle insurance documents (including green card). Your UK driving licence is valid for up to six months from

entry into Croatia. If you are staying longer, you need to apply for a Croatian licence. International Driving Licences are not valid in Croatia.

As you enter the country, get any existing damage to your car certified – you will have to pro-duce the certificate as you leave. If your car is damaged in an acci-dent while you're in Croatia, you must get a police report (again to get back out of the country).

When travelling by car you should ensure, before setting out, that your green card covers Croatia. Insurance can normally be purchased at the main border crossings, however some of the smaller crossings may not have this facility or have limited hours when the service is available. If you are driving to or through Bosnia and Herzegovina, includ-ing the 20-km strip of coastline at Neum on the Dalmatian coastal highway, you should ensure that your green card includes cover for Bosnia and Herzegovina. If this is not the case, temporary third-party insurance can be purchased at the main border posts, or in Split and other large Croatian cities. Insurance cannot be obtained at the Neum border.

For further advice on driving in Croatia, see 'Rules of the Road' below.

By Train Travelling to Croatia by train is certainly possible. It's even enjoyable. But it takes a lot longer than flying, and it's more expensive. However, if you want to give it a go (perhaps you're a family of train-spotters?), have a word with 'The Man in Seat 61' (*www.seat61.com* – one of *The Times* 100 best travel sites) and book onto the London–Paris Eurostar, then the Paris–Munich sleeper, followed by the Munich–Zagreb Eurocity train Mimara. You'll be walking out of Zagreb's splendid Orient Express era station around 27 hours after you started, and it'll have cost a fortune. If you're a train buff, it'll have been worth it.

Direct train services run from Austria, Bosnia-Herzegovina, Hungary, Italy, Switzerland, Slovenia and Serbia and Montenegro.

By Bus There's a pretty comprehensive network of coach routes covering the whole of Europe, and it is feasible to get from the UK to Croatia by bus. However, travel times are long (certainly longer than by train), and despite developments in on-board facilities and the growth of the European motorway system, coach travel is still one of the least comfortable forms of transport. For children, the novelty of travelling to Croatia by coach is likely to wear off long before you arrive. You can check out routes and prices at *www.eurolines.com*.

Package Deals & Escorted Tours

Croatia has a long history as a package holiday and escorted tour destination going back into the early years of the last century, and the market has certainly

gone from strength to strength during the early years of this one. Whether by luck or judgement, Croatia has by and large avoided the proliferation of high-rise hotels that afflict some countries – the big holiday complexes tend to be tucked discretely away from the gorgeous Adriatic towns that made Croatia a holiday hot-spot in the first place.

Package holidays (usually consisting of flights, accommodation and transfers) offer unbeatable value (because they're ordering in bulk, they can negotiate terrific rates), while escorted tours (involving detailed itineraries and the services of a guide) combine value-for-money, maximum coverage of attractions, and the peace-of-mind that comes from letting somebody else do all the organising and worrying. And if you're concerned that package holidays and tours inevitably include a factory-farming element of regimentation, think again – the degree of flexibility on offer these days is astounding.

The first step in choosing a package or escorted tour provider is to obtain the excellent information pamphlet, which is available from the Croatian National Tourist Office (*www.croatia.hr*). It includes a summary of companies offering hotel and villa based inclusive air holidays from the UK (43 of them, giving the resorts, holidays and flights), coach holidays (12 companies, with details of destinations), and a staggering 90 companies that arrange special-interest holidays in Croatia including city breaks, archaeology, art and culture, walking, cycling, adventure, sport, sailing, singing and cookery.

Of particular interest to families are:

Perfect Places Family self-catering apartments ☏ 0870-3667-567 *www.perfectplace sonline.co.uk*

Adventure Company Family adventure holidays ☏ 01420-541007 *www.adventurecompany. co.uk*

Activities Abroad Activities for families ☏ 01670-789991 *www. activitiesabroad.com*

Small Families Holidays
Single parent family holidays ☏ 01767-650312 *www.small families.co.uk*

Camping holidays can make an ideal break for families. There's lots of space for children to roam in a safe environment and a host of activities (often called animation) to get involved in. Popular camping operators have upped their game to provide easy to navigate websites with listing for family friendly campsites, those with toddler clubs, special offers for young families and extras such as free playcentres, travel cots and high chairs. From family discos to table tennis tournaments and children's fun packs sent out before the holiday, the camping option should be considered for families looking for a fun, adventurous and refreshing

outdoor trip together. Here's a selection of operators in Croatia:

Canvas Holidays *www.canvas holidays.co.uk*
Sites at: Camping Bi Village, Pula; Lanternacamp, Porec.

Eurocamp *www.eurocamp.co.uk*
Sites at: Camping Marenda, Porec; Lanternacamp, Porec; Camping Poljana, Lošinj.

Keycamp *www.keycamp.co.uk*
Sites at: Lanternacamp, Porec
For more information on operators to Croatia see (p.258).

see (p.258).

> **INSIDER TIP** ›
> Don't forget travel agents when looking for holiday discounts or specialist advice on Croatia. The Association of British Travel Agents (*www.abta.com*) has a list of specialist agents and operators on its site. A specialist on Croatia can save you an inordinate amount of time and hassle, compared with going online, and help you with special arrangements for families.

Getting Around

By Car The quality of Croatian roads varies from the excellent to the primitive. Zagreb is the hub of its 250km motorway (autocesta) system (blue signs, prefix 'A'), which is of international standard. (For main motorways, see map). They are relatively traffic free, thanks to the need to pay substantial tolls (Zagreb to Zadar, for example, is 105 Kuna (£ 10)). The motorway from Zagreb to Split, with spurs to

Rules of the Road

As with the rest of mainland Europe, you must drive on the right in Croatia. You must have lights on at all times – after a coffee or refuelling break, it's easy to forget to switch them back on.

Don't drink and drive – at all. Croatia's attitude to alcohol in the blood is zero tolerance. You even need to make sure you stop drinking early enough the night before to give your body time to get rid of the alcohol. The police administer spot-checks for alcohol, and breathalyser tests are automatic at even the slightest of accidents. A lot of Croatians objected when this policy was introduced, on the grounds that it stops you even having a glass of wine with your meal.

Speed limits in Croatia are 50 km/hour (30 mph) in built-up areas, 90 km/hour (56 mph) outside built-up areas, 110 km/hour (68 mph) on major routes and 130 km/hour (81 mph) on motorways. If you're towing, the limit is 80 km/hour (50 mph).

It is illegal to use a mobile phone while driving, unless you have hands-free kit.

You must have a fluorescent vest in the car at all times (in the car itself, not the boot), and wear it at any time when attending to a break-down – even changing the wheel. You must also carry spare bulbs, two warning triangles and a first aid kit.

The use of seat-belts for drivers and front passengers is mandatory, and rear passengers must use seat belts if fitted. Special seats for infants are also mandatory. Children under 12 must not sit in the front seat.

Apart from the new Zagreb to Split motorway (which is excellent), and parts of the rest of the motorway system, dual carriageways in Croatia are the exception rather than the rule. Many Croatian's solve the problem of two-lane roads by overtaking at times that may seem unwise – on sharp bends, for example, or on the brows of hills. Don't try to emulate them – the death rate on Croatia's roads is fairly high.

During the summer, English language traffic information is available on the radio at 98.5FM every hour from 6.30am to 8.30pm.

Zadar and Šibenik, was opened in 2005, and work has begun to extend it to Dubrovnik. There are also plans to bypass the Neum corridor in Bosnia by building a bridge between the mainland and the Pelješac peninsula. There is major road-building going on in Istria as well and eventually Croatia will be linked to the Italian motorway system. Apart from bona fide motorways, there are other three- and two-lane major roads. Both kinds are of good quality. The most picturesque route in Croatia is the Jadranska magistrala along the Adriatic coast

Driving Times

Zagreb–Pula:	3 hours
Zagreb–Zadar:	3 hours
Zagreb–Split:	4 hours
Zagreb–Dubrovnik	7–8 hours

from Rijeka and Dubrovnik. Don't plan to cover too much ground on it, though – it's two lanes, has lots of bends, and in summer becomes clogged with traffic. Away from the main roads, side roads vary from fair to dreadful – the worst are pot-holed gravel tracks.

Filling stations, offering petrol (95 and 98 octane) and diesel are widely available on the coast, less so as you move inland. LPG is obtainable only in Istria. Good maps are on sale in filling stations, and a useful map of Croatia (with a road map on one side and a pictorial tourist map on the other) is available from the Croatian National Tourist Board.

Two excellent websites, Croatian Auto Club *www.hak.hr* and Croatian Motorways *www.hac.hr*, are worth consult-ing before you drive in Croatia – both have lots of up-to-date information about routes, tolls, road conditions and so forth.

Renting a car in Croatia is easy, but can be expensive. Major car hire chains exist in Croatia, as well as local compa-nies. Most have offices in the larger Croatian towns and at airports.

Adriatica *www.adriatica.net*

Budget *www.budget.hr*

E-Sixt *www.e-sixt.co.uk*

Hertz *www.hertz.hr*

Kompas No. 1 *www.kompasno1.hr*

Mack Rent a Car *www.mack-concord.hr*

National *www.nationalcar.hr*

Rent a Car Matejuska *www.matejuskarent.hr*

Do shop around, though – you can sometimes get much better deals by going through the UK offices of rental compa-nies such as Avis *www.avis.co.uk* or Holiday Rentals *www.holiday rentals.co.uk*.

By Air As might be expected in such a long-drawn-out country, Croatia has a well-organised internal air transport system, with Zagreb at its hub. There are Croatia Airlines flights from Zagreb to Pula, Zadar, Split and Dubrovnik, together with sum-mer services to Brač – most internal flights take under an hour. Booking is simplicity itself at *www.croatiaairlines.com*, and single fares can start as low as 189 Kuna (£ 77).

By Train Travel by train is a viable option between major cities, and even between smaller centres in Zagreb and inland Croatia. For the Adriatic coast they are less useful. Croatian trains are clean, punctual and efficient. Intercity (IC) trains are air-conditioned, and have first and second-class carriages. Local passenger trains (putnički) are cheap, cheerful and slow. Tickets can be bought at railway stations, or, where there's no ticket office, off the guard/conductor. Singles are usually half the rate for returns, though on some intercity routes the return is cheaper. Timetables, ticket prices and so on are available in English, via the Croatian Railways website at *www.hznet.hr* (guide fare – Zagreb to Split, 126 Kuna (£ 11.80). Some Interrail type tickets are valid in Croatia, but are not really worth buying if you're just going to travel within the country.

By Bus Buses can be divided into intercity expresses and local – the former are faster and can be cheaper (fares are based on the distance travelled). At city bus stations you buy your ticket before boarding – be careful that you get on the right bus, since there is a profusion of companies. On local buses, simply get on and pay the driver. City buses and trams often require you to offer exact fares, and if you pre-purchase tickets (at kiosks or newsagents), they need to be validated when you get on.

Tips on Accommodation & Dining

Hotel tariffs in Croatia compare well with those in much of the rest of Western Europe, but when you're paying for a whole family it can still get pretty expensive. Croatia has adopted a star rating system (from 1 to 5 stars), though you need to remember that this relates to the range of facilities on offer, and not to quality, ambience or service. Many of the large turn-of-the-century hotels, and their 60s and 70s high-rise equivalents are being refurbished, and a lot of smaller boutique hotels, often family-run, are opening. Whether the hotels are new or refurbished, there now seems to be a fair degree of uniformity in what they offer.

You'll find a lot of variation in tariffs at different times of the year, especially in the more popular coastal resorts (inland there's far less seasonal variation). Different areas, too, have different tariff-ranges – expect to pay a lot more in Dubrovnik, a fair amount more in Zagreb. Some parts of Croatia seem to offer little in the way of budget hotel accommodation (Dubrovnik and Zagreb again).

Within hotels, too, you can pay widely different rates – facing the car park will be cheaper than overlooking the sea. You need to compare tariffs very carefully – it would take an accountant to factor in all the variations depending on room facilities and position, what extra charges are made for cots or additional beds and so on. And pay particular attention to the cut-off ages for child discounts: few hotels charge for infants, most allow 50% discount for younger children and 30% for older children. Breakfast is almost invariably included, half and full board is often also on offer. Some hotels charge per person, some by the room. For a family, suites are sometimes more economical than rooms. By the time you've allowed for all the variations, you'll need a holiday to recover. The least child-friendly hotels seem to be the mid-range medium sized hotels. The large expensive hotels, the resort hotels and the small family-run hotels and room providers seem to be the best bets for families.

Business hotels frequently offer discounts at weekends; tourist hotels will offer a cheaper rate if you're staying, say, for four or more nights. And it is often the case that buying a package holiday is cheaper that going it alone. Finally, for an often extremely economical alternative to hotels, why not try one of the thousands of rooms, apartments and villas available throughout the county? A very comprehensive guide to the agencies that provide such accommodation – called 'Private and Confidential: Private Accommodation, rooms, apartments and villas' – is available from the Tourist Office. Look also at the Association of Croatian Travel Agencies website at *www.croatia-travel.org*, where there's an extremely useful accommodation finder: just put in the details of the party, your itinerary and preferred type of accommodation, and Bob's your uncle!

Eating Out

Croatia offers a great chance for families to enjoy a different type of cuisine. From fresh, delicious seafood to more hearty, inland fare, if children are willing to be adventurous there's a huge amount to feast on. If, however, children are fussy, there's lots of familiar food to fall back on, too.

Croatians seem particularly keen on fresh ingredients and families are well catered for with a distinctive cuisine drawing on culinary traditions from the Mediterranean and Central Europe.

Although there are, of course, regional specialities (like truffles in Istria, or fish along the whole Dalmatian coast), they are actually widely available throughout Croatia. Some of the regional

Staying In A Lighthouse

During the 19th century the Austro–Hungarians built 48 lighthouses along the Croatian coast. No longer needed to help shipping navigate these dangerous waters, 12 of the more accessible ones have been converted into holiday accommodation. Not all would be suitable for families – the one on Palagruža, for example, is too remote – but others (including the one at Struga) have beaches suitable for children. So if you want something a little different from the usual, why not check them out? Various companies can arrange stays in Croatia's lighthouses: try Adriatica (☎ *012-405-611, www.adriatica.net*).

tourist boards produce excellent guides to the restaurants in their area (e.g. the Zadar Region Gastro Guide and Istria's 'Istragasto', each available from regional tourist offices).

Istria is widely recognised as the home of the best regional cooking with its heavy Italian influences.

Croatian starters (predjela) are often a home cured ham from Istria and Dalmatia – a delicious delicacy called pršut.

Meat dishes usually consist of a grilled meat or pan fried kotlet (chop) or odrezak (fillet or esca-lope). A popular way of cooking meat and vegetables together is 'ispod peke', which means 'under the lid' – the food is cov-ered by a metal lid, and hot embers are then heaped onto it.

The coast is a treasure trove for families with an overwhelm-ing range of seafood. Some of the most flavoursome fish comes from the kovač (John Dory), list (sole), orada (gilthead seabream) and škrpina (scorpion fish). The most common salads are zelena salata (green salad) and mješana salata (mixed salad).

Deserts you'll find in a typical Croatian restaurant include *sladoled* (ice cream), *torta* (cake) and *palacinke* (pancakes), usually served *sa marmeladom* (with marmalade), *s cokoladom* (with chocolate sauce) – a favourite with youngsters – or *s oresima* (with walnuts). In Dubrovnik try *rozata*, the locally produced version of crème caramel.

Vegetarianism isn't a signifi-cant part of Croatian culture and the choice of dishes in restau-rants reflects this accordingly. Even vegetarian looking options such as bean soups or rata-touilee-style *duvec* are often made with meat stock. Vegetarians can instead try mak-ing a meal out of the various meatless starters such as *omlet sa gljivama* (mushroom omelette) and *pohani sir* (cheese fried in breadcrumbs). Pizzerias and spaghetterias are often the best option offering vegetable pizzas and sometimes vegetable lasagne.

Croatian beer (*pivo*) is a light lager with good brands including Karlovacko and Ozujsko. Regional beers to taste are Tomislav from Zabgreb and Osijeck Crno from Osijek.

Croatia also has a strong range of good red and white wines (*vino*). Regional white wine varieties include Kastelet Grk and Posip from Korcula, Vrbnicka lahtina from Vrbnik on krk: Semion from Istria; and Vugava from Vis.

The reds include Dingac from the Peljesac peninsula, Babic from Primosten, Tehran from Istria and Viski plavac from Vis.

Relatively few restaurants have child seats and child menus, but most will bend over backwards to accommodate children. A willingness to provide extra help to families will be to you more important than child menus when you feel comfortable and are having an enjoyable time together. Restaurants are usually more than happy as well to divide meals up for youngsters and satisfy less adventurous tastes.

Few Croatian restaurants have children's toys, so try as far as possible to take your own diversions when eating out.

In terms of prices, Croatia in general is slightly cheaper than eating out in the UK.

INSIDER TIP ›
Tipping in Croatian restaurants is not obligatory, especially for something small such as a cup of coffee. However, for a round of drinks or a meal, rounding up the bill to a convenient figure is polite.

Suggested Itineraries

If you've got very young children

For holidaymakers with young children the best option is to go for a single centre holiday. Many of the main package operators offer holidays in Croatia. The larger and more expensive hotels tend to have better child facilities, as do the big resort hotels. Experience indicates that the hotels least sympathetic to children are medium-sized hotels with pretensions. Try to identify areas of the country with lots for adults to see and do without too much travelling – it's your holiday as well! You'll also need pleasant areas within easy walking distance of your accommodation, where you can take babies or toddlers. It helps if your chosen area is close to the airport, so that the transfer isn't too onerous, or if you prefer, to allow you to take a taxi.

Best bets: Fly to Dubrovnik Airport and stay at the Excelsior in Ploče (p.93), or the Kompas on the Lapad Peninsula (p.94). This will give you easy access to the Old Town, beaches, cafés and restaurants, pleasant walks and interesting excursions. It will also allow some personal time for each partner to get away from the family for a breather!

Fly to Pula Airport and stay at the Scaletta Hotel in Pula itself (p.168), or the Histria on the Verudela Peninsula (p.168), or the Katarina in Rovinj (p.175). Again, lots of interesting places to see, both nearby and on excursions further away, together with enough to be going on with in the immediate vicinity.

If you've got teenagers Two- or three-centre holidays can be a good bet for families with teenagers, or even a touring holiday in your own or a rented car. Look out for areas with lots of places to visit and lots of possible excursions. Good in-hotel entertainment is also useful.

If you're in Croatia for two or three weeks Best bets – several from: three to six days in Dubrovnik to explore the Old Town, the harbour and the Lapad Peninsula, Cavtat and Lokrum and the other islands (p.55).

Three to six days in Šibenik to visit the town (p.141), Split (p.101) and Trogir (p.116), the Blue and Red lakes of Imotski (p.124), the Cetina Gorge (p.147), the Krka National Park (p.128) and the islands of Brač, Hvar and Vis (p.153), the Zadar Archipelago (p.153) and the Kornati National Park (p.157).

Three to five days in Zagreb – a couple to explore the city and its immediate hinterland, a couple to take a look at the Zagorje.

Three to six days in Istria to drive up the west and east coasts, and to explore the interior. This would, at a pinch, enable you to cover virtually everything included in this book, since a stay in Šibenik would allow you to cherry-pick from both the

Central Dalmatia and Northern Dalmatia chapters. It would also involve no more than 320 km (200 miles) of driving on any one day. So fly to Dubrovnik, pick up a rented car there, drive up through Croatia, return the rented car and get your return flight home from Pula. Or vice versa. If you have to fly to and from the same Croatian airport, then the logistics might be a bit more difficult, and might have to include internal flights in Croatia. But you'd see a great deal of the country in your two or three weeks.

If you're in Croatia for a week Because Croatia's so long and thin, having just a week probably makes it wise to confine yourself to one region or other. Istria, for example, makes a good base for a week's holiday (see p.155). Alternatively you might explore the coast from Dubrovnik up to Split (p. 55 to 101), the coast from Split up to Zadar (p. 101 to 136) or Zagreb and its hinterland (p. 197).

The Adventurous Family's Holiday Planner

Walking/Hiking Most areas of the country have marked walks – ask at the local Tourist Information Office. In addition, there are lots of good walks, from the gentle to the challenging, in the National Parks (see p.45) especially the Plitvice Lakes and on the islands of Brijuni and Mljet. The most strenuous hiking is to

Croatia is one of the most diverse countries in Europe, both in its wildlife and in its geography and geology. As a relatively new nation, it is also very much aware of the need to prevent encroachment into its many areas of natural beauty, and of the need to preserve this heritage for its own future generations and as a way of attracting visitors to its increasingly important tourist industry. The result is that Croatia has 450 different protected areas covering around 10% of its land area, which includes eight national parks, as well as nature reserves, forest parks and some 70 protected landscapes. No-one could accuse Croatia of not taking its duty to the environment seriously. Wherever you are in Croatia, you're not far from one or probably more of its protected areas. Most of these parks, including the Kornati Archipelago (see p.153), the Brijuni Archipelago (see p.170) Krka National Park (p.147) and Mljet (see p.89), have been covered in this book. Of those that aren't covered in the main text, the best is Plitvice National Park.

Despite being some distance both from Croatia's largest cities and from its most popular holiday areas, the **Plitvice National Park** is the biggest tourist magnet in the country. Croatians and foreign visitors throng this region, which is made up of 16 lakes connected by numerous travertine (limestone sediment) rock waterfalls. Wherever you are in Croatia, the chances are that you will be able to join an organised excursion to these lakes, which are spectacularly beautiful. For the foot weary there are little trains and electric boats. There are also hotels and restaurants, a shop, post office and restaurant (near the southern entrance to the park), and loads of informative booklets, pamphlets and information boards. The lakes are easy to get to and are just off the Zagreb-Split motorway, about half way between Zagreb and Zadar. For more information visit **www.np-plitvička-jezera.hr**.

The **Krka National Park** (**www.npkrka.hr**), a short drive from Šibenik, is in many ways like a mini-Plitvice. It too has a series of travertine waterfalls, but also a number of man-made attractions. Easiest access is from Skradin, from which a pleasant boat ride brings you to Skradinski Buk, the lower of the three sets of waterfalls that make up the park (occurring in an 800 metre stretch of the river wide, dropping 46 metres and made up of 17 cascades). Paths and steps take you up beside the falls to a large viewing area overlooking the whole vista of broken water. There are the remains of a very early hydroelectric scheme, and several stone water mills. Unlike Plitvice, you are allowed to swim in the park, though only in the lowest pool of Skradinski Buk. Further up the river there's a Franciscan monastery on a tiny islet in the river, another set of cascades (Roški slap) and above that the impressive Krka Monastery. All are accessible by bus or boat – ask Park officials to help you plan your visit.

be had on Mount Biokovo (above Makarska) and the Velebit mountains (northern Dalmatia), but these are not for the novice. (For information on hiking in Croatia, try *www.findcroatia.com* or *www.croatiatraveller.com*.)

Cycling For general information about cycling in different parts of Croatia, go to *www.bicikl.hr/cikloturizam/*. A number of travel companies are involved in Croatian cycling holidays. The British company **2 Wheel Treks** (*www.2wheeltreks.co.uk/cycling_croatia.htm*) is one of the best and can arrange cycling holidays in the National Parks, and in Kvarner Gulf, southern Dalmatia and the Makarska Riviera. Some of their package deals combine cycling and cruising aboard a boat. After a morning spent cycling, you have the option of returning to the boat for lunch and relaxing on board or heading off for another spin in the afternoon, and returning back to the boat in time for your evening meal.

Horseback Riding Equestrian centres abound in northern Croatia, Slavonia, Istria and Dalmatia, which offer tuition and, for more experienced riders, the opportunity of hiring a horse and going on expeditions (try *www.horse-riding.net/vacations/Croatia/*, and the Tourist Board *www.croatia.hr*).

Tennis Since Goran Ivanisevic's success at Wimbledon in 2001, Croatia is associated in many people's minds with tennis (for a brief history of tennis in Croatia, go to *www.hr/croatia/sport/sports/tennis*). There are many tennis schools along the Adriatic coast, and several companies are happy to organise flights, accommodation and tuition (for tennis holidays, look at *www.jsttennis.com*).

Diving Diving is growing in popularity in Croatia, and it's no wonder. The Adriatic coast has some of the clearest and cleanest waters in the Mediterranean – a positive side effect of its lack of sandy beaches. Sea life is plentiful, and in several areas Ancient Greek and Roman artefacts add interest to the underwater explorations. Diving courses are widely available – virtually every seaside town has a diving centre – but even if you're sufficiently experienced not to need them, you'll still require a diving permit issued by the Croatian Diving Federation (the fee is around 100 Kuna (£ 9.50), and you will have to present recognised diving qualifications). Hiring gear can be difficult if you don't want to join the centre's staff for a dive, and you'll need to check out where you are and aren't allowed to dive. To sign up for diving tuition, there is a lower age restriction – usually 14. See *www.diving.hr* and have a look at *www.findcroatia.com* for further information.

Fishing Both sea and river fishing are popular in Croatia, but you'll need a Ministry of Agriculture and Forestry licence, available from Tourist Offices – a one-, three- or seven-day permit will cost you 60 Kuna (£ 5.60), 150 Kuna (£ 14.00) and 250 Kuna (£ 23.40) respectively, and covers a two-piece rod with a maximum of three hooks. Various other restrictions may apply in particular places, or for particular fish (see *www.find-croatia.com/fishing-croatia/*).

Kayaking, Rafting and Canoeing There has been an explosion in both fresh-water and salt-water kayaking and rafting in Croatia, with single or multi-day tours widely available. This should always be done through official white-water agencies, and you can check out the Croatian Rafting Association's website at *www.rasah.hr*. The most popular rivers for kayaking, rafting and canoeing are the Kupa, the Dobra, the Mreznica, the Korana, the Una, the Zrmanja, the Krka and the Cetina.

Sailing There can be few places on earth more suited to sailing holidays than Croatia's Adriatic coast. With a deeply indented coastline and over a thousand islands, you can drop anchor in a deserted bay or moor in an all-mod-cons marina. Sailing holidays can include instruction, from beginners to advanced, or you can simply hire a boat, with or without captain and crew. A wide range of companies offer sailing holidays and boat hire – the Croatia Holiday Information booklet (available from the Croatian National Tourist Office, 162–164 Fulham Palace Road, Hammersmith London W6 9ER(☏ 020-8563-7979, *www. croatia.hr*) contains details of no fewer than 31 companies, offering a wide variety of packages, from family 'learn-to-sail' holidays to luxury yacht charter, 'oldtimer' cruises to flotilla sailing to bareboat, skippered or crewed yacht hire. You can go for an off-the-peg or a bespoke package. And if you don't want to be all that hands-on, you can simply sign on for a cruise. (Look at *www.sailingholidays.com*, *www. setsail.co.uk*, *www.sail-croatia.com* and many, many more.)

Getting Children Interested In Croatia

For a smooth holiday with the family, getting everyone involved from the start in the planning and preparation stages is essential. It will help you gauge what may or may not be enjoyable abroad and what is realistic in terms of an itinerary, as well as building up interest and expectation before the trip:

● Involve the children in the planning, and give them some control over where you're going.

● Ask them to research Croatia: capital city, main regions, language, best buys and so on. Have family quizzes based on this information.

Croatian Beaches

There is no disguising the fact that Croatia is not really the place to go for traditional beach holidays – buckets and spades, sandcastles, donkeys on the beach, that sort of thing. The reason's quite simple – there are very few sandy beaches in Croatia. So where beaches are mentioned in brochures or guide books, you should picture in your mind, not miles of golden sand, but lots of rounded pebbles, or, all too often, lots of quite abrasive builders' gravel. Indeed, in many parts of Croatia there is simply rock, and in some places you'll see wooden platforms suspended above the rock on metal frames, or platforms and steps cut into the rock itself.

Although there is, then, a distinct absence of sand, being at the seaside in Croatia has many advantages. The coast is clean, and the sea in most places is crystal clear – at times you can't see the water at all, and it looks as if boats are suspended in mid air. This is partly because of the absence of sand (it's an ill wind and all that), and partly because the currents that sweep the Croatian coast come from relatively unpolluted areas like Albania, rather than from the highly polluted Italian coast across the Adriatic. As a result Croatia can boast 80 blue flag beaches. And because of building restrictions (no building is allowed within 100 metres of the Adriatic), the nightmare developments that have ruined beautiful coastlines in other parts of Europe have not been permitted here (Croatia looked at the experience of parts of Spain, and learned the lesson). There are no theme parks or massed holiday amusements either – which is boring or blissful, depending on your priorities.

The clear water along Croatia's coastline brings ideal conditions for snorkelling and diving (with wrecked ships and aeroplanes to look at) and encourages a wealth of marine life.

There are ideal conditions for other water sports along the Dalmatian and Istrian coasts. The usual flat calm, with the seaward protection of Croatia's many islands means that sea kayaking is popular all along the coast (and especially in Dubrovnik). Sports that depend on the existence of wind are also blessed – the Bura, the Mistral and the Jura ensure a regular supply of motive force for windsurfers. One of the most popular beaches for this activity is Zlatni Rat near Bol on Brač. Other beaches worth trying are Viganj near Orebić on the Pelješac Peninsula, Premantura near Pula.

For the best family beaches try Copacabana on the Babin kuk Peninsula just outside Dubrovnik (lots of water sports and sea slides), Brela on the Makarska Riviera (pebbles, but a gently sloping sea bottom), Rajska Plaža at Lopar on Rab (sandy beach and shallow sea) or any of several sandy beaches around Nin, north of Zadar. The islands of the Zadar Archipelago also have a good name.

● Let them help with drawing up lists for packing, and let each child have his/her own suitcase and back pack.

● Encourage children to put together a scrapbook of pictures and text about the places you'll be visiting – there's lots of material available in travel brochures and on the Internet, and from the tourist boards.

● Get the children to send to national and regional tourist boards for information and maps – they love getting mail.

● Suggest that they research the airline or ferry company with which you're travelling, find out the planes or boats you're likely to be on.

● Let them practice currency conversion and language pronunciation for Croatia.

● Get them to research any particular interest of their own as it applies in Croatia – football, horse riding, tennis, stamp collecting.

On holiday here's a few tips:

● If possible, let each child have a digital camera – they love taking pictures. If that's not possible, let them take pictures with the family camera.

● Have limerick competitions about the places you visit.

● Take your time – sounds simple but it isn't always the case.

● Let the children have a say in where you go next.

● Take addresses with you, so that the children can play their part in writing postcards home.

INSIDER TIP »

Croatia goes in for a lot of statues and imaginative public art – there always seems to be something interesting to see in its towns and cities. Research some statues and landmarks online or from the tourist board before you go and then see if can try spotting them once you've landed.

FAST FACTS: CROATIA

American Express Services can be accessed through the following Atlas Travel Agency offices:

Zrinjevac 17,
Zagreb, Croatia 10000;
📞 01-487-3064.

Sv. Djurdja 1,
Dubrovnik, Croatia 20000;
📞 020-442-574.

Eufrazijeva 63,
Porec, Croatia 52440;
📞 052-434-813.

Nepotova 4,
Split, Croatia 21000;
📞 021-343-055.

Business Hours Most shops are open Monday–Friday 8am–8pm, Saturdays 8am–2 or 3pm. Some shops retain the long mid-day break and close between noon and 4pm. Some shops work through during the winter, and change to the long mid-day break in the summer.

Hours can be longer in summer anyway, especially in holiday areas and in cities. Most shops are closed on Sundays, though some supermarkets and larger shops in bigger cities are open on Sunday mornings. Some supermarkets are open 24 hours a day. Office hours are generally 8am–4pm, Monday to Friday. For bank opening hours, see 'Money' earlier in this chapter.

Currency See 'Money'earlier in this chapter.

Drinking Laws Alcoholic drinks are served in *kavanas* (cafés) or, for the younger crowd, in *kafics* (café-bars) or pubs, as well as being available in supermarkets. Although some of them open very early (as early as 6am), they are not allowed to serve alcohol until 9am. Closing time is normally 11pm, though this is often extended in summer.

Electricity 220 volts 50 AC. Sockets are continental two-pin type, so UK and Irish visitors will need an adaptor.

Embassies and Consulates
Embassy of the United Kingdom of Great Britain and Northern Ireland:

I. Lučiśa 4,
10000 Zagreb;
☎ 01-600–9100.

Consulate General of Ireland:
Turinina 3,
10000 Zagreb;
☎ 01-667-4455 and 241-3900.

Emergencies Dial ☎ 92 for the police, ☎ 93 for the fire brigade, ☎ 94 for an ambulance, ☎ 987 for roadside assistance, ☎ 9155 for search and rescue. The Europe-wide emergency number is ☎ 112.

Internet Access Most towns and cities in the holiday areas have Internet access, whether in cyber-cafés, hotel lobbies or in hotel rooms. An increasing number of establishments have Wi-Fi. Using ordinary phones for dial-up connection, while OK in theory, can actually be a nightmare – it's probably better to use one of the public access points. Charges for Internet access vary enormously, from 20 Kuna (£ 1.90) upwards – best to check before you spend hours online.

Language English is widely spoken among tourist-board professionals, and hotel and bar staff in holiday areas. However, German (in the east) and Italian (in the west and south) are by far the most common second languages. Croatian is not as difficult to pronounce as it might appear from its fearsome clots of consonants, so a good phrase book and pocket dictionary will get you a long way. For the most common words and phrases and a guide to pronunciation see 'Language' on p.251.

Mail Stamps are available from Post Offices, newsagents and tobacco kiosks. Postcards cost 4 Kuna (36p) to EU countries, 5

E-Mail Monkeys

In Croatia, if you ask for an e-mail address, you'll soon hear them talking about monkeys. At first it's a bit confusing – I'd never come across the term before. What have cute little simians to do with cyberspace? But 'monkey' is their term for the '@' sign. And you can see why – doesn't it look like a little monkey, reaching over its head to scratch the opposite armpit? Don't you love it?

(45p) Kuna to the USA. Allow 4–10 days for delivery. Letters are priced by weight. If you are sending a parcel, staff will want to inspect the contents before you seal it. Post boxes – painted yellow – are situated in a variety of public places, and in most hotel foyers.

Maps The maps in this book are designed to help with orientation. To explore the country in any detail it is a good idea to invest in an up-to-date regional map before you arrive. These are widely available in the UK and will also be available at all major bookshops in Croatia and at Croatian filling stations, newsagents, and the Croatian National Tourist Office.

Mobile Phones See 'The 21st Century Traveller' (p.32).

Newspapers and Magazines Very few Croatian newsagents stock English language newspapers and magazines.

Pets Although dogs and cats can be taken into Croatia temporarily, it is a much better option to make sure that your pet is adequately housed and cared for at home while you are on holiday. If you do plan to take your pet with you make sure you have a valid International Certificate showing that their vaccinations are up-to-date, and they are fitted with a microchip or clearly marked with their International Certificate number. Possibly dangerous breeds (pit bull terriers, for example) will not be allowed into Croatia. Ask your local vet for advice on taking pets abroad.

Pharmacies Pharmacies (*ljekarna*) keep shop hours, but all those in a particular area will have a rota for out-of-hours opening, posted in their windows. As well as selling over-the-counter medicines, pharmacies will also offer first aid advice.

Police The Croatian police are polite and helpful to tourists, though few of them can speak English. Always have a means of identification on you such as a driving licence or passport. The emergency number is (℡ 92).

Smoking Smoking is widespread in Croatia, and most Croatians consider it one of their human rights to smoke where they like. So even in no-smoking areas, you may find that the international no-smoking sign is ignored.

Street Names Many addresses in the rural areas have 'BB' after the street name. This stands for 'Bez Broj' which means 'without number'.

Taxes VAT is charged on most goods at 22% (with a reduced rate of 8½% on food, books and accommodation). If your total receipt(s) for one day for a single retailer exceeds 500 Kuna (£ 46.80), ask for a form PDV-P form. This then needs to be stamped at the border as you leave Croatia, and returned to the shop with the number of the account into which you want the refund paid (by post, since you're hardly likely to be going back there yourself). Government literature claims that you will then get a refund within 15 days – I'd give it a year. There is also a non-refundable tax on excursions and hotel rooms. Further details can be found at *www.carina.hr*.

Telephones The country dialling code for Croatia is ☎ 385. When ringing from the UK you should use the international code followed by the local code without the zero and then the local number. For example, to phone the Zagreb tourist information office (☎ 01-481-4051) from the UK or Ireland, dial ☎ 00385-1-481-4051. To phone the UK from Croatia you should use the UK code (0044) followed by the regional code (minus the 0) and then the number. Within Croatia, dial the city/area code and number in full – including the zero.

Direct local, national or regional calls can be made from public telephones. Public telephone booths do not accept change – you'll need a magnetic-strip telephone card, available at Post Offices and newsagents. They come in 25, 50, 100, 200 and 500 units. Peak rate is from 7am–4pm, there's a slight reduction (5%) from 4pm–10pm, and the rest of the time is off-peak with a 50% reduction. For international calls, have a large

Area Codes in Croatia

Zagreb and region	01
Dubrovnik and region	020
Split and region	021
Šibenik and region	022
Zadar	023
Istria	052

Football has a place in the Croatian psyche with which UK and Irish football fans can sympathise. As iconic Liverpool manager Bill Shankley once said, 'Football's not a matter of life and death – it's more important than that'.

Croatia didn't exist as a footballing nation until 1992, but certainly made up for lost time, reaching the quarter finals of their first ever international tournament, the 1996 European Championships and, two years later, finishing in third place in the World Cup, with Davor Suker (see below) finishing as top scorer. They have qualified for every World Cup they've entered. And this with a population of less than five million! Eat your hearts out every other footballing country in the world!

Croatia's most famous player is Davor Suker (known affectionately as Sukerman – as in 'Superman': get it?) who played for, among others, Arsenal, West Ham and Real Madrid. During a career that spanned 20 years, Suker was included in Pele's top 125 players in the world and was voted the best Croatian player of the last 50 years in a UEFA-sponsored poll.

It is often said that the war between Croatia and Serbia Montenegro didn't begin in 1991, as the history books say, but on the 13th May 1990 when Red Star Belgrade played Dinamo Zagreb at the Maksimir Stadium. The Red Star visiting supporters (also known as Delije – 'tough guys') and the home supporters – the Zagreb ultras ('the Bad Blue Boys') – started laying into each other, and the police (whom many Croatians suspected sided with Red Star, since a disproportionate number of police were ethnic Serbs) had to call for back up – more men, armoured vehicles and water cannon.

The hostilities lasted 70 minutes and, while the Red Star players retreated to the dressing rooms, the Zagreb players remained on the pitch. The 21-year old Zagreb midfielder Zvonimir Boban, seeing a Zagreb supporter being attacked by a policeman with a truncheon, toppled the offending policeman over with a well-aimed Cantona-type kick, allowing the supporter time to escape. Boban became an overnight hero for Croat nationalists around the world. In terms of his career, the gesture cost him a six-month worldwide ban, though he later went on to play for nine seasons with AC Milan as well as to captain the national team in the 1996 European Championships and the 1998 World Cup.

Many Croats saw the battle as the first step in resisting what they saw as 70 years of Serbian rule. Many of the supporters present enrolled in the Croatian Police or Army, as their Serbian opposition on that day joined the Serbian militia. As one newspaper said, 'The Serbo-Croat war was a follow-up to the Yugoslav football league by military means'. So much for sport extending the hand of friendship across national borders!

denomination card available, or phone from a Post Office booth. Hotel telephone charges can make your eyes water.

Time Zone Croatia is on Central European Time – GMT plus one hour. Clocks go forward an hour on the last Sunday in March, back an hour on the last Sunday in October.

Tipping No tips are expected for minor purchases (a cup of coffee, a beer) but round up by around 10% for full meals, rounds of drinks and so on. Rounding up is also a good idea for taxi drivers.

Water All public water supplies are safe.

3 Dubrovnik

Ask most people in the rest of Europe to name a Croatian city, and the majority will say 'Dubrovnik'. It is the country's most famous and talismanic city. There are many beautiful settlements along Croatia's Adriatic coast, stunning poems in stone and tile against a brilliant blue sea. But Dubrovnik, with its ancient city walls, picturesque palaces and vibrant culture, is not first among equals – it's the best. Hence the deep shock that electrified the world when the Yugoslav army bombed the city in the winter of 1991–2.

Some 15 years on, it's remarkable how quickly the damage has been made good. Dubrovnik is, apart from the rawness of some of the replacement roof tiles and masonry, as good as new – and as fascinating, both historically and architecturally, as it ever was. Admittedly, the new roof tiles weren't shaped over their maker's thigh in soft clay as the old ones were in the Middle Ages, but they're still a pretty good fit.

There's far more to Dubrovnik than its beauty. It also contains, in Lapad, Babin kuk and even the port area of Gruz, three districts that together make up one of the most pleasant, family-friendly holiday areas on the whole coast. So where better to start a book on Croatia than with the city that Lord Byron described as the 'Pearl of the Adriatic', whose stunning medieval architecture and extensive tourist infrastructure provides attractions, facilities, hotels and restaurants to suit every possible taste – especially families.

ESSENTIALS

Getting There

By Air There are many scheduled and chartered flights to Dubrovnik from the UK and Ireland. Dubrovnik's airport, Zračna Luka (*www.airport-dubrovnik.hr*), is near the village of Čilipi, about 20 km (12½ miles) southeast of the city centre. The red-and-white check livery of Croatia Airlines (*www.croatiaairlines.hr*) is a common sight in all of Croatia's airports. They run international flights to Zagreb from several European cities, and their regular internal flights mean that you can get anywhere in the country from the capital in under an hour. In addition, more and more budget airlines are targeting Croatia for new routes (to research this book, I flew from Doncaster to Pula).

Croatia Airlines run buses to and from the airport for their own flight arrivals and departures, but that's often not a lot of help – greater Dubrovnik is very spread out, so there will still be the problem of getting to your accommodation from the bus terminal. And if you're with any other airline, as is quite likely, you'll have to wait for the next Croatian Airlines bus. Better to bite the bullet and cough up around 250 Kuna (£ 24) for a taxi – agree a price before getting in (*www.taxiservicedubrovnik.com*).

By Car The A1 motorway (autocesta) from Zagreb to Split

is a delight to drive – uncrowded, beautifully engineered (with spectacular viaducts and tunnels), and relatively cheap. There are regular motorway service stations, though annoyingly some have restaurants and some don't – which means that, unless you're happy to manage on sandwiches, you might have to stop twice, once to refuel the car, again to refuel the family. Services are clean, well-organised, have pleasant indoor and outdoor seating, and have small but reasonably well-equipped playgrounds to help younger children let off steam.

Beyond Split it's a different story. The motorway ends in a huge building site (where the next stage – Split to Dubrovnik – is under construction. You can drive in towards Split, and then follow the coast road (the E65). It's pleasant enough, but there are a lot of twists and turns and you go through a lot of small towns – you'll be lucky to average 40 mph. There's an alternative inland road (the route number is 60) actually signposted from the end of the motorway, which is a far better bet – it feels counter-intuitive (you start off heading for the mountains) but is in fact a fast, straight main road which runs parallel to the coast road. And certainly don't believe maps that show the A1 motorway extending from Split to just before the Neum Corridor – it's still being built.

By Ferry Ferries operate between Dubrovnik and the islands and cities up the Croatian coast, as well as local services to the Elafiti Islands and Mljet. Consult the Dubrovnik Jadrolinija office in Gruž (☎ 020-418-000) or at Jadroagent at Radiča 32 (☎ 020-419-000).

By Bus Bus services operate between the Dubrovnik ferry port at Gruž and Zagreb, Zadar, Split, Šibenik, Rijeka, Orebić, and Korčula in Croatia, together with Mostar and Sarajevo in Bosnia and Međugorje in Herzegovina. The main Dubrovnik bus terminal is at Put Republike 19 (☎ 020-357-020).

VISITOR INFORMATION

The **Dubrovnik Tourist Office** is across the road from the Hilton Imperial at Starčevića 7 (☎ 020-427-591), 50 metres or so up from the Pile Gate. It offers a good selection of brochures and pamphlets, and also computers with Internet connection for checking e-mails and surfing the net. There's another branch on the main street – Stradun, or Placa – but it's nowhere near as well-resourced. You'll get a complete list of tourist offices from the **Dubrovnik Tourist Board** at Cvijete Zuzorić 1/11 (☎ 020-323-887), (*www.tzdubrovnik.hr*).

In addition, private tourist agencies also fulfil some of the functions of the Tourist Office. Try **The Tourist Information Centre** at Placa 1 (☎ 020-323-350), **Atlas Travel Agency** at

Dubrovnik's Old Town

Cira Carica 3 (📞 *020-442-855*) and **Metro Tours** at Šetalisšte Kralja Zvonimira 40A (📞 *020-437-320*).

A free monthly listings magazine (Dubrovnik Guide) is also available at the Tourist Office.

City Layout

The part of the Dubrovnik rightly celebrated in a million postcards and in vast tracts of tourist information is the stunningly picturesque Old Town. Yet this is only a small part of the modern city – a mere 4,000 out of a total population of 44,000 live within its walls. Beyond it, to the east, the city has started to spread up the hillside towards the main coast road – an area, called Ploče, with the Museum of Modern Art and a sprinkling of very upmarket hotels. To the west, it has colonised the whole of the Lapad/Babin Kuk peninsula, which has become not only a dormitory area for the thousands who work in the tourist industry, but also has large numbers of shops, hotels, apartments and restaurants, the pleasant Lapad Beach, and the big hotel and campsite complex centred on the Hotel President. Finally, between this peninsula and the mainland, the port and ferry terminal of Gruz teems with boats against the background of the elegant Franjo Tuđman Bridge. Hilly and attractive, with a rocky coast and lots of trees, the whole city is a delight to the eye.

A word about Dubrovnik addresses: they work much as ours do, except that the street number comes after rather than before the name of the street. The only complication is that, as is the case across Croatia, streets sometimes have two completely different names. So, to give the most obvious example, the main street in the old town is sometimes called Stradun, and sometimes called Placa. Confusing, but it really keeps you on your toes! An excellent street map (with the Old Town on one side and Greater Dubrovnik on the other) is available free from Tourist Offices and most hotels.

As regards exploring Dubrovnik, it makes sense to start with the Old Town. Then, if you have to go back home or the world ends, at least you've seen it. The rest of the city, though, is also very pleasant, and could hold its own with any other holiday area on the Adriatic. Finally, if you've still got time, take a leaf out of the locals' book and drive out of the city for the day.

The Neighbourhoods in Brief

The delightful **Old Town** contained within the city walls lies at the heart of Greater Dubrovnik. It's why everybody's here. Flagged, traffic-free, sustained by hand trolleys, little electric cars pulling trailers and,

Stradun

for only the heaviest grunt-work, small diesel wagons, it contains all the historic buildings, museums, shops, cafés, bars and restaurants (from the unutterably posh to the cheap-and-cheerful) you could ever hope to visit.

The relatively wide main street – **Stradun**, sometimes called Placa – runs roughly east/west from the **Pile Gate** and **Onofrio's Large Fountain** to the main square **Luža**, around which cluster a number of palaces and **Onofrio's Little Fountain**. East of this is the **Old Port**, south the **Cathedral**. South of Stradun, along its length, is a maze of little alleys, and to the north a series of lanes, often stepped, which climb steeply to the north wall of the city. There are only two hotels within the walls of the Old Town, and they're at the top end of expensive. Though not particularly child friendly, it might be worth a night's stay, just to be slap bang in the heart of things.

Beyond the city's eastern gate is **Ploče**, notable mainly for the nearest beach to the Old Town (Banje) and for some very upmarket hotels.

Stretching westward from the Old Town are the two suburbs of **Lapad** and **Babin kuk**, on either side of Lapad Beach. This is the area where most visitors to Dubrovnik stay – it's a bustling mixture of shops, cafés and restaurants that serve not only the visitors staying at its many hotels and private rooms, but also the local people who work in the tourist industry and in the

Little Fountain of Dubrovnik

docks. It also has the only campsite in greater Dubrovnik. For any extended stay in Dubrovnik, this is the best area for families with children – there's a good selection of hotels, a passable beach, lots of children's play areas, some lovely excursions out to the Elafiti Islands, and a calm, laid-back atmosphere.

Gruž, which lies on the mainland facing the north coast of the Lapad and Babin kuk Peninsula, contains Dubrovnik's main dock, along which are moored pleasure craft, excursion boats, ferries and cruise ships. It also has hotels and restaurants. **Lokrum**, east of the Old Town, is an island covered in trees with just enough of interest to persuade holidaymakers and locals to undertake the 15-minute ferry crossing (9am–6pm from the Old Port, 35 Kuna).

Getting Around

By Public Transport
Dubrovnik's public transport system (i.e. buses) is fast, efficient and easy-to-use. Buy tickets at your hotel or at a newspaper kiosk – at 8 Kuna (70p), they're 2 Kuna (18p) cheaper than if you buy them from the driver. You can buy as many tickets as you think you'll need for the day (at least two per person, to cover the ride there and back). Each ticket entitles you to up to an hour's use of the bus, and you activate it by feeding it into a machine as you get on. There are plans to introduce a daily ticket – it should be in place by 2007.

By Car If you've arrived in Dubrovnik by car, once you've parked it in the hotel car park or garage (if you're lucky) or on the street (if you're not), the best advice is to leave it there, and use it only if you're taking the family on an excursion. For travelling within Greater Dubrovnik, use the excellent bus service, or you could hire a taxi. Car hire is also available in Dubrovnik, try Hertz (Frana Supila 9, 📞 *020-425-000, www. hertz.com*), Avis (Vladimira Nazora 9 📞 *020-422–043, www. avis.com* or Mack (Frana Supila 3 📞 *020-423–747, www.rentacar-croatia.com*.

By Taxi Although taxis are more expensive than buses, for a family it might well be worth paying the extra, just for the convenience, especially as the buses (particularly at the end of the afternoon from the Pile Gate) can get very crowded. There are taxi ranks at both town gates, the bus station, Gruž and near Lapad post office. Radio cabs are available by phone on 970, or there are numerous individual private companies that can be contacted direct. One of the city's best known is Radulovic Ltd 0-98-725-769, email: *info@ taxiservicedubrovnik.com*. Their taxis are large Mercedes saloons, and fares vary from 35 Kuna (about £ 3.20) to the central hotels to 200 Kuna (about £ 18) to Cavtat. For larger families or groups of friends, they also have 8-seater minibuses, 15-seater minibuses and even a 19-seater coach. All vehicles can accommodate push-chairs, and if vehicles are pre-booked they can provide child seats.

Planning Your Outings

For outings to the Old Town, take plenty of water (or cups – there are several public drinking fountains in the town, and they're safe), try not to wear leather soles – the flagstones of the Old Town and its walls have been polished slick by a million feet, and make the children wear a hat (more easily said than done if they're feeling mutinous). If you're intending to walk the walls, take into account the age of your children – a complete circuit would be too much for youngsters, but there are four access points, so you can plan to do just a section. It would be a mistake to try to walk the walls and then do some heavy duty sightseeing: far better to aim for a blend of different types of activities – a swim, perhaps, or a leisurely paddle in a canoe.

The moat on either side of the Pile Gate (see p.68) contains a shady public garden (it's even got some play equipment) where you can rest up or have a picnic. There's swimming at Banje Beach in Ploče, at Lapad Beach and off the rocks in places from the base of the walls of the Old Town. The best-known off-rocks swimming is from the terraces of two bars called Buža I and Buža II – a scattering of tables perched on ledges carved in the rock. To find Buža I walk from the Cathedral down Ilije Šarake, then go through the door numbered 8–20 (opposite Konoba Ekvinocijo). For Buža II follow the signs for 'Cold Drinks with the Most Beautiful View' behind the Jesuit Church. There are steps cut into the rocks, and metal ladders and steps. Outside

Pile Gate

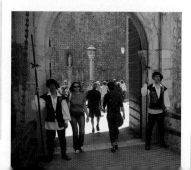

the city, the best swimming is off the island of Lokrum, though this is suitable only for older children who are strong swimmers. You can ring the changes by hiring canoes or rubber dinghies. (Kayaks can be hired from the cove between the Bokar Fortress and Lovrijenac, just down from the Pile Gate. ☎ *091-526-38-13, www.crochallenge.com*.)

Around the city there are lots of places where you can sit to catch your breath or breastfeed (perfectly acceptable in Croatia if you're discrete), and lots of pleasant outdoor cafés and restaurants at which to grab a drink or something to eat. Together with bus or railway stations, they are also the best bet for toilet visits. Public toilets as we know them in the UK are leg-crossingly rare. If you do find any, they'll be marked 'WC' or 'zahod'.

As for child-free evenings, most of the top-end hotels can arrange babysitting, though seem shy of sharing the practical details. All the parents of young children I've spoken to say that they would never consider using people they didn't know to look after their children abroad anyway, however well-qualified.

Dubrovnik Itineraries

If You Have 1 Day

If you have only one day, try to stand on the **gargoyle** and then walk around the **City Wall** (see p.66), starting as early as you can manage (they open at 8am). Have lunch in the Old Town, and in the afternoon take the ferry across to Lokrum (see p.78) and have a wander around.

If You Have 2 Days

Day 1 Spend Day 1 as above.

Day 2 Enjoy a round trip. Drive up the coast to **Trsteno** (see p.81) and have a look at the

The City Walls

The Old Town's Market

arboretum. Continue to Ston (p.82), wander around the village, the castle and the salt works, and grab some lunch. Continue to Trpanj (see p.82), get in line, buy tickets for the car ferry to Ploče (see p.82) then have a coffee in one of the cafés that look out on the ferry quay while waiting for the boat to arrive. From Ploče, return down the coast road to Dubrovnik, crossing a little bit of Bosnia-Herzegovina at Neum. You won't need a visa, but even though they often don't bother to ask for a passport, it's as well to have it available.

If You Have 3 Days

With 3 days you can do some of the heavier duty sightseeing in the Old Town, and see more of the rest of Greater Dubrovnik.

Days 1–2 Spend Days 1 and 2 as above.

Day 3 Join one of the guided tours of the Old Town, or better still, negotiate your own with the family. Your route might take in Onofrio's Large Fountain, the Franciscan Monastery, the Synagogue, Sponza Palace, Luža Square, Orlando's Column, Dubrovnik Cathedral (especially the Treasury), Dubrovnik Aquarium and Maritime Museum, Gundulićeva Poljana and the Old Port. Then make your way out to Lapad for a swim, and for the children to enjoy the rides, bouncy castles and so on near the beach.

If You Have 4 Days or More

Days 1–3 Spend Days 1–3 as above.

Day 4 On your fourth day you can do one of the following:
Spend a day in pleasant Cavtat (see p.84). You can get

there by car, and park in the centre of the village, or catch a boat from the Old Port (the hourly trip takes about 50 minutes, and costs 30 Kuna (£ 2.80).

Take a trip to the **Mljet National Park** (see p.89) or **Elafite Islands** (see p.88).

Watch the folk dancing in **Čilipi** (see p.86) if you happen to be around on a Sunday.

Try out one of the activities mentioned in 'For Active Families' (see p.90).

FAST FACTS: DUBROVNIK

(see also 'Fast Facts' in Chapter 2 (p.49))

American Express accessed through the Atlas Travel Agency at:

Sv. Djurdja 1, Dubrovnik, Croatia 20000, ☎ *020-442-574*.

ATMs there are cash machines through Greater Dubrovnik.

Banks open from 7.30am–7pm Monday to Friday and from 7.30– 11.30am Saturday. Some banks close for lunch.

Business Hours in Dubrovnik, food shops and department stores are usually open from 7:30am to 8pm. Non-government offices generally work 8:30am to 5pm Monday to Friday.

Credit Cards widely accepted at hotels and restaurants – look out

for the logo, or ask before you order.

Electricity as in the rest of Croatia, electricity in Dubrovnik is 220 volts, 50 AC, and sockets are continental two-pin (so UK and Irish nationals will need an adaptor).

Emergencies police ☎ *92*, Fire ☎ *93*, Ambulance ☎ *94*, Roadside assistance ☎ *987*, Search and Rescue ☎ *9155*, Europe-wide emergency number ☎ *112*.

Holidays see 'When to Go', p.25.

Hospital in emergencies, head for the Dubrovnik General Hospital (☎ *020-431-777*).

Internet Café Netcafe Internet Bar (no. 21 in the middle of Prijeko St.'s restaurant block). Open 9am to 11pm daily. Internet access is also available at the Dubrovnik Tourist Office opposite the Hilton Imperial.

Pharmacy Dubrovnik pharmacies have varied opening hours: they are open in the morning and afternoon Monday to Friday, but only in the morning Saturday. Almost all accept credit cards.

Telephone public telephone boxes accept only phone cards available from newspaper stands and post offices. They have a list of international codes posted (easily identified by the flag of the relevant countries), and the charge per minute (3.5 Kuna (33p) to the UK and Ireland).

Time Zone Dubrovnik, like the rest of Croatia, is on Central European Time (GMT plus 1 hour). Daylight saving time starts at the end of March and ends on the last Sunday of October.

Tipping generally not expected, though it is appreciated. Certainly, round bills up.

Tourist Information

Dubrovnik Tourist Board
Ante Starčićeva 7,
☎ 020-323-887.

Dubrovnik Neretva County Tourist Board
Cvijete Zuzoric 1/1,
20000 Dubrovnik
☎ 020-324–999.

Water tap water is safe in all parts of Croatia.

Weather the climate in Dubrovnik is similar to that of Greece, with mild winters and hot, dry summers. Daily forecasts are available at *www. dubrovnik-online.com/english/ weather.php*.

WHAT TO SEE AND DO

Children's Top 10 Attractions

Standing on the gargoyle
Great fun for young and old.

Indeed, the young are usually better at it, given their frequently lesser girth. See p.70.

Celebrity signatures in the Franciscan Monastery
Including, from the UK, the Queen, Margaret Thatcher and Prince Charles. See p.69.

Treasury of the Cathedral Not only glowing with jewels and precious metals, but choc-a-bloc with ghoulish body parts belonging to a variety of saints, plus the nappies of the infant Jesus! See p.73.

Aquarium Get up close and personal with thousands of sea creatures, from water-spitting archer fish to gruesome looking eels, at the Aquarium. See p.74.

Maritime Museum Just upstairs in St. John's Fortress from the Aquarium, the Maritime Museum illustrates Dubrovnik's fascinating naval history with hundreds of ship models and onboard artefacts. See p.74.

The docks at Gruž The bustle of small boats, the coming and going of Jadrolinija ferries and great cruise ships, and the chance to see reconstructed galleons like the Karaka moored at the quay. See p.79.

Lapad Beach amusements
All the fun of the fair, from bouncy castles to children's rides, merry-go-rounds to toy-stalls, ball-pools to inflatable slides. See p.78.

Elafite Islands By foot-ferry from Gruž, or on excursion boats from Lapad Beach, the Elafite Islands offer sparse population, lovely walks and secluded beaches. See p.88.

Mljet National Park Unspoiled nature, two stunning 'lakes' (actually salt water inlets), and miles of footpaths and cycle-tracks to explore. See p.89.

The fortifications at Ston The great fortifications built to protect the Republic of Dubrovnik's northern frontiers link two villages famous for salt production, oyster beds and fish restaurants.

The Old Town

City Wall ★ ★ ★ MOMENT ALL AGES

Walking around Dubrovnik's massive walls, you became aware of the summit of Mount Srđ, towering over the city to the north. This was where the Serbian army and its allies set up their artillery and, in November 1991, shocked the world by starting to bombard the Old Town. The assault lasted until May 1992. Now, looking over the roofs of the city, the only sign of the damage was the large areas of raw new tiles. Seeing the tourist-thronged streets, hearing the shouts of children swimming far below, it was difficult not to reflect on the indomitability of the human spirit.

Allow at least half a day for a complete circuit of the walls, including frequent rest stops.

By far the best way of getting an overview (literally) of Dubrovnik's Old Town is to walk around the city walls. There are four access points – the Pile Gate through the western wall, and Ploče Gate, St. John's Fortress and the fourth near the Rector's Palace along the eastern side. Older teens could probably manage the whole circuit, younger ones might manage a half circuit from (say) the Pile Gate to one of the others, whilst younger children could take advantage of the much more frequent access points, pleasant seaward views, and little cafés, along the eastern wall.

There's a 50 Kuna (£ 4.60) charge (20 Kuna £ 1.80) for children), and the point is made on the notices that the money is used for maintenance – you're not being rooked by a city with an eye for the main chance.

From the walls you get superb views across the city's roofs, down into the port and out to sea. But be warned: it gets very hot, there's a lot of step-climbing, and it seems a lot longer than its two or so kilometres. So take it easy, have plenty to drink and schedule in one or two stops along the way.

High spots of the walk (going clockwise from the Pile Gate) are the 15th century Minčeta Fortress, the Ploče Gate, St. John's Fortress and the Bokar Fortress.

> **INSIDER TIP**
>
> Avoid the mid-day heat. Access to the wall is from 8am and until 7.30pm, so a very early or late start means that the hottest part of the day can be spent elsewhere.

DUBROVNIK'S OLD TOWN

Attractions ●
City Wall 1
Dominican Monastery
  and Museum 2
Dubrovnik Aquarium
  and Maritime Museum 3
Dubrovnik Cathedral 4
Franciscan Monastery 5
Gargoyle 6
Gundulićeva Poljana 7
Luža Square 8
Old Port 9
Onofrio's Large Fountain 10
Onofrio's Small Fountain 11
Orlando's Column 12
Pile Gate 13
Rector's Palace 14
Sponza Palace 15
St. Saviour's Church 16
Stradun 17
Synagogue 18

Accommodation ■
Hotel Stari Grad 6
Hilton Imperial 7

Dining ◆
Mea Culpa 3
Restaurant Jadran 4
Restaurant Aquarius 6
Proto 7
Porat 8
Atlas Club Nautika 9

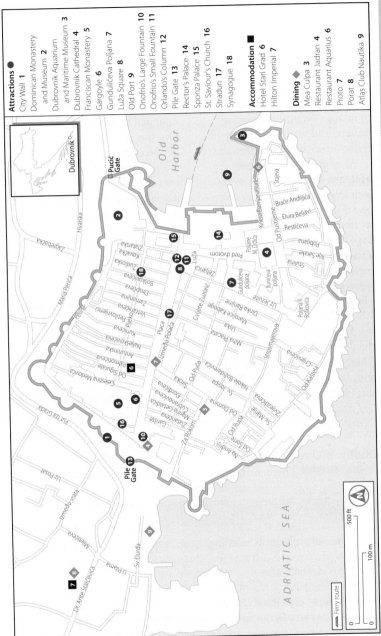

Pile Gate ★ **ALL AGES** Most visitors to the Old Town enter via the Pile Gate – the main bus routes terminate in the square just outside, and it's the main dropping off point for tour buses. The Tourist Office is just up the road, and there's a fountain in the square, so it would be as well to take on board information leaflets, and water the family liberally, before setting off into town.

After crossing the stone bridge to the outer gate, overseen during the season by a couple of sheepish guards in medieval costume (bound to set the children giggling), you'll see a statue of St. Blaise, the city's patron saint, looking down from between the drawbridge chains. Once through the gate, take a look up into the archway on the inside – all the gear for raising the drawbridge is still in place. There's an interior gate as well, with its own statue of St. Blaise, this time a 20th-century version by Croatian sculptor Ivan Meštrović (see p.72).

Onofrio's Large Fountain
★ ★ ★ **ALL AGES** The first thing you'll see on getting into the Old Town is Onofrio's Large Fountain, a circular colonnaded structure with a domed brick roof and 16 water spouts. Built in the mid 15th century to distribute water brought in from the Dubrovnik River (12 km away) by aqueduct, it was designed by water-engineer Onofrio de la Cava, principally to get people to wash before entering the city – a futile anti-plague measure. Fill your water bottles if you haven't already done so, the water is perfectly safe to drink. You can even soak the children's hats if it's a particularly hot day (assuming you've managed to get them to wear hats).

St. Saviour's Church **ALL AGES**
As you pass through the Pile Gate, the steps up onto the walls are immediately to your left. Next to them is St. Saviour's Church, an attractive little Renaissance building (note the typical trefoil gable over a rose window), which is now used for contemporary art displays, concerts and recitals. Built around 1520 as thanks to God for

A City That Was Once a Republic

At one time Dubrovnik was an island. Stradun, the spine of the Old Town, which runs east from Pile Gate to Luža Square, is the city's main street and marks where a channel once was when Dubrovnik was surrounded by water. In the 14th century Dubrovnik was called Ragusa and was actually a maritime city-state. The republic was founded on maritime trade and ruled an area of southern Dalmatia, including the islands of Lastovo and Mljet. It reached its peak in the 15th and 16th centuries before being conquered by Napoleon Bonaparte's army in 1808.

The 1667 Earthquake

Even by the standards of Adriatic earthquakes, the one that destroyed Dubrovnik in April 1667 was horrific. Not only did the first shock knock down most of the buildings in the city, but successive aftershocks also initially set fire to what was left, then created a series of tidal waves that smashed into the ruins, drowning many of the survivors. By the end of the day, 5000 people – over half the population – had perished.

Rebuilding was at first slow as the survivors had to negotiate to keep Turkish and Venetian vultures at bay, but when it got into its stride during the early decades of the 18th century, the city was rebuilt with a delightfully harmonious unity given to very few human settlements. So it could be said that Dubrovnik owes its fame and beauty to that 17th century disaster.

delivery from one of the area's periodic earthquakes, it's said that the citizens were so grateful that even snooty aristocratic ladies got their hands dirty by helping to carry building materials.

Between the Pile Gate and the Franciscan Monastery at Stradun 2. Daily 9am–7pm.

Franciscan Monastery

ALL AGES Next to St. Saviour's is an alley leading to the splendid Franciscan Monastery, which is not to be missed by those interested in musical notation (it has priceless manuscripts tracing its development). The monastery's museum also has what it claims is the oldest pharmacy in Europe (the modern-day shop at the entrance can still stock you up with medicines and pain-killers). Look out for the silver votive offerings submitted over the centuries as offerings for divine intervention to help with a variety of medical conditions. There

is one in the shape of a leg, which was (unsurprisingly) for a pain in the leg. Another is shaped like a woman with a big stomach that was to ensure the health of an unborn baby.

Within the complex there are peaceful cloisters where you can stretch your legs. Here, look out for the framed signatures of famous visitors to the monastery beneath pictures of their national

Franciscan Monastery

Can You Spot?

flag. The Union Jack appears three times, with the signatures of the Queen, Prince Charles and Margaret Thatcher.

Monastery museum: 10 Kuna (95p). Summer 9am–6pm. Hours during the rest of the year vary.

Balancing on the Gargoyle

★ ★ ★ MOMENT AGES 3 AND UP Back on Stradun, look at the wall to the right of the alley. Sticking out about 15 centimetres above the ground is a gargoyle-like feature – it looks a bit like an owl with a moustache – which has, over the years, provided Dubrovnik residents with hours of fun. It has become a tradition for people to try and balance on it, facing the wall, with their arms outstretched.

Depending on who you ask, it was either a rite of passage for testosterone-fuelled young men trying to outdo each other in how long they could stand on the stone before falling off, or it was a way of making your dreams come true: you had to make a wish, then balance on the gargoyle and remove your shirt without falling off. If you succeeded, your wish

would come true. Personally I'd take the latter with a pinch of salt – I don't think it would be physically possible to remove your shirt without stumbling. Whatever the truth, there are brilliant opportunities for a family competition here!

The Synagogue AGES 5 AND UP

Just off Stradun, up the narrow and atmospheric Jews' Street (Žudioska Ulica), is Dubrovnik's tiny synagogue – it's on the second floor of a little town house, with a small museum on the ground and first floors.

From the 16th century onwards Dubrovnik began to acquire a reputation as a haven of tolerance compared to most other places in Europe.

The city reaped its rewards on earth as well as in heaven – the Jews attracted to the city by its relative safety were highly educated, and began to exert an influence on its development, through the jewellery trade, finance and local government, out of all proportion to their numbers.

Monday–Friday, 9am to noon.

The Dominican Monastery and Museum ALL AGES

There's not much to detain you here unless there are any members of the family who are interested in 16th and 17th century religious art, though the Monastery church has a nice painting of St. Dominic by 19th century Cavtat painter Vlaho Bukovac, and a compelling statue of Motherhood by Ivan Meštrović (see box). There's also a delightful colonnaded cloister with an ornate well, which is a vision of cool leafy shade on a hot day.

Sv. Dominika 4. Museum admission 10 Kuna (95p). Daily 9am–6pm.

Sponza Palace ★★

AGES 5 AND UP On the corner of Luža Square, the Old Town's central meeting place, thronged with visitors and locals alike, is the 16th century Sponza Palace. Once the city's Custom House and Mint, it is now used for concerts and exhibitions, and is considered to be one of the city's most beautiful buildings.

One of the most affecting rooms in the palace is the 'Memorial Room of the Defenders of Dubrovnik'. There's probably no better way

Sponza Palace

to introduce children to the realities of war. When the city was bombarded by the Yugoslav Army in 1991–2, the casualty rate of 300 dead (around 200 members of the army and navy, and about 100 police) didn't sound that bad. But when you see portrait photographs of most of them, mounted in rows on the walls, it brings home the fact that these were real people – largely young men – who lost their lives in the war. Together with photographs of the bombardment, video clips, and written commentary, the exhibition is perhaps a useful antidote to the gung-ho sanitised version of war that children are so often subjected to.

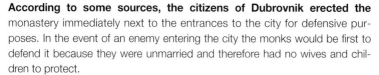

DID YOU KNOW? 〉〉 **Single Monks** 〈〈

According to some sources, the citizens of Dubrovnik erected the monastery immediately next to the entrances to the city for defensive purposes. In the event of an enemy entering the city the monks would be first to defend it because they were unmarried and therefore had no wives and children to protect.

Ivan Meštrović

It's difficult to go anywhere in Croatia without becoming aware of its greatest modern sculptor, Ivan Meštrović. And as you find out about his life, it is difficult to think of a more inspirational story for your children.

Born in 1883 into an impoverished working class family, he spent most of his formative years in the tough mid-Dalmatian heartland town of Otavice. Having taught himself to read, write and draw, he was taken on by a local stonemason and won, at the age of 18, a place at the Viennese Academy. He proved to be a gifted pupil and was fulfilling large-scale commissions by the time he was 22.

A great left-wing Croat and Yugoslav patriot, he attracted a following in Britain (he had a one-man show at the V&A in 1915), became a great supporter of the establishment of Yugoslavia after World War 1, and spent the period up to World War 2 working on commissions and as Rector of the Academy of Fine Arts in Zagreb (from 1923).

In 1941 Meštrović was imprisoned by Croatia's quisling Ustase government, but was quickly released as a result of ferocious international pressure. He paused briefly in Italy, then Switzerland, finally settling in the USA, where he spent the rest of his life as a sculptor and academic.

On his death in 1962, his body was returned to his homeland, where it is buried in an Otavice mausoleum, which he designed himself.

Look out for his work – it's everywhere!

Luža. 📞 020-321-032. Free admission, except for some exhibitions. Daily 9am–2pm, though times vary during exhibitions.

Luža Square ALL AGES In Luža Square, which marks the end point of Stradun, you can see Onofrio's Little Fountain (whose big brother stands at the other end of Stradun), and the lofty 15th century Bell Tower. Outside St. Blaise Church is

Orlando's Column AGES 5 AND UP Topped by a statue of Roland (or Orlando) in full armour, the column was erected in 1418–19 as a tribute to Orlando for defeating the Saracens after they besieged the city (including a

duel with the memorably named pirate 'Smelly Breath').

Orlando must have been quite old, though – the siege of Dubrovnik took place over a century after his time.

The column became in many ways a symbol of the Old Town, and a rallying point where notices were posted, announcements made, meetings held, and punishments meted out. Later, it was used as the emblem of Dubrovnik as an independent city-state – an emblem that took on new life during the Patriotic War (see p.248) in the 1990s, when a freedom ('Libertas') banner was flown from the top. This is now done each year at the beginning of Dubrovnik's famous Summer Festival (see p.27).

The Rector's Palace ALL AGES

A short walk from Orlando's Column down Pred Dvorom brings you to the Rector's Palace. Much rebuilt (it was used as a gunpowder store in the 15th century and blew up twice) the Rector's Palace was once Dubrovnik's seat of government, where the elected Rector governed the city. He wasn't allowed long to settle into his role, however, and served for only one month in office, separated from his family and virtually imprisoned. Following this, he could relax for a while – he was given a get-out-of-jail-free card that lasted for two years, exempting him from service for that period. Today, the palace houses the City Museum, and has lots of furniture and displays relating to the time of the Ragusa Republic. Much of the furniture is from the correct period but not original to the building. Concerts are also held in the lovely courtyard – hence the presence of a shrouded grand piano. The palace is also a popular venue for weddings.

Pred Dvorom 3. ☎ *020-321-497. Admission 15 Kuna (£ 1.40). Summer daily 9am–7pm; winter Mon–Sat 9am–2pm.*

Dubrovnik Cathedral (Church of the Assumption) ★ ★ ★

ALL AGES Dubrovnik's 17th–18th century cathedral is understated and plain compared to many.

It is the last in a line of three (the previous one was destroyed by the great earthquake of 1667), and the city plans to restore the remains of the previous two and install information boards to explain the history of the building. Legend has it that the original cathedral was built using a donation by Englishman King Richard the Lionheart, which was made as an offering to God for his delivery from shipwreck in the vicinity on his way home from the Third Crusade. Killjoy archaeologists, however, say that the foundations of the original cathedral pre-date Richard's time.

While the Cathedral should be of interest to British schoolchildren because of its Lionheart connection, the contents of its **Treasury** should be of interest to children everywhere. Glowing with precious metals (especially gold), it is stuffed full of reliquaries, containing the bones or mummified body parts of a variety of saints. Since the reliquaries are often in the shape of the bones or body parts they contain, the treasury looks like nothing so much as a storeroom for prosthetic limbs, with elaborately decorated arms, legs, and heads scattered about. Pride of place goes to one containing (allegedly) the skeletons of two of the children murdered during Herod's 'slaughter of the innocents', and another which houses one of Jesus's nappies! What small child could fail to be enchanted?

*Poljana Marina Drižca. Treasury 10
Kuna (95p). Mon–Sat 9am–5:30pm;
Sun 11am–5:30pm.*

Dubrovnik Aquarium and
Maritime Museum ★ ALL AGES

Down an alley opposite the
entrance to the Cathedral stands
the massive St. John's Fortress,
which looks out across the Old
Port it was designed to protect.
It now houses, on the ground
floor, a really nice, if limited,
aquarium – limited because it
has quite rightly confined itself
to species that are found in the
southern Adriatic. So unless you
intend to spend most of your
holiday under water, this is the
best way of seeing indigenous
marine life.

Sure-fire hits with children
of all ages are live examples of
the fish they are otherwise most
likely to encounter on a plate,
together with massive moray eels,
the smaller congers, a fascinating
octopus, and the most celebrated
and, at an alleged 300 years of
age, certainly oldest inhabitant of
the aquarium, a huge sea turtle
that environmental groups want
released into the wild (where,

aquarium-supporters counter, it
would almost certainly perish).
All tanks are fed by water from
the sea.

On the next two floors
of the fortress a well-presented
Maritime Museum stretches
away under barrel vaulting.
Tools, weapons, flags of all
nations, along with numerous
models of ships from different
eras make for an interesting
half hour.

*Damjana Jude 2, St. John's Fortress.
📞 021-427-937. Admission to both
museum and aquarium 20 Kuna
(£ 1.90) adults, 10 Kuna (95p)
children. Aquarium summer daily
9am–9pm; winter Mon–Sat
9am–1pm. Maritime Museum
summer daily 9am–6pm; winter
Tues–Sun 9am–6pm. The Aquarium
and Museum are also accessible
from the City Walls.*

Down another alley at the back
of the Cathedral lies

Gundulićeva Poljana ALL AGES

If you venture down an alley at
the back of Dubrovnik Cathedral
you will find this open-air market, selling fruit and vegetables,
lavender products, lace and a

Carrying Stuff In Old Dubrovnik

Dubrovnik's Old Town is traffic-free. Yet huge volumes of food, drink
materials and goods have to be delivered to its cafés, bars, restaurants,
hotels and shops. Similarly, thousands of tons of waste have to be
removed, and heavy materials like stone delivered to the many renovation projects currently underway in the city.

So how do they carry all this stuff? And what type of power do they
use?

I have spotted at least three types of conveyance, using three different types of power, being used in the old city. How many can you spot?

The Old Port

variety of multi-coloured beverages in oddly shaped bottles. The stalls, sheltered under red and white parasols cluster around a statue of Ivan Gundulić, the 16th–17th century poet whose likeness you can find on the 50 Kuna note. Look out for old-fashioned scales in use, and an elegant flight of steps at the southern end of the square.

Žudioska Ulica 5. Summer daily 10am–8pm; winter Mon–Fri 10am–1pm.

The Old Port ALL AGES The Old Port, behind the Rector's Palace (see p.73), is a pleasant place to stroll where you can watch the island ferries come and go, as well small fishing boats and excursion launches plying their trade. There are plenty of benches, which are shaded at the right time of day (especially during the afternoon), as well as cafés and restaurants galore.

Beyond the Ploče Gate

Beyond the Old Town's eastern gate are the 16th century Revelin Fortress, and the Lazareti – a group of houses and courtyards once used for quarantining approaching visitors during times of plague, and now an arts-and-crafts complex which is also used for displays of folk music and dancing. Beyond the Lazareti is the Modern Art Museum.

📞 *020-426–590. 15 Kuna (£ 1.40). Tues–Sun 10am–1pm, 2pm–5pm.*

Top 10 Family Experiences

Walking the walls of the Old Town: terrific views inland to Mount Srđ, up and down the coast, out to sea, and above all, across the tumbled rooftops, towers and cupolas of the Old Town. See p.67.

Seeing and discussing the Memorial Room of the

Defenders of Dubrovnik: sombre and sobering, but a focus perhaps for family discussion of what Dubrovnik has been through in recent times. See p.71.

Wandering around the market in Gundulićeva Poljana: there are few better places to absorb the everyday sights and sounds of the city, tucked away from the main tourist thoroughfares. See p.74.

Getting a ferry out to Lokrum: a delightful fifteen minute boat trip, then a refreshing potter around the island, and, perhaps, a swim. See p.87.

Walking along the path on the north side of Lapad bay: leave busy Lapad beach behind, and walk under the trees above the rocks to the Levanat café/restaurant for a drink or a meal. And don't worry if the sun sets – the path is lit. See p.78.

Enjoy Trsteno's arboretum: lush woodland, orchards and fruit trees, ponds and Victorian follies. See p.81.

Watching the Moreška Sword Dance in Korčula Town: with its roots in the Middle Ages, its clashing swords and loud brass band music are a big attraction. See p.82.

Driving along the Pelješac peninsula to Trpanj and catching the car ferry to Ploče: an exhilarating drive through rolling countryside past mussel and oyster farms and palm-thatched fish restaurants, and a beautiful crossing from pretty Trpanj against a majestic backdrop of mountains. See p.82.

Having a swim at Klek, or off the rocks in the Old Town: pretty village and broad crescent of beach. See p.84.

Visiting Čilipi for the Folklore show: every Sunday, after Mass, a colourful 40 minutes of song and dance put on by the local Folklore Society. See p.86.

The Rest of Greater Dubrovnik

Although Dubrovnik's Old Town is certainly the main reason for coming to Southern Dalmatia, the rest of the city is a well-appointed holiday area very much geared to families, with enough of a life of its own to stop that 'living in a bubble' feeling you can sometimes get where you've spent a week or a fortnight in a country without in any way touching its everyday life or culture. The beautiful Lapad and Babin kuk peninsula, a couple of kilometres to the west, with all its restaurants, bars, beaches and boat rides, should not be missed. It also has a good number of hotels and makes an ideal holiday destination in its own right. Next to it, the modern port of Gruz is a lively place, busy with ferries to the islands, palatial cruise ships, and throngs of small boats and

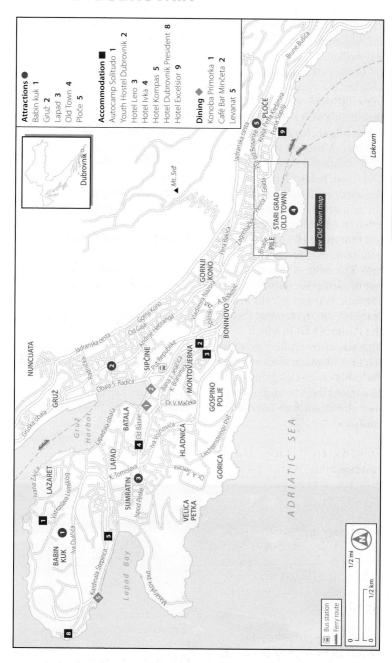

Attractions ●
Babin kuk **1**
Gruž **2**
Lapad **3**
Old Town **4**
Ploče **5**

Accommodation ■
Autocamp Solitudo **1**
Youth Hostel Dubrovnik **2**
Hotel Lero **3**
Hotel Ivka **4**
Hotel Kompas **5**
Hotel Dubrovnik President **8**
Hotel Excelsior **9**

Dining ◆
Konoba Primorka **1**
Café Bar Minčeta **2**
Levanat **5**

STARI GRAD (OLD TOWN) **4**
see Old Town map

Bus station
Ferry route

0   1/2 mi
0   1/2 km

ADRIATIC SEA

Lokrum

ocean-going yachts all contained in the bay between the Lapad/Babin kuk peninsula and the elegant modern coastal highway bridge.

To the east, the island of **Lokrum** is a pleasant 15-minute ferry ride away, while on the mainland a series of up-market hotels hug the coast, and the road south rises up steeply to offer wonderful views of the Old Town below. Finally, towering above it all to the north, the mountain of **Srđ** offers those intrepid enough to climb it (on foot or by car) a terrific panorama of this whole coastline. The cable car has alas been out of commission since the Patriotic War (see p.248) in the early 1990s – remember, this is the mountain from which Yugoslav army artillery pounded the city. Plans are afoot to get the cable car going again, and to convert the fort at the top into a museum cum restaurant complex.

The only fly in Dubrovnik's ointment is the level of its own success – it is hugely popular, and therefore very crowded, especially in July and August. You can spend a lot of your time in the Old Town dodging tour groups that are being addressed in most of the world's languages by guides holding up coloured cards, flowers, or (most popular) extended but rolled up folding umbrellas, so that their charges don't accidentally get tagged onto somebody else's tour.

Lapad ★★★ **FIND** **ALL AGES** If you're looking for reasonable prices (for Dubrovnik that is; prices are still expensive by the standards of the rest of the country) and enough activities to keep the children occupied, then look no further than Lapad, to the west of the Old Town. Lapad lies on its peninsula, stretching uphill from Lapad Beach, then downhill on the other side to the ferry port at Gruž. There are lots of shops, cafés, restaurants and

Lapad Beach

hotels, and the bus (Number 6) to the Old Town takes no more than 10 to 15 minutes. Lapad Beach is not very long – a couple of hundred metres at most – and is, as is usual on the Croatian mainland, made of gravel, not sand. But it has lots of sun loungers and parasols, a slightly iffy sea-slide, and crystal-clear water.

Stretching up to the centre of Lapad from the beach, a pleasant pedestrianised street is lined with all manner of entertainment including arcades, a playground, tennis courts, children's rides, bouncy castles, inflatable ball pools, and stalls selling every-thing you could conceivably need for a day on the beach. It is also lined with people selling boat excursions to the islands. Add a number of hotels, restau-rants and bars, and a beautiful meandering footpath along the northern arm of the bay giving access to lots of off-the-rocks bathing, and you have not only a great chill-out area for the whole family, but one of the best home-bases for exploration of this part of Croatia. Highly recommended.

Babin kuk ALL AGES Beyond Lapad, occupying the northwest of the peninsula, Babin kuk offers two totally different kinds of holiday experience. On its western flank it has a group of related hotels – the President, the Argosy, the Minčeta, the Tirena and the Plakir, all on one huge site interspersed with restaurants, coffee bars, a disco, pools and sports facilities. All are managed by Valamar Hotels and Resorts. On the north side of the peninsula is the only campsite in Greater Dubrovnik – also run by Valamar (see 'Family Friendly Accommodation' below).

Gruž ★ ALL AGES Situated on the mainland between the coast road and the sea, facing the Lapad peninsula, the port of Gruž is a pleasant area of the city packed with interest. Starting from the elegant Franja Tuđmana bridge that carries the main coast highway – the *magistrala* – over the river Dubrovnik on the bridge, you come first to the quays where the big cruise ships and ferries dock, then to the quays and moorings where a thousand small boats, rubber dinghies and private yachts rub gunwhales (the upper edge of the ship's sides) with a police launch, two reconstructed galleons and a steady stream of water taxis, all surrounded by the steep mansion-and-apart-ment-dotted slopes of the main-land on one side and the Lapad peninsula on the other.

Along the southern edge of the port (Nikole Tesle) there's a small shopping centre with a café terrace thronged with local people, some nice shops and restaurants, the Sveti Vlaho, 'the first battleship of the Croatian Navy' (don't get too excited – it's a gunboat!), and a children's playground. Just behind Nikole Tesle is the bus station.

TRIPS OUT

Cavtat **1**
Čilipi **2**
Elafite Islands **3**
Gruda **4**
Klek **5**
Koločep **6**
Korčula Town **7**
Lokrum **8**
Lopud **9**
Mali Ston and Veliki Ston **10**
Mljet **11**
Neum Corridor **12**
Orebić **13**
Ploče **14**
Šipan **15**
Trpanj **16**
Trsteno **17**

Trips Out

There are only three directions in which to go on trips out of Dubrovnik – up the coast, down the coast and out to sea. This is because, if you drive inland, by the time you get into top gear you'll be entering Bosnia-Herzegovina. Not that you can't do this – a lot of tours go to Mostar and beyond – but this book is about Croatia.

There are plenty of organised excursions out of Dubrovnik, although it often makes more sense to hire a car and plan your own trips. Dubrovnik is easy to get out of – if you're going up the coast, head for Gruž, travel along the dockside, and then drive under the splendid suspension bridge that can be seen for miles. The road then turns back on itself and brings you out onto the coastal highway at the start of the bridge.

If you're heading down the coast, just follow the signs for Cavtat. The road skirts the north wall of the Old Town, takes you through Ploče, then swings upwards (narrow, but one-way) to the coastal highway. And the views back towards the Old Town are out of this world.

A Tour up the Coast

A very popular family day out for the citizens of Dubrovnik involves driving to Ston, at the base of the Pelješac peninsula. You can make this a part of the round trip that has everything:

Trsteno ★ **ALL AGES** A visit to Trsteno is a lovely way to start your family day out, or, if you decide to stop on the return journey, to bring it to a close. After going under, then onto, the Franja Tuđmana bridge just outside Dubrovnik, drive north along the *magistrala* the 20 km or so (12½ miles) to Trsteno. You'll immediately see that the village is heavily wooded between the highway and the sea, and herein lies a story.

Back in the 16th century, a local nobleman Ivan Gučetić built a summer villa here, which he then surrounded with delightful formal gardens, spreading across a terrace above the sea. Maintained and developed by successive generations of the family, the communist government of Yugoslavia eventually confiscated it in 1948 – tough on the family, I suppose, but, being a communist government, you could see their point.

Since then, the gardens have been developed by the Croatian Academy of Sciences and Arts into an arboretum for the enjoyment of all. Despite the earthquake of 1667, the considerable damage caused by gunboat attacks from the sea in 1991 and an accidental fire in 2000, the main buildings and the oldest trees have survived. The whole 26 hectares (63 acres) is a haven of peace and quiet, with lush trees, shrubs and flowers spilling down around a pavilion, aqueduct, chapel, fountain, mill and loggia towards the balustraded steps that lead down onto a rocky beach and tiny harbour.

http://mahazu.hazu.hr/ENG/ arboretum.html 12 Kuna (£ 1.10). Open May to October 7am–7pm, November to April 8am–3pm.

The Arboretum at Trsteno

Mali Ston and Veliki Ston ★

AGES 4 AND UP Some 25 km (15 miles) beyond Trsteno are Mali Ston and Veliki Ston (little and large respectively), which are perched on the edge of crystal clear waters. The two villages guard the entrance to Peljesac Peninsula, and were founded in the 14th century. These small communities have a special flavour imparted to them by the local salt pans and oyster farms. Within their walls both towns reveal a small grid of streets that are ideal for exploring.

Mali Ston's massive fortifications date back to the 14th century, when they were built as the northern defences of the Republic of Dubrovnik. From a castle beside the salt pans, the astonishing walls climb the hillside behind the village, while down at sea level the rectangles of the salt pans, and the rails and trucks that are used to transport the salt, stretch off into the distance.

Walls at Ston

Long a destination for local school trips, Mali Ston is also becoming something of a mecca for couples intent on a romantic weekend and there are a number of top class restaurants serving the local oysters.

Continuing along the Peljesac peninsula, every kilometre or so you are exhorted to eat and buy shellfish, or taste and buy wine – the two great crops of the area.

From Mali Ston you have a choice. You can take the road down the spine of the peninsula to the little port of Orebić for the short ferry hop across to the island of Korčula (**the long tour**) or turn right off the main Pelješac road before getting to Orebić, and head for the equally small ferry port of Trpanj for trips across to the mainland at Ploče (**the short tour**).

The long tour takes you swooping along the road that traverses the spine of the peninsula to the little port of Orebić for the short ferry hop across to the island of (and its main town) Korčula. Ferries depart roughly every hour, so just get in line, buy your ticket and wait.

Korčula Town ★ ★ ALL AGES

is very pretty, with narrow medieval streets, 14th century walls and towers, and a variety of palaces and churches. Once you've climbed the steps from the market square and entered the old town through the Land Gate, the oval street plan has been compared to the skeleton of a fish, with a string of narrow lanes emanating from the main

Korcula Town at Night

at 6am, 9am, 11.15am, noon, 4.30pm, 6.45pm and 9pm.

It is a lovely crossing, with the mountains of the Pelješac peninsula receding behind you and the mountains of the mainland increasingly dominating the skyline ahead. It's a nice break from driving, too, and a good opportunity to get the children fed and watered – you can sit in the air-conditioned lounge and have a drink and an ice-cream, visit the toilets, sunbathe on the upper deck at the rear (though it gets very hot), or stand on the walkway above the car deck and cool off in the breeze created by the boat's passage. As you come into the busy working port of Ploče there is a lot of activity (ships being loaded and unloaded, cranes working, cruise ships docking) to keep the children occupied.

The return drive from Ploče to Dubrovnik along the *magistrala* will take you first on a short detour inland through the distinctly odd yet attractive landscape of the delta of the Neretva river: wetlands, reed-girt lakes,

street that crosses the town, interrupted only by the square which holds St. Mark's Cathedral. There's nothing specific to aim to see, but the small scale and ambience are bound to appeal to children.

The short tour involves turning right off the main Pelješac road from Mali Ston before getting to Orebić, and heading for the equally small ferry port of Trpanj. Again, drive down to the dock, get in line, then leave the car and walk to the Jadrolinija office to buy a ticket. **The ferries** ★★★ across to the mainland at Ploče take about three quarters of an hour, and depart

Moreška Sword Dance

While in Korčula you should try and see this famous dance that was once a common sight across the Mediterranean. Probably originating in Spain, the Moorish dance was originally performed only on St. Theodore's Day (29th July), but now, owing to popular demand, it is recreated every Thursday evening between May and September just outside the Land Gate (or, if wet, in the local cinema). You have to buy tickets (60 Kuna (£ 5.60). The skilful dance is very colourful and noisy, and should appeal to children (though don't tell them its roots are probably the same as the more genteel English Morris Dancing – definitely not cool!).

Polo Was Here?

Residents of Korčula Town like to claim that this is the birthplace of the 13th century explorer Marco Polo. It's a nice story, but there is no evidence and the citizens of Venice have more right to claim Marco Polo than do the citizens of Korčula. Nevertheless, evidence suggests that Marco Polo did at least visit the island during his travels and a festival in his honour is held every May to celebrate what islanders like to think was the homecoming of the great explorer.

riverside settlements, all mixed up with railway sidings and patches of industry. You can stop to buy fruit or wine at roadside stalls.

Klek ALL AGES When you get back to the coast, there's a nice beach at Klek, should the family be gasping for a swim. After it, almost immediately, you have to (briefly) leave Croatia. When the shape of federal Yugoslavia was agreed after the World War 2, a little stretch of coastline (about 15km long) that logically should have been part of Croatia was tacked onto Bosnia-Herzegovina to give it access to the sea. You may have to stop to show passports, and even open the boot for inspection. The town of Neum is a mass of holiday hotels, restaurants and so on – if you've only got 15km of coastline, you've got to pack 'em in! Beyond the Neum Corridor, it's about 35km (21 miles) back to Dubrovnik.

Down the Coast

An even more popular day out for Dubrovnik families is to head down the coast and in particular spend some time in Cavtat. Just three kilometres off the coast road and about 20 km (12½ miles) from Dubrovnik, you can drive there in 20 minutes. Alternatively, you can get a boat across the bay from Dubrovnik's Old Port.

Cavtat ★ ★ ★ ALL AGES The main appeal of Cavtat is that, compared to Dubrovnik, it has a peaceful and relaxed atmosphere. Cavtat sits astride a beautiful strip of land. Its yacht-thronged harbour curves around a gorgeous horseshoe-shaped bay dotted with houses peeking out of heavily-wooded hillsides. And although Cavtat is now a major tourist-magnet, don't think it has become totally separated from its fishing-village roots: its quayside still hosts loads of little fishing boats, and you'll find yourself stepping over piles of cork-floated nets. Apart from being a really nice place to stroll, have a swim and stop for a drink or a meal, Cavtat has got just enough other attractions to make a trip there worthwhile.

Cavtat Waterfront

The Račić Mausoleum

AGES 5 AND UP was designed by Ivan Meštrović (see p.72) in 1921 as a mausoleum for a local ship-owning family. Take a pleasant walk up through the trees onto the hill behind the town to get there.

The **Vlaho Bukovak Gallery**

(5, Bukovčeva) **AGES 4 AND UP** has a wide selection of work by the local-born painter Vlaha Bukovak (1834–1908), who went on to become a professor at the Prague Academy of Fine Art. His work is displayed in the house that belonged to his father, and in which he spent a lot of time. There's plenty to appeal to children, particularly pictures of animals and birds, and, more frighteningly a vivid depiction of heaven, purgatory and hell.

Tues–Sat 9am–5pm (closed 1pm–2pm), Sun 2pm–5pm, 20 Kuna (£ 1.80).

A number of monuments can be seen in Cavtat along the quayside, including **a bust of Frano Supilo (1870– 1917)** **AGES 8 AND UP**, a Cavtat-born politician and journalist and a great Yugoslav/Croatian patriot, and a **Statue of Baltazar Bogišić (1834–1908)** **AGES 8 AND UP**, another local boy made good. Bogišić was a famous scientist who lived most of his later life in Paris. After his death, his books, manuscripts, graphics and coins were lodged in the **Rector's Palace** in Cavtat. In addition to the Bogišić Collection, the palace also contains some notable paintings – look out in particular for a huge one, again by Bukovac, of a local carnival celebration.

Palace open Mon–Sat 9am–1pm, 10 Kuna (90p) (children 5 Kuna (45p))

Statues in the Park

Croatians commemorate their local heroes more than most. Every town has its memorials to local people or events, usually but not always in parks or gardens, from full statues to busts on plinths to understated memorial tablets. These are rarely mentioned in guidebooks, or in local tourist board literature. Yet they can offer a real insight into the life, past and present, of that community, into what it thinks is important and is worth celebrating.

Čilipi ★ **ALL AGES** Beyond Cavtat, after passing Dubrovnik airport, you drive across the broad agricultural valley called the Konavle to the little village of Čilipi, six kilometres (four miles) from Cavtat. It is known for a Folklore Show, organised by the local folklore society, which takes place in front of the Church of Saint Nicholas every Sunday at 11.15am. The three-quarter-hour song and dance medley includes the linđo,

a courtship dance accompanied by a Croatian stringed instrument called the lirica. There's also a market that sells embroidery and textiles.

Just before the village of Gruda, 10 kilometres (6 miles) south of Čilipi, a left turn and a three kilometre drive brings you to the Konavoski dvori restaurant, the final destination of many a trip by locals to the area south of Dubrovnik (see 'Family-Friendly Dining' below).

The Sunday Morning Folklore Show, Cilipi

DID YOU KNOW? ⟫ **Understand the land** ⟨⟨

Here's a way of increasing both adult's and children's understanding of the towns and villages that you've visited on holiday: take a digital picture of each memorial, making sure the name and dates are clearly visible on the picture (they are almost always that simple – a name and date). When you get home, bring history to life with the Internet to find out more about them.

To the Islands

In Dubrovnik, as in most parts of coastal Croatia, one of the most popular short trips is to take a boat to one of the offshore islands. All are accessible from Dubrovnik as day trips.

Lokrum ★★★ **ALL AGES** The closest island to Dubrovnik is Lokrum, a wooded islet that is clearly visible from the mainland. Boats shuttle back and forth from the Old Port in Dubrovnik (9am to 9pm, every half hour, 35 Kuna (£ 3.25)), and also from Cavtat.

The island's two main claims to fame are that it is meant to be where Richard the Lionheart was shipwrecked, and that Maximilian von Habsburg once

Curse of the Monks

In 1808 the Benedictine Monastery on Lokrum was closed and the monks displaced. On their last night on the island, legend has it that the monks put a curse on the island, and on anybody who had dealings with it in the future. The curse didn't take long to kick in. The three men who brought the news of the monastery's dissolution all died violently – one drowned, one was stabbed, and one was thrown through a high window. In 1859 the island was bought by Maximilian, brother of Franz Josef, the Austro-Hungarian Emperor. Maximilian became the Emperor of Mexico and was executed by rebels. The island was offered to the Dubrovnik authorities, but they wouldn't touch it. Instead it passed to a wealthy businessman (who was quickly ruined) a lawyer (who was ruined and disgraced), and the lawyer's nephew (who drowned on his way to look at his inheritance). Reverting to the Emperor, it was passed on to Franz Josef's only son Rudolf, who honeymooned on the island, fell in love with another woman, and together they committed suicide. Franz Josef's wife Sisi tried to get rid of the accursed island, to no avail, and she was assassinated by an anarchist in 1889. Finally, her nephew Franz Ferdinand intended to spend the summer of 1914 on the island with his wife Sophie. Instead they went to Sarajevo – and were assassinated! So by all means visit the island, but under no circumstances let anyone persuade you to buy it!

Lopud, Elafite Islands

owned it (before he became Emperor of Mexico and was executed by firing squad for his pains.

Today there's not much to do on Lokrum. You can take a look at the cloister of the island's monastery (though not the monastery itself), wander around Maximilian's Botanical Garden, or explore the paths that meander across the northern part of the island. There are a couple of rocky beaches where you can swim in the crystal-clear water, and that's about it. Lokrum's main recommendation is that it's quiet and tree-covered (a nice contrast to the busy, hot city that you've just left), and that visiting it involves an enjoyable 10–15 minute boat ride with lovely views back towards the Old Town.

The Elafite Islands ★★

ALL AGES Probably the most popular boat trips from Dubrovnik are to the Elafite Islands

(Koločep, Lopud and Šipan). You'll find loads of boat trips on offer along the dock in Gruž, on the road up from the beach at Lapad, in the Old Port of Dubrovnik, and in any port up and down the coast. There is also a ferry, four times a day in summer. Each operator offers slightly different packages, so you'll need to talk to the reps and choose one that suits your family's needs. Of the 14 or so islands, only three are inhabited, and most trips offer some time on each of them. They're very pleasant to explore, though you'll have to do it on foot – motor transport is not allowed. Refreshments including drinks and snacks are available on all three islands.

Koločep, at around 2½ square kilometres (under a square mile) is the smallest of the Elafite Islands, and is about half an hour from Dubrovnik (the ferry costs 11 Kuna (£ 1.00). It has a tiny population (about 200 inhabitants) that is mostly based in two hamlets: Donje Čelo and Gornje Čelo. There's a single shop and a post office, both with limited opening hours, and during the summer the three-star hotel (the Ville Koločep) and several restaurants and bars are open. There's not a lot to do but walk along meandering paths through the pine trees and olive groves or go for a swim.

Lopud, at twice the size and twice the population of Koločep is also a lot more popular, because there's more to do. It has several beaches (Šunj, the best known, and sandy to boot, is a couple of kilometres south of Lopud village along an asphalt path), a Franciscan monastery and church, the ruined palace of Miho Pracat, a local boy-made-good who became fabulously wealthy as a result of services to the Spain of Charles V, and the Đorđić-Mayer Park, together with a ruined fortress, an ethnographic museum and a number of hotels, shops, cafés and restaurants stretching along the front. Interestingly, the altarpiece in the church at Šunj is English – bought during Henry VIII's great fund-raising sale after the Dissolution of the Monasteries. The trip to Lopud takes just under an hour from Dubrovnik (ferry – 20 Kuna (£ 1.80).

Šipan is the largest of the group, and the furthest from Dubrovnik (getting on for two hours on the ferry). It is therefore the one that attracts fewest visitors. Like the other two, Šipan offers peace and quiet and some good walks. There are ruined manor houses, a couple of churches, vineyards and olive groves. There are only two villages – Šipanska Luka and Suđurađ – and the ferry calls at both.

Mljet ☆ ALL AGES One of the most popular days out from Dubrovnik is to the island of Mljet, and in particular to the Mljet National Park (*www.np-mljet.hr*), which occupies the western end of the island. It's accessible by a variety of routes – on excursion boats from any of the usual places in Dubrovnik, for example, or by hydrofoil from Orebić. There's also a passenger-only catamaran (the *Nona Maria*), which, in summertime, sails each day directly from Dubrovnik to the National Park – it takes 1½ hours, and costs around 50 Kuna (£ 4.50).

Linked in legend with both Ulysses and St. Paul, the island was settled by the Illyrians and the Romans. The Benedictine Order took it over in 1151, building a monastery on St Mary's Island in Veliko Jezero, one of two salt water lakes (they're actually inlets attached to the sea) in what is today the National Park – the other is Malo Jezero. The two salt water lakes are linked by forest paths to the villages of Polače and Pomena. The park is a haven for wildlife, and for walking, swimming, snorkelling and sunbathing. You can rent bikes in Polače harbour, the Hotel Odisej, in Pomena ☎ 020-744-022, or from National Park offices. Canoes and rowing boats can be hired at Mali most. If you're looking for nightlife, though, go somewhere else.

INSIDER TIP
'Most' in Croatian means 'bridge'.

For Active Families

Apart from seeing the sights in and around Dubrovnik under your own steam, there's an increasing choice of activities to choose from in the area.

Walks. A wide range of guided walks are available; you can pick up leaflets at the Tourist Office. With most tours, you don't have to book; simply turn up at the meeting point and pay the guide. Walks are usually based around a theme, such as the Old Jewish Quarter, the City's Defences, Hidden Treasure, and cost between 90 and 140 Kuna (£ 8–12.50), depending on how many of the attractions visited have an entrance fee. Walks last anything from 45 minutes to two hours, again depending on what's included. One company offering walks with an English-speaking guide is Dubrovnik Walks. Details can be found at *www.dubrovnikwalks.com*.

Sea Kayaking. As you walk the walls of Dubrovnik, you'll undoubtedly see people paddling brightly-coloured kayaks. These can be hired, with all the appropriate instruction, from several sources. Adriatic Sea Kayaking offers a 9am–1pm session, including a light meal on the island of Lokrum for 250 Kuna (£ 22.90) (*www.adriatic-sea-kayak.com*). Adventure Dalmatia can provide a three-hour session, which includes snacks and use of a mask and snorkel for around 230 Kuna (£ 21.00)

(*www.adventuredalmatia.com*). No previous experience is necessary, though you do need to be reasonably fit. A range of discounts is available for children. Or try 'Adventure Croatia' for sea kayaking and snorkelling (☎ *091-526-3813*).

Jeep-safari. A nice way for the whole family to see the countryside. The fee usually includes the vehicle for an eight-hour drive in convoy, instruction and lunch. There is also usually the opportunity to have a swim, and many companies will arrange complimentary pick-up at your hotel. Prices are not cheap, and start from around 550 Kuna (£ 52.50) per adult, and 270 Kuna (£ 25.80) per child (usually aged 4–12). The nearest area where jeep safaris go is the Konavle Valley, just south of Dubrovnik: summer only. One company offering tours such as these is Magical Journeys (*www.magicaljourneys.com*).

Horseback riding. Another nice way to see the countryside is from the back of a horse. Again, the Konavle is a popular destination. A typical package, from a company such as Magical Journeys, includes instruction (no previous experience necessary), the riding tour and a snack or light lunch. Prices start from 450 Kuna (£ 43) for adults and 225 Kuna (£ 21.50) for children 4–12. The ride normally lasts for five hours – and that's plenty, especially if you're not experienced!

Other activities include **mountain biking** and **free climbing** (again in the Konavle). It is even possible to book a whole holiday based around these activities – try *www.responsibletravel.com*.

Shopping with Kids

Most of the merchandise on sale in Dubrovnik is not particularly aimed at children. It's a major tourist town, after all, so the bulk of shops in the Old Town (all small – strict planning laws apply) sell souvenirs of varying quality, local costume and lace, and gold, silver and coral jewellery (mainly along Stradun and the lanes that herringbone off it). There's a smattering of clothes and shoe shops – the Ronchi Hat Factory in the Old Town is good fun (Lučarica 2, ℰ 020-323-699) and a good range of CDs, Croatian and International, is available at Aquarius (Poljana Paskala Miličevića 4), plus you can buy English Language books at Algebra (Stradun 9) and Algoritam (Stradun 8). For local embroidery you could do no better than visit stalls on the quayside in the Old Port. And as we have seen, there's an open-air market at Gundulićeva Poljana – mainly fruit and veg, but also a range of other merchandise. In the Lapad/Gruž area you'll find all the shops that you'd expect in a small UK city (this is where the locals do their shopping). In particular, visit Lapad's main street (Kralja Tomislava).

Between Lapad and Gruž, just before the harbour (near the bus station), is a supermarket (on Put Republike) and, around the corner on Nikole Telse, there's a small shopping mall with a first-rate pizzeria (see Café Bar Minčeta, p.98).

Family Entertainment

Dubrovnik's cinema (Kino Sloboda, on Luža ℰ 020-321-425) shows lots of English language films (almost exclusively American), and since they're invariably subtitled rather than dubbed, they are accessible to UK families. There's a theatre Marin Držić Theatre (Pred Dvorom 3, ℰ 020-426-437), but be warned, its productions are almost always in Croatian. As for music, the Dubrovnik Symphony Orchestra performs regularly, often at the Rectors Palace (*www.dso.hr*), whilst less highbrow (rock and jazz) fare is sometimes available at the Lazareti, or at Klub Orlando (*www.klub-orlando.com*). Watch out too for live music nights at Latino Club Fuego (at Brsalje 11, near the Pile Gate). The best way of finding out what's going on is to keep an eye on fly-posters around the city.

As regards festivals, the big beast in Dubrovnik's entertainment forest is without doubt the Summer Festival (see 'Children's Favourite Croatian Events, p.26). Having said that, it is heavily highbrow, with classical concerts in various venues across the city, so the degree to which it might appeal to your children depends on their age and their interests. You can't, though, go wrong with the spectacular opening firework display.

Another festival that might be of interest – the Karantena Festival – takes place at the Lazareti during August. It consists of alternative theatre and other types of performance art, and might well appeal to teenagers. The Lazareti also hosts twice-weekly traditional song and dance performances by famous local group Linđo (Tues and Fri, 9.30pm, summer only), and the occasional rock or jazz concert.

FAMILY-FRIENDLY ACCOMMODATION

Dubrovnik has very little in the way of budget accommodation – the whole area is infamous, in the rest of Croatia, for being expensive (a taxi driver in Pula told me to expect to pay 40% more in Dubrovnik than in the rest of the country). If you don't fancy staying in a hotel then it's worth getting a copy of the booklet 'Private and Confidential – private accommodation, rooms, apartments and villas', which is available from the Tourist Board. This booklet has detailed lists of agencies offering private accommodation. What this means is that you'll usually be occupying perhaps an upper floor of a family home – a lovely way of getting

to know Croatians, if that's your kind of thing.

As for hotels, the ones inside the Old Town are expensive but luxurious – if you can afford it, they'd make for a nice day or two in the thick of things. However, it wouldn't be possible to recommend longer than that as they're not really cut out for children. Outside the Old Town, there's a huge range of expensive to moderate hotels, and most are very good. However, the best choice for families with children is to be found on the peninsula northwest of the Old Town, in Lapad and Babin kuk. Here you have beaches (if only of the gravel-and-concrete variety), plenty to do, and easy access to excursion boats, while still being only a 10 to 15 minute bus ride away from the Pile Gate (see p.68).

EXPENSIVE

Hilton Imperial ★ ★ ★ Almost completely destroyed by shelling during the Patriotic War in 1991 (see p.248), what is now the Hilton Imperial reopened in 2005 as the first Hilton in Croatia. Its position just outside the Pile Gate is perfect for exploring the Old Town, and, set back in its own grounds much higher than the road, it is amazingly quiet. Although mainly a business hotel, the management is making great efforts to adapt to families with children – they'll put in extra beds, free for up to 12 year olds, and cots are available, also free of charge. Children's menus and high chairs are available in the restaurant, and there are a few toys in the indoor pool. And there are substantial grounds in which to walk around. Although the hotel has the unmistakable feel of palatial luxury, the staff couldn't be nicer – you'll never feel that the children are a nuisance. A number of special offers are often available such as second room half price or free breakfasts for children, so it pays to ask.

Marijana Blažića 2, at the Pile Gate. ☎ 020-320-320. Fax 020-320-220. www.hilton.com. 147 rooms, including eight junior suites. From 1700 Kuna (£ 153) double; from 2460 Kuna (£ 221) suite. Amenities: Restaurant, piano bar, pool, sauna, steam bath, elevator, garage, non-smoking rooms, room for those w/limited mobility. In room: A/C, TV, Wi-Fi, minibar, hair dryer, safe.

Hotel Dubrovnik President

★★★ This is the most palatial of a group of hotels on the Babin kuk peninsula (Minčeta, Tirena, Argosy) that are owned by the same company. The President has been refurbished over the last four years, all rooms have balconies and sea views, and the hotel is well-adapted to children, with six family rooms and double rooms with divans or pull-out beds. You can order extra beds, and cots are available free of charge. The restaurant has high chairs, and the kitchen is happy to adapt meals to children. There's a children's playground, a programme of entertainment for youngsters, a mini club, and competitive

Hotel Dubrovnik President

games and sport. You can swim (in the pool or off the beach), or take part in a wide variety of sports including tennis, diving, water-polo, mini-golf and a lot more. Entertainment is put on in the evenings, and there are buses and water-buses to the Old Town. There are lovely views to be had from the hotel's lift down to the beach.

Iva Dulčića 39, 20000 Dubrovnik. ☎ 020-441-100. Fax 020-435-600. www.valamar.com. 181 rooms. 1120–2320 Kuna (£ 110–225) double, 1960–4350 Kuna (£ 190–425) apartment. (Look out for offers, though, or try one of the other hotels in the group). Amenities: 'wellness' suite, fitness centre, diving centre, tennis courts, boat hire, water skiing, three beaches, indoor pool. In room: Sat TV, A/C, mini bar, direct phone line, hair dryer, non-smoking rooms, Internet connection, safe, room service.

Hotel Excelsior ★★★ One of

several expensive Ploče hotels, the Excelsior has all the facilities and luxuries you'd expect for the money, it's close to the beach, and it has superb views of Dubrovnik's Old Town. It has a number of features that make it a good choice for (prosperous) families – there's a children's indoor swimming pool, a pool table, babysitting can be arranged by appointment, and of its 164 rooms, 18 are suites. The hotel was built in 1913, and it still has echoes of the upper class lifestyle that was to be swept away by World War 1.

Frana supila 12, Ploče. 020-353-300. Fax: 020-414-214. www.hotel-excelsior.hr. 164 rooms. From 2165 Kuna (£ 204) double with sea view and balcony; from 4265 Kuna (£ 402) suite. Rates include breakfast and stay the same all year. Half-board available. Amenities: two restaurants, piano bar, indoor pool, children's indoor pool, elevator, sauna, access for those with disabilities, garage, Internet access. In room: A/C, TV, fax, dial-up Internet connection, minibar, hair dryer, safe.

Hotel Kompas ★★★ Right next to Lapad Beach, the Hotel Kompas is one of the best places to stay for families in Dubrovnik. It has a curious upside-down feel (it's built into the hillside, so Reception's on the 9th floor) but has everything you need including eight connecting rooms, 30 rooms with an extra bed (a sofa bed that can easily sleep two children), and cots available at no extra charge. The restaurant has high chairs and a children's menu, while the outdoor pool has a good selection of large children's toys. Entertainment on the terrace can be noisy, but it finishes at 11.30pm (hint: if you've got young children, ask for a room at the top of the hotel). Within a five minute (traffic free) walk, there's the beach itself, plus all the children's rides, arcade games, bouncy castles, inflatable slides and ball pools you could wish for. Buses depart regularly to the Old Town.

Šetalitše Kralja Zvonimira 56, Lapad. 020-352-113. www.hotel-kompas.hr. 115 rooms. Doubles from 1400 Kuna (£ 135). Amenities: Restaurants; bar; indoor and outdoor pools; elevator, entertainment (June–October), gym, sauna, massage, Jacuzzi, fitness centre, salon, laundry and ironing service, books and board games available, games room, parking. In room: A/C, TV, minibar.

Hotel Stari Grad ★★ A beautiful but tiny hotel within the walls of the Old Town, the Hotel Stari Grad isn't really cut out for children. But although it couldn't be a recommendation for a long family stay, it can make a lovely alternative for one or two nights – it's pretty luxurious, the roof terrace is stunning, and you're right in the thick of things, just off Stradun, the city's main street. Each floor has two rooms, so you could book two rooms on the same floor or a double room with extra bed/cot. If you do stay for three nights or more, there's a 10% discount.

Od Sigurate 4, Old Town. 020-322-244. Fax 020-321-256. www.hotel starigrad.com. Eight rooms. From 1400 Kuna (£ 132) double. Extra bed 420 Kuna (£ 40) Cot 108 Kuna (£ 10) Amenities: Restaurant, valet, safe-deposit box, babysitting options. In room: A/C, TV, dataport, minibar, hydro-massage shower, hair dryer.

MODERATE

Hotel Ivka ★★ **FIND** First impressions of the Ivka can be that it is the architectural equivalent of painting by numbers – it has everything you need, but it perhaps lacks character. Indeed the bar and restaurant have a really cold, institutional feel. And the info you're given in the room is distinctly flimsy. Look a little closer, though, and it begins to improve. First of all, the in-room facilities are exceptional. Then there are the roomy balconies (though the existing chairs would be enhanced by the addition of a table). But above all, the family rooms (made up of two pairs of rooms with connecting doors) and the single suite are truly enormous – you could play five-a-side football if you had enough children. Cots are available. The location, too, is good – on a leafy hill (one-way, downhill, so cars are always coasting quietly) five minutes walk from the inlet that contains Dubrovnik's port, a nice little children's playground, and two of the best no-frills eating places you could hope to frequent. And youngsters will just love the speedboats, cruise liners, replica galleons (honestly!), yachts and excursion boats that throng the port.

Put Sv. Mihajla 21, 20000 Dubrovnik. 020-362-600. www.hotel-ivka. com. 72 rooms (one suite and six family rooms). From 960 Kuna (£ 92) per double room. Parking (free), bar, two restaurants, laundry. In room: Sat TV, hair dryer, air conditioning, safe, data port.

Hotel Lero At the entrance to the Lapad peninsula, Hotel Lero is just over a kilometre from the Pile Gate. A modern hotel done out in contemporary décor, it has eight family suites with connecting rooms sharing a bathroom. An extra bed can be put into double rooms (at 50% the normal per person rate), and cots are available free of charge. Rooms have either a sea view or look out over a local park. There's a hotel car park, a souvenir shop, coin-operated Internet access and a pleasant café. There's also a beach, sports hall and tennis courts nearby.

Iva Vojnovića 14, Dubrovnik. 020-341-333. Fax 020-332–123. www. hotel-lero.hr. 160 rooms (152 doubles, eight family suites). 1015 Kuna (£ 100) double and suites, extra bed 50%, cots free. Amenities: Hairdresser, massage room, souvenir shop, Internet access, parking. In room: A/C, Sat TV, mini bar, and hairdryer.

INEXPENSIVE

Autocamp Solitudo ★ ★ By far the best way of staying in Dubrovnik cheaply is this large campsite on the northern side of the Babin kuk peninsula – the only campsite within easy reach of Dubrovnik's Old Town (buses leave from just outside the site entrance). In many ways it is ideal for families. It is just 300 metres to the nearest beach, and guests are given a pass for the pool at the nearby hotel complex, which is owned by the same company. There's a shop, restaurant, take-away, and minigolf. The toilet and shower blocks are immaculate. Excursions and canoe safaris can be booked at the campsite. Although the website says that there's a minimum stay of five days, the site itself does not enforce this and your stay can be as short as one night.

Vatroslava Lisinskog 17, Babin Kuk. 📞 *020-448-686. Fax 020-448-688.* **www.babinkuk.com**. *166 pitches. Pitch with electricity and two persons 115 Kuna (£ 11). Seasonal closing. Amenities: Restaurant, market, pool, excursions, laundry.*

FAMILY-FRIENDLY DINING

Dubrovnik is packed with restaurants. Exploring the city and trying to find your own hidden gems is part of the fun. But don't expect lots of high chairs, booster seats and children's corners – even if the inclination were present, there just isn't the room. What you *will* get in almost all of them, though, is a cheerful willingness to provide extra plates, divide meals between the children, and allow you reasonable latitude in negotiating the menu to satisfy picky appetites. You won't come across much really poor food as the competition is so keen that survival depends on achieving reasonable standards. So sometimes the deciding factor in choosing somewhere to eat is not the food, but the setting and the view. And if they are exceptional, then you'll pay for the privilege.

EXPENSIVE

Atlas Club Nautika ★ ★ ★
DALMATIAN Run by the same people who manage the Proto (see below) and the Konavoski Dvori (see below), the Atlas Club Nautika is one of the most famous restaurants in Croatia. Past patrons have included Pope John Paul II and, it is claimed, Edward VIII and Mrs. Simpson. The food is of a very high quality with terrifically high prices to match. Much is made of the view of the Bokar Fortress and Lovrijenac from the terrace, though you'll see backpackers enjoying the same view, munching burgers on the public benches next to the restaurant. The Atlas Club Nautika has something of a reputation for being haughty, and some reviewers seek to take it down a peg or two, but I saw no evidence of this – indeed, I felt that the attitude of staff to children was gravely courteous.

Brsalje 3, Old Town. 📞 *020-442-526.* **www.esculap-teo.hr**. *Dinner entrees 148–380 Kuna (£ 14–36). AE, DC, MC, V at dinner only. Noon–midnight; light lunch served noon–4pm).*

Konavoski Dvori ★ ★ ★ FIND
CROATIAN One of the most spectacularly sited restaurants in Croatia, the Konavoski Dvori is in an old water mill, out in the pleasant countryside of Konavle, some 33km (20 miles) south of Dubrovnik. The water rushes past on all sides as you sit on the terrace and watch the two waterwheels turn, or look at the fish in the huge holding tank. You do need a car to get there, though – it's a long 40 minutes by bus.

20217 Ljuta, Konavle-Croatia. 020-791-039. Main courses 60–190 Kuna (£ 6–18). AE DC MC V. Phone for times.

Porat ★★★

CONTINENTAL/DALMATIAN With its wide, varied and imaginative menu, and its relaxed, unthreatening atmosphere, the Hilton Imperial's restaurant is a great place to dine out with the family. I'm rapidly warming to the Hilton chain. Whether from good recruitment, good training or both, their staff are brilliant at combining friendliness and helpfulness – nothing is too much trouble, and they seem to actually like children. You don't need to be a resident to dine here. Children's menus and high chairs are available, and if you're a big party and you think things might get a bit raucous, there's a private dining room available free of charge.

At the Hilton Imperial. Marijana Blažića 2. 020-320-320. Fax 020-320-220. www.hilton.com. Reservations required for dinner. Main courses 140–190 Kuna (£ 13.50–18); lunch and breakfast 70–120 Kuna (£ 7–11.50). AE, DC, MC, V. 7–10:30am for breakfast; 12:30–2:30pm for lunch; 7–11pm for dinner.

Proto ★★ CROATIAN/SEAFOOD This is an A-list restaurant, which, though known for the excellence of its fish menu, actually provides equally good meat-based dishes. It's not cheap, though they do a moderately-priced 'light lunch' from 11am–6pm. You can sit outside, although it is on a busy corner so you'll have floods of people passing by, or you can sit inside in the formal restaurant, or on the really nice roof terrace.

Korčula,Široka 1, Old Town. 020-323-234. www.esculap-teo.hr. Reservations recommended. Main courses 74–110 Kuna (£ 7–10.50). AE, DC, MC, V. Daily 11am–11pm.

MODERATE

Levanat ★★
DALMATIAN/DUBROVNIK REGION
Wonderfully set on the rocky headland about a kilometre along the coastal path from Lapad Beach, and accessible on foot too from Babin kuk's hotel-and-campsite complex, the Levanat is a family-run restaurant offering delightful views across the bay and out to sea, a lovely terrace with a good balance of sun and shade, and excellent food and wine. Drinks and snacks are served on the terrace across the path, meals in the restaurant or on the restaurant terrace. And if you walk out there in the evening, it's nice to know that the path is well lit for your return.

Nika I Meda Putcića 15, 20000 Dubrovnik. 020-435-352. e-mail levanat@dubrovnik-online.com.

Restaurant Aquarius ★ FIND
SEAFOOD This little fish restaurant is in the narrow alley that leads to the Aquarium (and no, there's no connection regarding fish supply). There's a wide selection of fish on the menu, which varies in price from the inexpensive to the pretty hefty. There's a

non-nonsense seating area outside, where its position wedged between the restaurant and the harbour wall gives it a nice cool ambience. However, you do have to get used to aquarium-bound tourists threading their way past you.

VL Miljenko Jelčić, Kneza Damjana Jude 4, Dubrovnik.

Restaurant Jadran DALMATIAN

A beautiful setting (in the cloisters of the Convent of St. Clare) and solid, if rather pedestrian food – the usual Croatian selection of fish and meat dishes, with some pasta, risotto and salads. Nice, accepting attitude to children.

Paska Miličevića 1, Old Town. ☏ 020-323-403. Fax 020-323-403. Main courses 19–49 Kuna (£ 1.80–4.60). AE, DC, MC, V. 10am–midnight.

INEXPENSIVE

Café Bar Minčeta ★★★ FIND

ITALIAN Just along from Konoba Primorka, and on the same side of the street, is this lovely café cum pizzeria. It looks out across the harbour. Heavily patronised by local people, the Minčeta is on the ground floor of a shopping centre. Pizzas range from 22–38 Kuna (£ 2–3.50) depending on the size and toppings, and sandwiches from 12–16 Kuna (£ 1–1.50). The service is excellent.

On Nikole Tesle. No phone. Open 7am to 10 pm, closed in November.

Konoba Primorka ★ FIND

CROATIAN On the front facing the harbour and docks at Gruž, the Konoba Primorka has an indoor restaurant, a paved terrace under a very substantial marquee, and a beautiful lush garden with lots of shade. It offers largely Croatian meat- and fish-based food. Most are around 30–60 Kuna (£ 2.80–5.60), though some of the fish meals are a lot more – a mixed fish plate will set you back 130 Kuna (£ 12). There's plenty of room for youngsters to move around, and the owners are very laid back and tolerant of children – their own are usually somewhere around. Just across the street are lovely views of the harbour (which you don't get in the restaurant's walled garden), and a children's playground.

Nikole Tesle 7, 20000 Dubrovnik. ☏ 020-356-176. Fax 020-356-186. Open daily 10am to 11pm.

Mea Culpa ★★ ITALIAN In the

middle of the maze of streets off Stradun, this is where young Dubrovnik meets to eat and drink. The food is unpretentious and uniformly good. A huge selection of CDs behind the bar ensures a varied musical accompaniment to your meal. If you can't find a table (it *is* very popular), *Restaurant Ilirija* (and its pizzeria manifestation *Prego* next door) is a perfectly adequate, if not so fashionable, alternative.

Za Rokom 3, 20000 Dubrovnik. ☏ 020-424-819. Main courses 30–80 Kuna (£ 3–7.50). Open 8am to midnight.

4 Central Dalmatia

Central Dalmatia is a region of beaches (largely rock and gravel), rivers, waterfalls and gorges, grapevines and olive trees, and stunning coastal towns. It also boasts, in Split, the country's second city (with one of its most famous football clubs), in the Makarska Riviera one of the country's principal destinations for family holidays, in Trogir and Primošten two of the most beautiful towns and in Krka one of Croatia's prime national parks, together with a host of well-known and popular islands. It is also (and not many people know this) a hotbed of Croatian Rugby Football!

A Note about Nomenclature The region containing Split and its hinterland is sometimes defined as Southern or Lower Dalmatia – although the reasons for this remain obscure. The only practice to make sense is to call Dubrovnik and its area of influence 'Southern Dalmatia', Split and environs 'Central Dalmatia', and Zadar and surrounds 'Northern Dalmatia'. So these are the definitions followed in this book.

TOP 10 FAMILY EXPERIENCES

❶ **Walking along the palm-fringed, boat-lined Riva** in Split and in Trogir, or sitting at one of their myriad pleasant cafés, watching the world go by. See p.105 and 116.

❷ **Deciphering the carvings** on the heavy, wooden doors of Split Cathedral, trying to decide which of the episodes in the life of Christ the 28 cartoon-like illustrations depict. See p.109.

❸ **Rubbing the big toe** of Grgur Ninsky's giant statue, outside the Golden Gate, and making a wish. See p.110.

❹ **Running under** the 'Fist and Funnel' fountain in Split, trying to get through without getting wet. See p.111.

❺ **Exploring the paths, playgrounds and breathtaking panoramas** of the Marjan Forest Park in Split, from whose highest point – Telegrin – you can see for miles. See p.111.

❻ **Having a picnic** and bouncing on the trampolines next to the Kamerlengo Fortress, at the western end of the picturesque island upon which the town of Trogir stands. See p.116.

❼ **Rafting** on the exhilarating Cetina river, which tumbles down from Knin in the karst highlands through the Cetina Gorge to Omis on the coast. See p.124).

❽ **Climbing down** vertiginous paths to vivid Modro Jezero, or the Blue Lake in Imotski. See p.125.

❾ **Enjoying a day** at one of the sweeping beaches and pleasant seaside towns on the Makarska Riviera – Brela, Baška Voda, Promajna, Krvavica, Bratuš Makarska itself, Tučepi, or Podgora. See p.125.

🔟 **Visiting the islands** of Brač, source of white marble for many famous buildings, fashionable and lavender-carpeted Hvar and distant Vis, whose naval base kept it foreigner-free until 1989. See p.128.

SPLIT

Split is both a desirable destination in itself, and a gateway to the rest of Central Dalmatia and its islands. The city is some 225 km (140 miles) northwest of Dubrovnik. A fast new motorway, opened in 2005, links the city to Zagreb (see p.193), which is 365 km (228 miles) to the north.

Heading for Split provides ample scope for child and adolescent humour – 'this car/bus/plane is going to Split. I am going to Split' and so on – as well as almost limitless word games – split infinitive, banana split, split your sides, split the difference. But Split is, of course, more than just a name that can provide little Anglophones with a few moments diversion. It's Croatia's second city, with around a quarter of a million inhabitants who are renowned for their very strong self image and sense of independence, and in particular their contempt for the metropolitans of the capital. And it is one of the most fascinating Roman cities on earth, centred around the retirement home of a Roman Emperor.

The approach to modern Split can be a little intimidating. It's a sprawling industrial and maritime city, swollen by post World War 2 and Patriotic War (see p.248) refugees, whose huge banks of flats dominate the skyline. But be not faint of heart – when you get to its

Split

Roman and Medieval centre, it's like walking into another world: chaotic, it's true, a bit like a rabbit warren or an ant hill, but vibrant, hectic and colourful. Probably not a sensible prospect for a long term stay, especially if you have young children, but certainly worth a full day's visit, if not a couple of nights. A word of warning, though: if you're looking for anything specific – a restaurant, a hotel – in the old part of Split it can be a nightmare as the part of the city centre bounded by the walls of Diocletian's palace is such a maze of alleys, and is often so badly signed, that you're on a hiding to nothing. So the best advice, if you're getting nowhere with the map, is to ask a local.

Essentials

Getting There

By Air The airport for Split ((021-203-171, *www.split-airport.tel.hr*) lies just 26 km (16 miles) to the northwest, just outside Trogir. There are frequent internal and external flights, and the airport is accessible using the shuttle bus (30 Kuna (£ 2.80)) each way.

By Car Split's position on the *magistrala* (the road that closely follows the Croatian coastline), and the narrowness of the country at this point, has always made it not only relatively easy to get to, but also virtually unavoidable. The building of the new Zagreb to Split *autocesta* has made the city even easier to get

to, and when the motorway extension to Dubrovnik has been completed, you'll be able to get to Split if you want or need to, but otherwise be able to avoid it.

By Ferry The city's ferry and hydrofoil berths are ranged along Obala kneza Domagoja, close to the railway and intercity bus stations. A bewildering range of international, local and island ferries throng the quay, and there are also fast hydrofoils to Brač Hvar, Vis, Korčula, Lastovo, and Šolta, as well as the massive Adriatic ferries that make overnight runs across to Italy. Contact the local Jadrolinija office (021-338-333), Semmarina (021-338-292), or Adriatica (021-338-335) for details.

By Train Split is linked by rail to Šibenik and Zagreb. Consult the Split train station (021-338-535) or the national train office (060-333-444, *www.hznet.hr*) for timetables and fares.

By Bus Split is a hub for the road transport system and consequently there are extensive local, national and international routes, including a weekly service to the UK (021-338-483 for details).

Visitor Information

The first time that you're likely to experience difficulties in Split is in finding the Tourist Information Centre. It's in the

Chapel of St. Rock on the Peristyle (☎ 021-342-666, *www. visitsplit.com*). It's not easy to spot and is surrounded by a confusing riot of Roman remains, later buildings, modern developments, all shot through with alleyways, tunnels and steps. If you can't find the Tourist Information Centre, ask. And when you do finally arrive, make sure you get a copy of 'VisitSPLIT, the excellent official calendar of events produced by the Tourist Board.

In addition to the Tourist Board, the Turist Buro at Riva 12 (☎ 021-347-100) is worth a visit, and there are numerous private tourist agencies and tour companies – 33 are listed in 'VisitSPLIT'.

Getting Around

The city centre is small enough for everything to be within easy walking distance. Even the Marjan peninsula, depending on the age of the children, is easily walkable – it takes about 20 minutes. For car hire, several big companies are represented in the city: Budget, Obala Kneza Branimira 8 ☎ 021-399-214 *www.budget.hr*; Hertz, Tomića stine 9 ☎ 021-360-455 *www. hertz.hr*; together with a number of more specifically Croatian ones – for example, MACK, Hotel Split, Put Trstenika 19, ☎ 098-601-727.

Otherwise your best bet is a taxi – there are ranks at either end of the Riva, or you can use

Radio Taxi Split ☎ *970*, or *021-475-343*.

Split has a comprehensive city bus system, with the main bus station in the centre of the city, next to the harbour and the railway station. For details, contact ☎ *060-327-777*, or have a look at their excellent website at *www. ak-split.hr*.

Split Itineraries

If You Have 1 Day

Morning explore the city's main sights including Diocletian's Palace (see p.108), the Cathedral/Mausoleum of Diocletian (see p.109) and the Baptistry/Temple of Jupiter (see p.109). Rub the toe of Grgur Ninsky's statue just outside the Golden Gate and make a wish (see p.110). Have lunch in the city.

Afternoon go out to the Marjan Peninsula (see p.111) so the youngsters can let off some steam at the Marjan Forest Park, take a look at the Museum of Croatian Archaeological Monuments (see p.111) and enjoy the statues in the Ivan Meštrović Gallery (see p.111) and the Kaštelet (see p.113).

Diocletian's Palace, Split

If You Have 2 Days

Day 1 Spend Day 1 as above.

Day 2 Drive south along the coast road to Omiš (see p.122). Climb up to the Mirabela Fortress and enjoy the view. Then head up the Cetina Gorge (see p.124). Stop for lunch then either try a spot of rafting, or continue along the road to Imotski (see p.124) to have a look at the Red and Blue Lakes, and if you've got time and energy to spare, climb down to the water.

If You Have 3 Days

Days 1–2 Spend Days 1 and 2 as above.

Day 3 Drive north through the villages of the Kaštela to Trogir (see p.116). Spend the morning looking around the town. The children might like to have a go on the trampolines at the end of the island, and, if you stop off at the market or the supermarket when you first arrive, you could have a picnic. Press on to Primošten (see p.121) and have a quick look round before returning to your hotel.

If You Have 4 Days or More

Days 1–3 as above and also do one of the following. Take a leisurely drive down to the Makarska Riviera (see p.125), explore the region, have a swim and, if you're feeling adventurous, go on a jeep trip up Mount Biokovo (see p.127). Or go on an excursion to one of the islands accessible from Split, such as Brač (see p.129), Hvar (see p.129) or Vis (see p.130).

What To See & Do

Split is the most extraordinary amalgam of the Roman, the Medieval and the modern you're ever likely to come across. Most of this Mediterranean port city was originally built within the walls of Diocletian's Palace. Much of the city, in fact, was actually constructed using masonry scavenged *from* the palace, when masons in the Middle Ages couldn't see the point of quarrying stone when it was just lying around, waiting to be used. Remember the last scene in the original *Planet of the Apes* film? When Charlton Heston (and therefore we, the viewers) become aware that this alien planet is in fact Earth, that he is standing above the ruins of New York City? You get a similar feeling in Split – you can take in the city's almost 2,000-year history at a glance.

Diocletian's Palace ★★★

MOMENT AGES 4 AND UP My first sight of Diocletian's Palace in Split was a revelation. The guide books tend to play down its impressiveness. Yet its ruined grandeur, and the way that later building has encroached on its remains and blurred its outline, give a far better idea of the centuries that have passed since it was built than any number of

SPLIT CITY CENTRE

Split

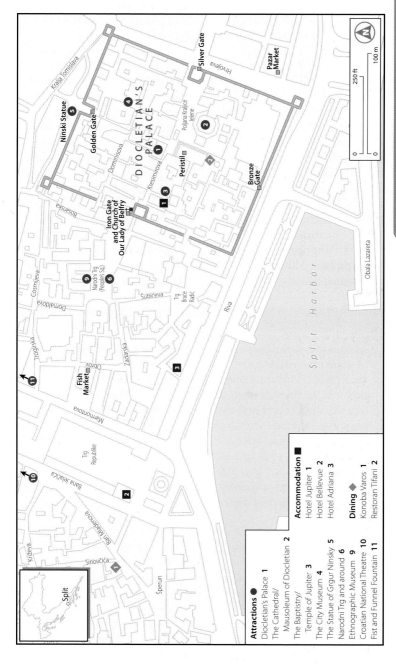

Attractions ●
Diocletian's Palace **1**
The Cathedral/
Mausoleum of Diocletian **2**
The Baptistry/
Temple of Jupiter **3**
The City Museum **4**
The Statue of Grgur Ninsky **5**
Narodni Trg and around **6**
Ethnographic Museum **9**
Croatian National Theatre **10**
Fist and Funnel Fountain **11**

Accommodation ■
Hotel Jupiter **1**
Hotel Bellevue **2**
Hotel Adriana **3**

Dining ◆
Konoba Varos **1**
Restoran Tifani **2**

better-preserved archaeological sites.

Any visit to Split must start with Diocletian's Palace. The Roman Emperor Diocletian (c245–c312AD) was a great rarity for his day in that he took early retirement voluntarily, rather than courtesy of coup or assassination. Upon retirement, Diocletian needed somewhere to live once he'd relinquished the reins of power. The general consensus is that he was born in the town of Salona, which is just outside modern-day Split, so the chances are that he decided to build this huge palace close to his birthplace. Although most of the original palace complex is a crumbling ruin, there is still much to see and the site has been placed on UNESCO's World Heritage List.

The best place to start is on the 'Quay of the Croatian National Revival' (known to all the locals, thank heavens, as the Riva). This long waterfront street, all cafés, restaurants and hotels, lies at the heart of Split's street life, and is thronged with young people passing the time of day. Goran Ivanišević, Split's 2001 Wimbledon hero, was welcomed home here. Have a good look at the excellent reconstruction of what the palace must have looked like, in a huge glazed display case under

Goran Ivanišević

As Goran Ivanišević grew up in Split, it might have been expected that he would become some form of engineer – his father was a professor of the subject, his mother a chemical engineer. However, it soon became clear that the boy was a natural athlete: he was a keen footballer and basketball player, and won the city's cross country championship no fewer than five times.

But it was in tennis that Goran excelled. Having started to play when he was seven, 10 years later in 1988 he was good enough to turn professional. Four years after that he was ranked second in the world. Despite considerable success all over the world in the 1990s, at Wimbledon he seemed destined only for disappointments and near misses.

In 2001, however, Goran achieved national hero status by winning the Wimbledon men's singles title. Having got into the tournament on a wild card, he beat Australian Pat Rafter 6-3, 3-6, 6-3, 2-6, 9-7 in a riveting and emotional final. His good looks, aggressive style and sense of humour made him the darling of the crowd – he is still widely popular throughout the world.

In Croatia, though, and even more so in his home city of Split, it goes further than this – to his compatriots and especially his fellow Splićani – Goran Ivanišević is little short of a god.

Diocletian (245AD–312AD)

Diocletian is a difficult man to pin down. He's principally remembered as one of the greatest saint-creators of all time. And this is not a good thing – he created them, of course, by killing early Christians. Indeed, under Diocletian, persecution of Christians progressed from being a hobby to becoming part of state policy. From 303AD, when the 'Edict against the Christians' was issued, Christians in the army were expelled, church property was confiscated and Christian texts were destroyed. Eventually, Christians had to choose between renouncing their faith or being executed. As Christianity spread, with even the Roman Empire eventually adopting it, Diocletian was bound to get a bad press.

Careful inspection, however, shows that he was more than the unmitigated scoundrel and all-purpose bogey-man that he is often portrayed as. For a start, he was a self-made man. Born to slaves in nearby Salona, in 245AD, he rose through the ranks of the army, finally becoming Emperor in 284AD. That's a terrific achievement in anybody's book.

Then again, he was a very successful Emperor. He put to an end 50 years of chaos in the Roman Empire, and restored respect for its rulers. He reformed the financial system and the army. He secured the Empire's borders against the Persians. And far from being a megalomaniac dictator, he introduced the Tetrarchy – rule by four men instead of one.

Above all, he did what virtually no other Emperor had managed, or even tried, to do – he retired! He had a superb palace built in what is now Split, and retired to it in 305AD, spending the last seven years of his life growing cabbages. He even declined to return to government when begged to by his failing successors.

the palm trees. Then enter the remains of the palace through its unassuming Bronze Gate (enticingly emblazoned with the legend 'The substructure of Diocletian's Palace'), which once gave the inhabitants access to the sea.

Stretching away to the left and right is the 'basement' (summer 8am to 8pm, winter 8am to noon, 4pm to 7pm; 10 Kuna (90p), the huge vaulted underpinning of what once was (from west to east) the Emperor's living quarters, the main reception room, and the dining room (which as every schoolchild knows, based on the three couches on which the diners reclined, is called the Triclinium). You'll get no better feel for the massive scale of the palace. There are multi-lingual displays with information on the palace, the development of the town, the four gates (Golden, Silver, Bronze and Iron) and the temples.

In the Central Hall, between the two basement wings, there are lots of stalls selling jewellery,

Diocletian's Palace

The palace built for Diocletian's retirement was a wonder of its age. Covering some 30,000 square metres at the edge of the sea in what is today the city of Split, no expense was spared in its construction – materials flooded in from all over the Balkans, and as far afield as Greece and Egypt. The layout of the palace was essentially similar to that of the villas of prosperous Romans throughout the Empire – rectangular in outline, with public rooms at the front, private apartments to the rear, all clustered around open courtyards to provide light and fresh air. The palace was on such a gigantic scale that it required four entrance gates, their names reflecting their importance – golden, silver, bronze and iron.

The whole of the current frontage, lining the Riva, marks the southern edge of the palace. On first entering through the Bronze Gate, you are actually in the basement of the building, the vaults that held up the Cryproporticus or Great Gallery, the Triclinium or Dining Room, the Central Hall, Main Reception and possibly Diocletian's living quarters. There's nothing to see of the actual rooms, but the scale of these subterranean spaces gives a clue to their size. Beyond this, a flight of steps leads up to the Peristyle, off which opened Diocletian's mausoleum (now the Cathedral) and the Temple of Jupiter (now the Baptistry). This is the most interesting part, where a great deal remains of the palace, but with many incursions and additions from later ages. There's little left of the northern half of the palace, though the magnificent Golden Gate can still be seen.

The palace's heyday lasted for 300 years. Then it slowly sank into obscurity as it was first colonised by a wave of refugees fleeing the destruction of the nearby city of Salona in 615, then slowly absorbed by the city of Split as it grew up around and through it, with local people helping themselves to ready-cut masonry for their buildings.

The surprising thing is how much of the palace remains. It is now pure solidified history, and in its ruined magnificence is one of the most affecting monuments I have ever seen. Its influence has also travelled far and wide – architect Robert Adam visited the site in the mid-18th century and made extensive sketches and notes which inspired and influenced architects all over the UK and Europe.

souvenirs, handbags, framed pictures, ceramics and textiles. Then you can climb the steps up into the light of the Peristyle, which was once the central square of the palace, and is now a raucous meeting place surrounded by impressive Roman remains. The Cathedral (once Diocletian's mausoleum) is on one side and the Baptistry (once the Temple of Jupiter) on the other. The area also has a jumble of café tables, hawkers selling stuff and, if you're lucky, very superior street performers.

World's Smallest Street <<

Inside the remains of Diocletian's Palace in Split is what is said to be the world's smallest street. Called 'Pusti me proći' (Let Me Pass), it is only wide enough for one person to walk along it at a time.

INSIDER TIP >>

Keep a tight hold on younger children – it would be very easy to get lost down there, and each chamber looks much like the other.

The Cathedral of St Domnius/Tomb of Emperor Diocletian AGES 4 AND UP

Split's Cathedral was once the tomb of the Emperor Diocletian, which is somewhat ironic as during his reign he was a zealous persecutor of Christians. The first thing to notice is the black sphinx to the right of the Cathedral entrance – it's over 2,000 years old, and was once one of a pair that guarded the entrance to Diocletian's mausoleum. Next, take a look at the Cathedral doors – they date from 1214, are made from walnut and oak, and have vivid carvings of 28 scenes from the life of Christ. The children will love deciphering them – always assuming, of course, that they know something about the life of Christ.

Inside the Cathedral, the most interesting thing is probably the Altar of St. Anastasius, who met his untimely end by being sent to sleep with the fishes: Diocletian ordered that he be thrown into a river with a boulder tied round his neck. The altar's statuary shows Christ being roughed up by a couple of hard men (the Flagellation of Christ), and Anastasius with the rope around his neck clearly visible. The saint's bones are apparently still buried under the altar.

In other parts of the Cathedral are commemorations of Split's two other famous Christian martyrs – St. Domnius (beheaded in 304AD) and St. Arnerius (stoned to death in 1180).

For those with the energy and a strong head for heights, for a nominal 5 Kuna (45p) you can climb the six-storey bell tower for wonderful views across the city.

The Baptistry/Temple of Jupiter AGES 4 AND UP

Directly across the Peristyle from the Cathedral, down a narrow alley in which baulks of timber prevent the buildings on either side of it from leaning wearily towards each other, is the Baptistry, built by Diocletian as a temple to Jupiter (or maybe Janus). The temple, together with other parts of the Palace, were visited by the Scottish architect Robert Adam in 1757, who felt that the 18th century

Revolution Art

In 1968, the year of youth revolution across Europe, three students painted the Peristyle of Diocletian's Palace red. It was hailed both as a political act (red being the colour of the left) and as a bold piece of conceptual art. A deadpan Yugoslav government, however, condemned 'Red Peristyle' as simple vandalism. In 1998, the anniversary of Red Peristyle was celebrated by Igor Grubić by painting a black circle in the middle of the Peristyle – again a political statement (black is the colour of fascism) and a piece of conceptual art. A deadpan Croatian government condemned it as simple vandalism

had a lot to learn about proportion, and about building techniques, from the ancient Romans. He recorded everything he saw, and the book of engravings that he produced was hugely influential in the European-wide classical revival. His description of Split could be applied to the modern-day city: 'the people are vastly polite, everything vastly cheap; a most wholesome air and glorious situation'. Today the temple has a warm, honey-coloured vaulted roof, a famous baptismal font portraying a Croatian king with a supplicant at his feet, and a modern statue of John the Baptist by (guess who) Ivan Meštrović (see p.72).

The City Museum AGES 5 AND UP
North of the Peristyle a maze of little lanes, once one of the worst slums in Split, are now clean and attractively decked out in painted shutters and potted plants. Tucked away on Papalićeva, just off the main street to the northern Golden Gate, is the City Museum – nicely laid out, with weapons, ships' figureheads and documents relating to the city.

The Statue of Grgur Ninsky
★★★ AGES 2 AND UP Beyond the splendid northern Golden Gate (swathed in fabric-covered scaffolding when I visited) stands yet another Meštrović statue: the enormous representation of Bishop Grgur Ninsky. A great patriotic figure in Croatia's history, Grgur was a tenth century bishop of Nin (north of Zadar) who fought for the right of Croatians to use their own language instead of Latin. You'll find other versions of the statue elsewhere in Croatia. It's a popular local belief that touching his big toe brings good luck, so the whole family should take it in turns to do so while making a wish.

Narodni Trg and around
AGES 5 AND UP Beyond and largely to the west of Diocletian's Palace, the rest of Medieval Split

Meštrović 's Statue of Grgur Ninsky

outside edge of the pavement – you can walk underneath the arch of water.

The Marjan Peninsula ★★

ALL AGES The centre of Split can, after a few hours, become very tiring, especially for children. The nearest help is a kilometre or so away – 15 minutes on foot, or a five minute drive, will bring you to the start of the Marjan Peninsula, which is worth a visit in its own right. It's one of the main recreation areas available to Split's residents and visitors alike. Known officially as the Marjan Forest Park, it has nature paths, viewing points, playgrounds and a small zoo, as well as absolutely terrific views to the north and south, and across the city. The southern cliffs are used by mountaineers and free climbers.

On the south side of the park are the **Museum of Croatian Archaeological Monuments** **ADULTS** and the **Ivan Meštrović Gallery** **AGES 5 AND UP**. The latter is housed in a building that the sculptor (see p.72) originally intended to make his home, but he'd only lived there for two years when he had to flee to the capital to avoid the Fascist occupation of Dalmatia in 1941.

is clustered around the main square – Narodni Trg. In the vicinity are the Town Hall (now the Ethnographic Museum), the fish market (smelly enough to cause distress to the carvings on the building next door), the city council building (the Prokurative) and, further north, the Croatian National Theatre. Also look out for an imaginative modern **fountain** ★★★ where the water squirts from a hand mounted in the city wall just to the west of the Grgur Ninsky statue, into a receptacle on the

GREATER **SPLIT**

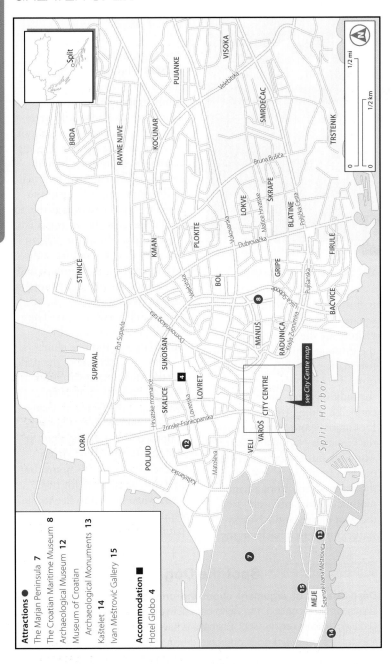

Split

Attractions ●
The Marjan Peninsula **7**
The Croatian Maritime Museum **8**
Archaeological Museum **12**
Museum of Croatian
Archaeological Monuments **13**
Kaštelet **14**
Ivan Meštrović Gallery **15**

Accommodation ■
Hotel Globo **4**

VISOKA

PUJANKE

BRDA

RAVNE NJIVE

KOCUNAR

Velebitska

SMRDEČAC

TRSTENIK

Bruna Bušića

SKRAPE

KMAN

PLOKITE

LOKVE

Vukovarska

Matice Hrvatske

BLATINE

Poljička Cesta

FIRULE

STINICE

Dubrovačka

BOL

GRIPE

Pujišanska

Velebitska

Ulica Slobode

MANUŠ

BAČVICE

RADUNICA

Kralja Zvonimira

8

Put Supavla

SUPAVAL

Domovinskog rata

SUKOIŠAN

4

LOVRET

CITY CENTRE

see City Centre map

LORA

SKALICE

Hrvatske mornarice

Lovretska

Zrinske-Frankopanska

VAROŠ

Split Harbor

POLJUD

12

Matoševa

VELI

Kaštelanska

7

13

MEJE

15

Šetanste Ivana Meštrovića

14

½ mi

½ km

Hajduk Split

All round the city there are graffiti tributes to Hajduk Split, the city's local football team. If you walk north from the Old Town, you'll come first to their old ground (Stari plac), then after the Archaeological Museum, their new home the Poljud Stadium. Formed in 1911 by university students returning to Split from abroad, Hajduk Split are famous not only for the standard of their football (though they're undoubtedly one of the great European football clubs) but also for the fervour of their support. Proudly Croatian during times when the country was subsumed into Austria-Hungary and later Yugoslavia, they were shipped by the partisans en masse to Italy towards the end of World War 2 to play demonstration matches as an identifiably anti-fascist team. Already known for their enthusiasm, their supporters reached new heights after the war as they copied the chanting, singing and flag-waving of the Brazilian supporters in the 1950 World Cup. The name 'Torcida' remains, in tribute.

Tickets are on sale at the ground (from kiosks outside the south stand) at a fraction of the cost of tickets to see top class football in the UK. Avoid the north stand (that's where the Torcida hang out). If you'd prefer the posher seats, try the west stand. The supporters club has its own website (***www.torcida.org***), and although it's all in Croatian, the pictures alone give a taste of what all the fuss is about.

There's more of his work in the nearby **Kaštelet** (little castle) AGES 5 AND UP but the works are aesthetic and religious, and perhaps less interesting to the modern world than those in which he follows the political, historic and patriotic themes for which he is best known.

The Croatian Maritime Museum AGES 5 AND UP The

Croatian Maritime Museum is located to the northeast of Split, in the shadow of Tvrđava Gripe – a massive 17th century Venetian fortress designed to repel the Turks.

The Maritime Museum contains a wide variety of naval bits and pieces, including lots of model ships, and a good display of torpedoes built for the Austro-Hungarian navy (by, incidentally, a Croatian engineer who was helped by Englishman Robert Whitehead). Pride of place goes to an absolutely enormous Roman storage vessel – probably used to store fish.

Shopping with Children

Split's main shopping street is the pleasant and pedestrianised Marmontova – this is where to go for branches of international chains (like Benetton, which seems to be ubiquitous in Croatia). However, for the most enjoyable shopping experience head for the small shops hidden away in the labyrinthine streets and alleys within the walls of Diocletian's Palace, and the souvenir, clothes, picture, handicraft and ceramics stalls that throng the Palace basement. Specialist food and wines can be bought at the daily market east of the Silver Gate, and at Vinoteka Bouquet (Riva 3) and Vinoteka Sv. Martin (Majstora Jurja 17.

Family Entertainment

Split has a flourishing arts scene, and is especially strong in drama, ballet, classical music and opera. Much of this revolves around the highly regarded Croatian National Theatre (HNK), Trg Gaje Bulata1, *021-363-014*, *www.hnk-split.hr*. There is also a very active youth drama scene at the City Youth Theatre (Trg Republike 1, *021-344-979*), with performances, and workshops for song and dance. Worth consulting for coming events is the Split branch of the Croatian Heritage Foundation, Nodilova 1, *021-321-904, www.matis.hr*, and the listings in the city's local paper 'Slobodna Dalmacija'. The cinema is Kino Produzeće Ekran, Trg Republike 1/III *021-348-676* – films are usually English language with subtitles in Croatian.

From mid-July to mid-August, the Split Summer Festival mounts music and drama at venues throughout the city (details from the Croatian National Theatre). In contrast to the mainstream of the Summer Festival, the International

Fist and Funnel, Split

Festival of New Film (*www.split filmfestival.hr*), at the end of September, attracts alternative film from all over the world.

For information regarding the bar and club scene in the city, get a copy of free listings magazines 'Splitski Navigator ' and 'Scena' from the Tourist Bureau at Riva 12. The beach used by all the locals is Blue Flag winner Bačvice, just across the railway tracks from the harbour, bus and railway station – it has showers, changing facilities, and an excellent bar (the Tropic Club Equador).

Family-Friendly Accommodation

There aren't many hotels in the centre of Split, though those that exist are not only pleasant, but also seem to be on the up. Until recently Split wasn't seen by most holidaymakers as part of Croatia's tourist industry, but its many attractions – particularly Diocletian's Palace – have started to draw in a growing number of visitors.

Hotel Adriana ★★ A quality small hotel, the Adriana, is situated just down the Riva from the Bellevue (see below). It is easy to miss, as the sign is just a small plaque on the wall. Look out for its popular restaurant with bar tables to the left, dining tables to the right, and newspapers hanging in a frame to the left of the door. The rooms are bright and functional, with a nice cool, dark interior. Most rooms are fine for families – there are double rooms and apartments available. Ask for one with a view.

Preporoda 8. ☎ *021-340-000.* **www. hotel-adriana.hr.** *five rooms; two apts. Mid-Apr to mid-Oct: from 850 Kuna (£ 80) double. 1200 Kuna (£ 115) apt (1400 Kuna (£ 132 with terrace). AE, DC, MC, V. Amenities: restaurant. In room: A/C, TV, minibar.*

Hotel Bellevue ★ A staid, slightly old-fashioned hotel, the Bellevue is nevertheless cool and pleasant, with a nice covered terrace under the colonnades facing Trg Republike. It was once quite upmarket (the French President François Mitterand stayed here during peace talks in 1992), but has accepted a more humble role since then. Although not obviously family friendly, it does have family rooms, and Trg Republike is traffic-free and therefore safe. The hotel is within a 10-minute walk of the

railway and bus stations, as well as the ferry port.

Bana josipa jelačļića 2. ☎ *021-345-644 or 021-347-499. Fax 021-362-382.* **www.hotel-bellevue-split.hr.** *50 rooms. From 750 Kuna (£ 71) double; 900 Kuna (£ 85) triple, from 1000 Kuna (£ 95) suite. 10% discount for children up to age 10. Rates include breakfast. Limited free parking. AE, DC, MC, V. Amenities: restaurant/bar, coffee-shop, concierge, money exchange, room service, laundry. In room: TV, minibar (suites only), hair dryer.*

Hotel Globo A nice hotel that is unfortunately in a rather scruffy and run down area, though it is only a 10-minute walk from the centre. The rooms available adapt well to families with a wide range of doubles and triples. Extra beds/cots are available, and there's a family room with two bedrooms. The restaurant has child portions, but no high chairs.

Lovretska 18. ☎ *021-481-111. Fax 021-481-118.* **www.hotelglobo.com.** *25 rooms. From 1100 Kuna (£ 105) double, 1340 Kuna (£ 127) triple, 1710 Kuna (£ 162) family. AE, DC, MC, V. Limited free parking. Amenities: breakfast room, elevator. In room: A/C, TV, minibar, Internet access.*

Hotel Jupiter ★ Wonderfully located in the maze of alleys directly behind the temple of the same name, the Hotel Jupiter has recently been renovated and provides clean, fresh rooms at extremely reasonable rates. With no breakfasts (but a really nice café-restaurant in the courtyard), and shared bathrooms, the

Jupiter is perhaps suitable only for shortish stays, but it's got a really pleasant feel – modern, bright, with an iced-water dispenser in the lobby – and is well-disposed towards families. It has double and triple rooms, but is open to negotiation to fit more children into the triple.

Grabočvevаširina 1. 📞 *021-344-801. www.hotel-jupiter.info. 25 rooms (three singles, 10 doubles, 12 triples). 250 Kuna (£ 24) per person flat rate (children 0–5 free, 5–18 150 Kuna (£ 14). Rates do not include breakfast. No credit cards. Amenities: cafe/bar, Sat TV room. In room: A/C double and triple rooms, fans in singles. Towels supplied but bring soap.*

Family-Friendly Dining

There is no shortage of eating places in Split, though there's a tendency for them all to be competing for the same market.

Konoba Varoš ★★★ DALMATIAN

Just west of the Bellevue (see above), the Konoba Varoš doesn't look too promising – the street frontage isn't very extensive, and there are usually locals playing cards at the two outside tables. Don't be dismayed. Inside, this is a large and comfortably air-conditioned restaurant with a varied menu and wine list. Among the specialties of the house are the *peka* – meats cooked under a lid. There are different sized tables, and there's a lot of bench seating too.

Ban mladenova 7. 📞 *021-396-138. Main courses 60–80 Kuna (£ 6–8). AE, DC, MC, V. Daily 11am–midnight.*

Restoran Tifani ★★ DALMATIAN

The great attraction of this restaurant, apart from its position right in the centre of Diocletian's Palace, is the variety and quirkiness of its menu. No immediate thought is given to the needs of children, but there is a willingness to bend over backwards to comply with even the most eccentric choices of the young. It can get very busy, so probably a good choice outside rush times.

Poljana kraljice jelene 5. 📞 *021-329/ 070. Fax 021-329-088. www.hotel peristil.com. Entrees 45–160 Kuna (£ 4.30–15). AE, DC, MC, V. Daily 7am–midnight.*

TROGIR

Some 22km (14 miles) along the coast northwest of Split, after a series of villages collectively called the Kaštela (each has its own little castle – in fact, fortified houses intended to defend the local lord's lands and act as summer retreats), you come to another Adriatic gem – Trogir, one of Croatia's seemingly endless supply of walled towns attached to the mainland by a bridge, or in this case, both to the mainland and to another island. It's as enchanting as Dubrovnik, but on a much smaller, and therefore more human, scale. It was added to the UNESCO list of World Heritage Sites in 1997.

TROGIR

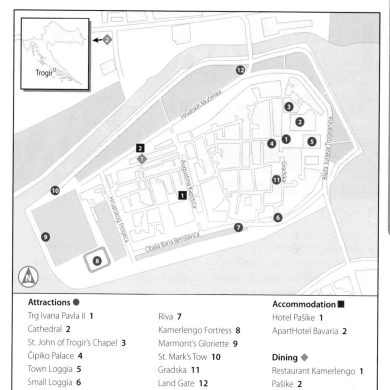

Attractions ●

Trg Ivana Pavla II **1**
Cathedral **2**
St. John of Trogir's Chapel **3**
Čipiko Palace **4**
Town Loggia **5**
Small Loggia **6**

Riva **7**
Kamerlengo Fortress **8**
Marmont's Gloriette **9**
St. Mark's Tow **10**
Gradska **11**
Land Gate **12**

Accommodation ■

Hotel Pašike **1**
ApartHotel Bavaria **2**

Dining ◆

Restaurant Kamerlengo **1**
Pašike **2**

Essentials

Getting There

The bus station is just outside the city gate next to the outdoor market. Split's airport, a kilometre or so down the road, is actually closer to Trogir than to Split.

Getting Around

You'll need to explore Trogir on foot – it's tiny, and you can walk right around the island in about 15 minutes.

Visitor Information

The tourist office in Trogir is on the main square at Trg Ivana Pavla II/I (☎ *021-885-628*; fax: *021-881-412*; *www.dalmacija.net/trogir.htm*; 8am–9pm June–Sept and 8am–2pm other times.

Things To See & Do

You'll almost certainly approach the town from the mainland bus station, which is next to an open air market and the local Konzum supermarket. So if you're intent on a family picnic, what could

Old Town, Trogir

be more convenient? The stretch of water between the mainland is incredibly narrow (it looks more like a minor canal than a stretch of sea), and is spanned by a little three-arched bridge. At the island end of this bridge is the **Land Gate**, topped by the town's patron St. John of Trogir, which gives access to the (pedestrianised) Old Town. The main street – Gradska – would in most towns qualify as an alley!

INSIDER TIP
As you walk through Trogir, notice the little stone eyelets sticking out from first floor walls. It's thought that they were anchor-points for pulleys used to haul heavy furniture up to upstairs rooms. They may also have been used to erect screens to deflect the sun.

Trogir is ideal for pottering around – older children can follow their own inclinations, and meet up with the family

at a pre-arranged rendezvous. But some things are worth taking a look at together. In particular, on the central square, **Trg Ivana Pavla II the Cathedral ALL AGES** has elements likely to be fascinating to people of all ages, whether devout Christians or without a religious bone in their body. Take the West Portal's amazing riot of carving, created in 1240 by master-mason Radovan. In addition to the usual saints and apostles, you'll also identify a whole host of ordinary people from the Middle Ages – farmers slaughtering pigs, another making sausages, a man pruning vines, another chasing a hare, woodcutters, leather workers, Jews and Turks, all intertwined with a range of animals from mundane sheep to mythical beasts and mermaids.

Within the cathedral is **St. John of Trogir's Chapel ★ ★ ★ ALL AGES**, which has a barrel-vaulted ceiling covered with sculpted heads of saints, angels and cherubs. At the centre God peers down, as if to see what's going on. At ground level, life-sized statues of saints stand around in niches, below which more cherubs, holding torches, peer cheekily through half-opened doors, presumably representing the passage between life and death. It can't help but bring a smile to the face.

Still on the square, the **Čipiko Palace** ADULTS is well worth visiting (look out for the typical Venetian triple windows) and the cool 15th century **Town Loggia** AGES 5 AND UP in whose shade justice was once dispensed - acting as an open-air court where criminals were tried and disputes settled - topped by a handsome clock tower. There's a relief on the east wall of St. John of Trogir and St. Lawrence (holding the grill on which he was roasted to death) – there used to be a Venetian lion, but it was blown up in 1932 by anti-Italian Croat nationalists, provoking Mussolini into threats severe enough to bring a grovelling Yugoslav apology. On the back (south) wall is a rather nice relief by Meštrović, of Petar Berislavić (he struggled against the Turks).

Beyond the square you eventually pass the remains of the town walls and the '**Small Loggia**', and step through the **Town Gate** (topped by a little UNESCO sign) out onto the **Riva**, the seafront promenade that faces the island of Čiovo (which is linked to Trogir by a bridge). The Riva is a pleasant, palm-lined street, with restaurants on one side and yachts on the other. There are lots of attractive buildings, including the 15th century **Kamerlengo Fortress** (impressive, but just a shell in the process of being renovated) and the six-columned **Marmont's Gloriette**, a tribute to the Napoleonic governor of Trogir. Look out for **St. Mark's Tower**, now 'The House of Croatian Music', which is topped by little umbrellas, like

Trogir Cathedral

Trampoline, Trogir

cocktail sticks. Next to the Kamerlengo Fortress are four individual trampolines and a huge eight-bay communal one ★★.

Beyond St. Mark's Tower – and you're now approaching the Land Gate again, having done a complete circuit of the town – there's an elegant pedestrian bridge across to the mainland. In the small park **ALL AGES** there are some public toilets. Here, you are very likely to see men playing the Croatian version of *boules*.

Family-Friendly Accommodation

ApartHotel Bavaria ★★ If you'd rather not be on the relatively cramped island of Trogir itself, your best bet is the town's seaside suburb about 4km to the northwest. It has a number of hotels, of which the Bavaria is probably the most useful for families. The hotel is convenient for the local beach, and there is also a range of sports nearby.

The apartments, some of which have kitchenettes, are ideal for families. Yet you're still only five minutes drive from Trogir. One apartment has two bedrooms, two bathrooms, and a sofa bed in the lounge. Further camp beds can be added. Cots available at no extra charge.

Hrvatskih Žrtava 133, 21220 Trogir-Seget Donji. ☎ *021-880-601. Fax: 021-880-553. www.hotel-bavaria.hr. 18 rooms. 435 Kuna (£ 40) per person (double), 544 Kuna (£ 52) pp (with balcony, 870 Kuna (£ 84) to 1450 Kuna (£138) (apartments). Children up to age three free, children 3–7 50% discount, children 7–12 30% discount. Rates include breakfast. AE, DC, MC, V. Free parking. Amenities: Restaurant, bar. In room: A/C, TV.*

Hotel Pašike ★★ Trogir has several good hotels, of which the newest is the delightful Pašike, which opened in 2004. Situated in a traditional house in one of Trogir's narrow streets the hotel has seven rooms and an apartment. The interiors are restored stone, with antique furniture and wooden floors. Staff wear regional costume, which you might feel is edging over into the twee, but children are likely not only to love the hotel, but also perhaps learn something about the area from staying in it. The apartment has large beds in the bedroom and a large sofa bed in the lounge. Cots can be pre-ordered and will be in your room on arrival.

Sinjska bb, HR- 21210 Trogir ☎ 021-88-51-85. Fax 021-79-77-29. www.hotelpasike.com. Seven rooms plus apartment. 700 Kuna (£ 65) double, 1000 Kuna (£ 95) apartment. Rates include breakfast. Discount for children aged 3–12. Restaurant 10% discount for hotel guests.

Family-Friendly Dining

You've got a lot of choice over where to eat in Trogir. If funds are running low, you can visit the open market and the Konzum supermarket on the landward side of the bridge attaching the island to the mainland, and put together a picnic. Then you could sit on the Riva, or the bit of grassland on the western end of the island, or the park near the Land Gate, and enjoy an al fresco dining experience. However, if you feeling flush, there are many good restaurants. Here are two of the best.

Restaurant Kamerlengo ★★
CROATIAN Although not as close to the Kamerlengo Fortress as you

might expect, the Kamerlengo does a nice range of meat and fish cooked on an outdoor grill in the courtyard.

Vukovarska 2. ☎ 021-884-772. www. kamerlengo.hr. Main courses 30–150 Kuna (£3–14). AE, DC, MC, V. Daily 10am–midnight or 1am from early July to end of Aug.

Pašike ★★★ DALMATIAN
Attached to the hotel (see above), the Pašike is well known for its traditional food, especially its anchovy recipes and black risotto. The restaurant's Dalmatian food and wine is excellent, the waiters and waitresses are dressed in local costume, and there's often live regional folk music to entertain diners.

SOUTH OF SPLIT

The area south of Split is worth exploring, and can provide a number of day trips and excursions if you fancy a bit of fresh air.

Primošten AGES 5 AND UP

Lovely from afar, Primošten is a bit more prosaic once you get closer in. Yet another (it gets boring to say it) town on an island attached to the mainland by a causeway, it really does take your breath away when you see it from the coast road. Tourist buses often stop for five-minute photo-opportunities. And, alas, that's probably all its worth. Look at those photos you took,

SOUTH OF **SPLIT**

Primošten **1**
Omiš **2**
Cetina Gorge **3**
Imotski **4**
Makarska **5**
Mount Biokovo **6**
Brač **7**
Hvar **8**
Vis **9**
Korčula **10**

and you'll notice an inordinate number of grey houses with grey roofs, or bright white ones with vivid orange tiles – not the picturesque medieval houses you'd hoped for, but a lot of modern dwellings. Having said that, I could live there (old houses can be a pain). But those tour operators know a thing or two: if you stopped in Primošten, there really would be nothing to see or do. It's said of a lot of places, 'nice to visit, but I couldn't live there', but of Primošten, the opposite applies.

Omiš ALL AGES

An odd little town that straddles the end of the Cetina Gorge, Omiš was once a pirate stronghold. Many, including the Pope, attempted to clear the miscreants out but to no avail. It has two ruined Venetian fortresses poised on pinnacles above the town: the first, Mirabela, is accessed by a zig-zag path that starts behind the church, and is definitely worth a look (June–Sept, 8am till noon, then 4.30pm to 8.30pm; 10 Kuna (90p)) – the

Primošten

Piracy

The Adriatic has always had a reputation for piracy – right into the late 20th century, ships passing through the straits between the heel of Italy and the Balkan coast were attacked and boarded by Albanian pirates.

The pirates of Omiš were early second-millennium Corsairs, whose fast boats and skilled seamanship made them widely feared. They would prey on passing ships, darting out of the mouth of the Cetinal Gorge to attack, then quickly return to their impregnable base. They even formed alliances with tribes on the surrounding mainland, to prevent sudden attack from behind. Many attempts were made to clear them out of Omiš over the centuries (including one, in 1221 by the Pope), but no record exists of any final defeat.

A later, and different, thread of Croatian piracy is represented by the Uskoks, who were dispossessed 16th century Roman Catholic Bosnians and Croatians driven off their land in the interior by the advance of the Turkish Ottoman Empire. Many settled on the coast, especially at Senj and turned to piracy – ostensibly at the expense of their Turkish enemies, but in reality involving attacks on Venetian ships (because they were carrying Turkish goods), and those of any (often Orthodox Christian) subjects of the expanding Ottoman Empire. Highly successful pirates in their fast, 15-metre long rowing boats, they were tolerated by Austria (in whose territory Senj was) until in 1615 a thoroughly fed-up Venice declared war on both the pirates and on Austria (the so-called Uskok War).

The Uskoks initially did remarkably well, but when Austria came to terms with Venice, they were forced to surrender.

Omis

view from the tower roof is spectacular. The other – the Fortica – is only for goats, or for the really intrepid, needing an hour and a half or more of steep scrambling.

The main reason for visiting Omiš, though, is for access to the Cetina Gorge **ALL AGES**. Just before the bridge across the Cetina river (if you're approaching from the south), a right turn brings you immediately to a couple of tunnels that give you access to the gorge. The reed-lined river moves slowly between steep cliffs, speeding up the higher up the gorge you go. Every few hundred metres there are adverts for 'rafting'. The Cetina Gorge is pretty, and there's a lot of tourist infrastructure, with some nice hotels and restaurants: a good day out. If you want to extend the excursion, you can push on to Imotski.

Imotski ★★★ MOMENT
ALL AGES

After a couple of kilometres driving along the Cetina Gorge, you hit a series of z-bends that soar upwards into the mountains. The road-surface deteriorates, the road gets narrower – it's not quite wide enough for two converging cars to pass abreast, though locals gunning it clearly disagree. Soon, you find yourself and your family feeling a million miles from the tourist circuit – a really nice feeling.

Then, just when you're muttering that this is totally beyond the pale, you come out on a main road at Zadvarje, and bowl along, via Šestanovac, to Imotski.

You're now hard up against the border with Bosnia-Herzegovina, and heading for a town that is famous for holes in the ground (see below). Probably better not mention this to adolescent family-members: they may not be overwhelmed and can be quite cruel. But wait till they see the holes!

After driving along the Adriatic Coast, which can get a bit samey, it is a pleasure to arrive at this no-nonsense provincial Balkan hill town, sunny but cooled by altitude. There is a series of parallel streets that follow the contour lines, and a take-it-or-leave-it impression that you're welcome, but that they don't depend on you.

Imotski's holes are actually two lakes, famous throughout Croatia. One is called the **Blue**

Lake, the other is known as the **Red Lake**. The first is on the edge of the town centre, the other about a kilometre away and they're joined by a paved promenade, with lots of benches for a sit down.

The geology of the two lakes is fascinating. Created by the collapse of underground caverns in the karst (see p.21) they are incredibly deep. The Blue Lake is 300 metres (980 feet) deep, while the Red Lake sinks to an amazing 500 metres (1,640 feet). Fissures keep the lakes fed with water whenever the surrounding land is waterlogged. The Blue Lake is so called because the water is an astonishingly deep and vivid shade of blue. The Red Lake's water is also blue – the name derives from the red colour of the surrounding cliffs.

The Blue Lake has become a magnet for Croatian tourists and school groups and the natural amphitheatre that surrounds the lake has been landscaped with a variety of steps, paths and vantage points from which to enjoy the view. When I was there, a school group accompanied by a teacher and a nun were ooing and ahhing (and surreptitiously talking on their mobile phones) against the backdrop of this phenomenal lunar landscape. It is difficult to comprehend the scale of what you're looking at – a boat in the Blue Lake looks like an ant. The mature trees on the lip of the Red Lake resemble the tiniest fringe of hair on the bald head of a very old man.

THE MAKARSKA RIVIERA ALL AGES

If, instead of heading up the Cetina Gorge at Omiš, you continue down the *magistrala*, you come to one of Croatia's principal sea and surf holiday areas – a string of villages, squeezed between the Biokovo Mountains and the sea, known as the Makarska Riviera. The villages all have sweeping beaches (pebbles, I'm afraid), and seem to be divided in two: a business section along the coast road, and beach plus hotels down by the sea. In detail there may not be much to write home about, but the general effect of the string of orange-roofed villages curving around the deep blue Adriatic, against the spectacular backdrop of the towering, pale grey Biokovo Ridge, is breathtaking.

Essentials

Visitor Information

The Brela city tourist office is at Trg Alojzija Stepinca bb (☏ 021-618-455; *fax: 021-618-337; www.brela.hr*). The Makarska city tourist office is at Obala Kralja Tomislava 16 (☏ 021-612-002; *www.makarska.com*).

Getting There

The coastal bus route from Split to Dubrovnik through the Makarska Riviera, or the local services to Split, Zagreb and Ploče are your only real alternatives if you don't have a car

(Makarska Bus Company 📞 *021-612-333*).

What To See & Do

The only reason for staying on the Makarska Riviera is sun, sea and – well – pebbles. With a good choice of hotels and lots of water sports, it's an area to lie back and do nothing, sit on the beach, or spend time out on, above or under the water. It's certainly not much good as a base for exploring anywhere else – except, perhaps, for Mount Biokovo (see below), and that's not recommended unless you really know what you're doing, or you've booked an organised trip.

Starting from the north, the first village is **Brela**, and it's a pretty mixture of old and new houses, pine woods and loads of beach. Brela, you can't help feeling, sees itself as a cut above the rest of its Riviera neighbours. Next is **Baška Voda**, populist and packed, Southend to Brela's Brighton. The next two villages – **Promajna** and **Krvavica** – are much quieter. Look out, too, for **Bratuš**, a pretty little fishing village that the Riviera throng seems to have passed by.

However, the heart of the Makarska Riviera is, as you'd expect, the town of **Makarska** itself. Birthplace of footballer Alen Bokšić, who played for clubs in Croatia, Italy and England, and home to Croatia's best rugby team (set up by returning antipodean exiles), Markaska somehow has more historical ballast than the other towns along this coast. It has been ruled at different times by the Romans, the Turks, the Venetians and the Austrians, and the influence of the last two can be seen in the lovely Venetian mansions and dignified Habsburg-era hotels that stand out next to the drifts of modern apartments, restaurants, tourist agencies, banks and shops. Although there's a Town Museum, a monastery and an excellent **seashell museum** **ALL AGES** (1st May–30th September, 10am–noon, 5pm–7pm, but times vary), the main reason for coming to Makarska is to swim, soak up the sun, and possibly do a bit of walking.

Beyond Makarska, the villages and beaches of the Riviera – Tučepi, Podgora, Igrane, Drvenik, Zaostrog – stretch down towards **Ploče**, ending at **Gradac**. All are pleasant, none hold any great interest outside the normal beach holiday. But the hotels are comfortable, and they do all they can to bring some idea of Croatia's music culture to their guests.

For quiet and pleasant beaches on the Makarska Riviera (but, I'm afraid, little sand), at the northern end try Brela, whilst to the south there's Drvenik and Zaostrog.

Family-Friendly Accommodation

On the assumption that you're here for a beach holiday, your best choice of hotel is one of the many, dotted along the length of the Makarska Riviera, which are given over largely to package holidays. Although there's not much to choose between them, the most recently renovated (2004), and the one with the most apartments (seven) and facilities is the Meteor.

Hotel Meteor ★★ The Meteor is what Prince Charles would no doubt call a 'monstrous carbuncle': a huge 525-bed concrete house of cards spilling down the hillside, which has every conceivable type of room and variety of entertainment. Consequently, it can accommodate a wide variety of family sizes and tastes. As a major package summer-holiday destination, the hotel is used to children, and there's a full programme of activities for

them – what is usually called, in Croatia, as in France, 'animation'. *Kralja P. Krešimira IV bb, Makarska. 021-615-344. Fax: 021-611-419. www.hoteli-makarska.hr. 277 rooms. July–Aug: from 940 Kuna (£90) double; from 1015 Kuna (£100) suite. AE, DC, MC, V. Rates include breakfast. Half- and full board extra. Amenities: Restaurant, tavern, disco, snack bar, two pools, whirlpool, sauna. In room: A/C, TV, minibar.*

Family-Friendly Dining

Given that the holidaymakers who visit the Makarska Riviera tend to be on package holidays, with relatively few independent travellers, the food on offer in the area tends to be much the same from restaurant to restaurant because they're all competing for the same customers – there wouldn't be much percentage in trying to cater for

Mount Biokovo

The Biokovo ridge shadows the Makarska Riviera for 50 km or more. Its massive, grey eminence is always in view above the coast. At 1,762 metres (5,800 feet), Sveti Jure is the highest coastal mountain on the Adriatic. The ridge largely makes up the Biokovo National Park, established to preserve this whole area of Mediterranean scrub, pine forests and arid rock escarpment.

As a holiday resource, Biokovo is limited. It's a hard five-hour plus climb, and should only be attempted by those who know what they're doing. There is an incredibly steep track up to the top that will take a vehicle, but your driving needs to be of professional rally-driving standard, your nerves must be of steel, and you'll need a head for heights. If you don't fit the bill, but are still keen to see the terrific views, there are both guided walks and jeep trips up the mountain – have a look at *www.biokovo.net*, the website of Biokovo Active Holidays.

The view from the top is incredible. On a good day you can see Monte Gargano, 252 km (150 miles) away in Italy.

minority tastes. As a general rule, prices rise the closer you get to the sea. Of the hundreds of places available, here are a couple of the best.

Jez ★ ★ DALMATIAN Renowned for the fish and an excellent wine list, Jez is not a place for a quick snack – it's formal and it's pricy. But you get the service and the attitude you expect for the money, and for a special family occasion it's worth the cost.

Petra Kreišmira IV 90, Makarska. 📞 *021-611-741. Reservations recommended. Main courses: 60–130 Kuna (£ 6–12). MC. Daily 11am–midnight.*

Riva ★ DALMATIAN Equally well-reckoned, Riva is a pleasant setting, whether indoors or on its leafy terrace. Hearty fish and meat dishes are on the menu.

Obala Kralja Tomislava 6, Makarska. 📞 *021-616-829. Fax: 021-615-422.* ***restoran.riva@htnet.hr.*** *Main courses: 75–180 Kuna (£ 7–17). AE, DC, MC, V. Daily 11am–midnight.*

For Active Families

Because of the rugged nature of the countryside in the vicinity of Split – especially the Cetina Gorge and the Biokovo ridge, the area around Split is rich in activities and adventure holidays – for single day activities consult the nearest Tourist Office. There are also complete package holidays offering families a wide variety of physical activities in the area. For example, Adriatic Sunshine (***www.adriaticsunshine. com/adventure.htm***) has

combined packages that include canoeing, mountain biking, kayaking, camping, rafting and horseriding in the Split area for 5345 Kuna (around £ 500) per person, with a 50% discount for children up to 12 (minimum age 8). Alternatively, try ***www. activitiesabroad.com/family/ package12.htm***) or simply surf the Internet.

THE ISLANDS

Split is the gateway to a trio of islands that lie due south of the city – Brač, Hvar and Vis. Each has its own distinct charm.

Getting There

Ferries leave Split for all three islands, though there are also boats from Makarska (to Sumartin, on Brač) and Drvenik (to the eastern end of Hvar). During the summer there are additional boats and catamarans. Consult Jadrolinija's excellent website at ***www.jadrolinija.hr***.

The Split–Supetar (Brač) crossing takes approximately 55 minutes, and tickets are around 29 Kuna (£ 2.70) per person and 130 Kuna (£ 12) per car.

The Split–Stari Grad (Hvar) crossing takes about 1¾ hours, and 38 Kuna (£ 3.50) per person and 254 Kuna (£ 23.50) per car.

The Split–Vis takes 2½ hours and costs 41 Kuna (£ 3.75) per person and 268 Kuna (£ 24.60) per car.

Brač ★★ ALL AGES

Brač has two towns, Supetar and Bol, both of which have excellent beaches. Inland, the terrain is marked by piles of white stones (grubbed out of the earth over generations by farmers). Pockets of lush vines and olive and orange groves flourish in depressions in the *karst* (see p.21). Brač's famous for its stone, which was used not only to build Diocletian's Palace in Split (see p.108), but also Berlin's Reichstag, the White House in Washington DC and even the high altar in Liverpool Cathedral. Brač has also developed a reputation as a windsurfers Shangri-la.

Supetar, Brac's biggest town, has a golden, honey look, and is pleasant and unspoiled, with good beaches and restaurants, and a relaxed, family feel.

Its other town is Bol, on the south coast. It was once a sleepy fishing village made up of little stone houses until two things happened: its terrific double-bayed beach Zlatni rat (Golden Cape) was discovered by holidaymakers and by the Croatian Tourist Board (it's on all the tourist literature) and the airport

for the island was built a couple of kilometres outside the town. So it now gets very busy during July and August.

There really are no 'must-sees' on the island, though there are a number of unassuming museums, churches and villages to visit if you need a little diversion. But the *point* of Brač, as a holiday destination, is that it's the perfect place to chill out. It's easy to get to, there's not much to do, there's nothing that'd make you feel guilty if you missed it, and it's got a fine tourist infrastructure. Indeed, a straw poll of Croatians in different parts of the country came up time and time again with Brač as the best island for families to head for.

Hvar ★ ALL AGES

Hvar is one of the most beautiful islands in the Adriatic, famous for its long history, its lavender, and above all its climate (it snowed there in January 2005, and a number of hotels had to put their money where their mouths were and cough up refunds to their guests). Initially a nest for pirates, Hvar Town was cleared out eventually by the

Bol Beach

Makarska

Venetians, who resettled it and developed it as the island's capital. It is now the centrepiece of Hvar's tourist industry – sitting on a curved, south-facing bay dotted with islands, backed by 700-year old walls and fortifications, a jumble of orange-tiled roofs and pale yellow walls. Its harbour is a constant hum of activity, and the town itself has a certain air of chic – it's the most popular destination for the Croatian *cognoscenti* after Dubrovnik. Try to be there on 2nd August (St. Stephen's Day), which commemorates the diocese's patron saint.

Vis ALL AGES

The most far-flung of the three islands, Vis is considered by many to be one of the country's best-kept secrets. The island is remarkably unspoiled. This is mainly due to its military history. Tito (see p.226) lived in a cave on the island for part of World War 2, and a military base kept the island off limits until 1989.

It boasts two attractive villages (Vis Town and Komiža), produces excellent wine, and has nice beaches and clean seas. To add to its charms, there are some good Croatian restaurants and a handful of museums and archaeological sites. The island's gentle, unspoiled character makes it a place that it would be better to visit sooner rather than later. You don't know how long it's going to last.

What's in a Name?

When it was inhabited by a Greek colony in 385BC the island of Hvar was known as Pharos. Under Roman rule it became known as Pharia and later Fara. In the 8th century Slavs settlers arrived, who renamed it Hvar, before the resident Roman population decided to have a change of heart and call it Quarra. In the 11th century the Italians got poetical and called the island Lesina, meaning forest (the island was covered with trees at the time). This name remained in use until the 19th century.

5 Northern Dalmatia

It is difficult to summarise northern Dalmatia. In Zadar, its principal settlement, it has a relatively urbane city that looks seawards towards the inevitable islands and north to the ancient town of Nin, which has claims to being one of Croatia's most important towns. The surrounding holiday areas have the benefit of sandy beaches (rare for Croatia), while the Velebit Mountains, to the east, must be one of the most barren places on earth. Šibenik, to the south of Zadar, is northern Dalmatia's second city and is worth a visit, if only for the views of the city from St. Anne's Fortress (see p.145).

TOP 10 FAMILY EXPERIENCES

1 Listening to the extraordinary music of the Sea Organ on the quayside at Zadar, as wavelets or the wakes of passing boats force air through its subterranean pipes.

2 People-watching in Zadar's central square Narodni trg (trg means square), against the backdrop of the 16th century guard house and the Town Loggia – there's no better place to skim pamphlets picked up from the Tourist Office on the square.

3 Exploring the pedestrianised and paved lanes of Varoš, Zadar's medieval quarter.

4 Looking at the carved heads on Šibenik's cathedral, and making up stories about who they were and what they did for a living.

5 Climbing up to Šibenik's St. Anne's Fortress – all roads in Šibenik seem to lead there eventually – and taking in the superb view.

6 Swimming in the lower pool of the Krka National Park's Skradinski Buk – the only place in its 800 metres length, and 17 cascades, where this is allowed. Follow this up with a meal at one of the restaurants at the entrance to the park.

7 Climbing to the top of the waterfalls in Skradinski Buk, and buying local produce from one of the stalls under the trees on the way down.

8 Walking through Nin, enjoying its churches and the sense of a once great town sleeping in the sun.

9 Visiting the donkey farm just outside Nin.

10 Enjoying the beach activities, sports, cafés, restaurants and shops in Zaton Holiday Village.

ZADAR

Zadar is the capital of the region and has a population of about 80,000. Ever since the new Zagreb–Split motorway opened, the city is less dominated by through traffic, and now feels a great deal more relaxed and laid back than it was. Zadar was ruled for most of the period between the two World Wars by Italy and there is still a lot of Italian spoken here, especially by older people.

Although it does have its mountains – particularly that other-worldly Velebit range some distance away to the northeast – you're far less conscious of being overlooked by nearby highlands than in most Croatian coastal towns and cities. This adds to its peaceful, easy-going atmosphere.

It has to be said that many of Zadar's attractions are of limited general interest, being mainly of an ecclesiastical nature. The Old Town, as in most Croatian coastal settlements, is fortified and built on a narrow peninsula. If you're driving, it's best to park in the area called Jazine, near the basketball stadium, and walk the final half a kilometre. The city centre itself is traffic free, and the squares are filled with café tables and outdoor seating for restaurants. Unusually, the focal point of the city is a square – Narodni Trg – rather than the more common Riva or promenade. Zadar's Riva, despite a certain amount of life in the evenings, is relatively empty. It does, however, have one of the most extraordinary musical instruments cum art installations cum conversation pieces you're ever likely to come across – a stunningly beautiful sea organ (see p.139).

Should you tire of the city, the Kornati National Park (see p.153) is just off the coast.

Essentials

Getting There

By Air Croatia Airlines flights land at Zadar Airport, which is about 12 km (7½ miles) southeast of the city. There's a bus into town (20 Kuna (£ 18).

Croatia Airlines in Zadar, Poljana Natka Nodila 7 (☎ 023-250-094; fax: 023-250-109; *Zadto@ croatiaairlines.hr*), is open 8am to 4pm Monday to Friday, 9am to noon Saturday, closed Sunday.

By Car the new Zagreb–Split motorway has halved the driving time between the capital and northern Dalmatia, and Zadar is now tied far more closely to the capital, and to the rest of northern Croatia. It is relatively easy to get to from most parts of Croatia and is 288 km (180 miles) from Zagreb (around three hours) and 169 km (105 miles) from Split (under two hours). Dubrovnik is 377 km (235 miles) to the southeast, but it seems further and takes longer, because the motorway ends near Split. It's a fairly hard five-hour drive, or even more in summer when the traffic is heavy.

By Boat Ferries arrive along Luburnska obala, the road that goes along the harbour side, and marks the northern edge of the city centre. So you're delivered to the heart of Zadar, and are just minutes away from the square. There are ferry connections to virtually all the islands and cities along Croatia's coast, as well as to Bari and Ancona in Italy.

By Bus and Rail The bus and railway stations in Zadar are about a kilometre east of the city centre, in a remarkably clean and user-friendly area that is thronged with shops, cash machines and other necessities. The city centre is a 20-minute walk or five minutes on the local No. 5 bus.

Zadar Coach Station is at Ante Starčevića 2 (023-211-555; *www.liburnija-zadar.hr*). The Zadar railway station is next to it, at Ante Starčevića 4 (060-333-444; *www.htnet.hr*)

Visitor Information

The main city Tourist Information Centre is at Narodni Trg 5 (023-316-166). The County Tourist Board, covering the surrounding area, is at Sv. Leopolda B. Mandića 1 (023-315-107; *www.zadar.hr*).

Getting Around

Zadar city centre is pedestrianised, so you'll have to travel by Shanks's pony. Away from the centre, the buses run along Liburnska obala, where there is also a taxi rank.

Northern Dalmatia Itineraries

If You Have 1 Day

Morning: spend the morning looking around Zadar. Start at Narodni Trg, where you can have a drink at one of the tables that crowd the square, and browse through the information in the Tourist Office. Walk along the main street, dip into the Archaeological Museum (see p.136), then let the children have a run around on the Forum. Pay a quick visit to the Cathedral (see p.136) and St. Donat's Church (see p.136), then walk through and out onto the Riva. Sit on the steps of the Sea Organ, and be calmed by the wonderful sounds. Continue round the peninsula to the market near the footbridge across to the rest of the city. Do some shopping. Have lunch.

Afternoon: drive north to Nin (see p.149). Park outside the Tourist Office on the mainland side of the bridge, then walk across the bridge and look around this peaceful, sleepy little town (look out for the little Church of the Holy Cross). Stop off, on your way into or out of the town to look at the Church of St. Nicholas, sitting on its mound in a field. Spend the rest of the afternoon on one of the nearby (sandy) beaches, or walk or drive across to Zaton Holiday Village (see p.150).

If You Have 2 Days

Day 1 Spend Day 1 as above.

Day 2 Drive south along the coast road (and take your swimming things). Park as close to Šibenik's Old Town (see p.142) as you can. Explore the narrow alleys and steps of the Old Town. Stop at the Bunari Museum (see p.144), then walk down onto the quay and let younger children play in the

St Donat's Church and the Campanile of the cathedral

playground, while older children/teenagers can go further along and have a drink in one of the pavement cafés. Drive to Skradin (see p.147) (about 20 minutes), then have lunch in the village, or catch the boat to the Krka National Park (see p.147) (25 minutes) and eat at one of the park's entrance restaurants. Either way, you'll then have the afternoon to explore the waterfalls and mills of Skradinski Buk (see p.147), and have a swim in the lower pool.

On the way to Šibenik, you could make two short detours. If you've got bird watchers in the party, they might want to take a look at Vransko Jezero, Croatia's largest natural lake, and a well-known bird sanctuary. It's a couple of kilometres off the coast

road, to the left (see p.152). Animal-loving family members might appreciate turning off to the right, a bit further down the coast road, to visit Tribunj and its donkey sanctuary (see p.152).

If you do either or both of these, it's probably better to eat in Šibenik, and leave the Krka National Park for a full day's visit, which would give you time to explore the Roški slap waterfalls further upstream, and visit the atmospheric Krka Monastery as well.

If You Have 3 Days

Days 1–2 Spend Days 1 and 2 as above.

Day 3 Explore the Zadar Archipelago. The easiest islands to get to are Ugljan (see p.153) (25 minutes) and Dugi otok (see p.153) (1–1½ hours)

If You Have 4 Days or More

Days 1–3 Spend Days 1–3 as above.

Day 4 Visit the Kornati National Park (see p.153). There are lots of companies authorised to organise excursions into the park (they're in Murtur, Primošten, Split, Šibenik and Vodice). The park's website (*www.kornati.hr*) has a complete list.

What To See & Do

As you enter Zadar, notice the Winged Lion of St. Mark above the main city gate – indicating that the Venetian Republic once ruled Zadar (see box).

The Forum AGES 2 AND UP The remains of the Roman Forum have a battered and neglected air. There's a wide expanse of flagstones, a single Corinthian column (allegedly used in the Middle Ages as the 'Pillar of Disgrace,' or pillory), a few carved faces, which certainly look distressed, and odd bits of masonry, often used as stalls for selling embroidery. On the other hand, local youngsters use its open spaces to hone their skate-boarding and roller-blading skills, giving the area a certain clattering vitality. And even if children have got no equipment, it is a good place to just run about and let off steam.

Clustered around the Forum are several buildings that are worth a look. The **Archaeological Museum** AGES 5 AND UP is a modern concrete building with some very old bits of masonry inside. The Museum traces the history of the area from the Neolithic times to the Middle Ages and has a series of well-captioned displays. Close by is the **Church and Monastery of St. Mary** ADULTS. The 11th century church, along with its 12th century bell tower were both severely damaged by Allied bombardment during World War 2, and renovation has been slow in making good the damage. To the inexpert eye, though, they are attractive old buildings.

St. Donat's Church ADULTS One of the most impressive buildings in the Forum is St. Donat's Church. Its name is bound to raise a laugh from the children, especially as it's round. The 9th century building was commissioned by St. Donat, an Irish Saint who was, for a time, Bishop of Zadar. The church was actually deconsecrated in 1797, and has since been pressed into a variety of uses – museum, sales area, military storehouse and iconic image for the city. Even today, it is still looking for its role in the life of Zadar, though it's occasionally used for musical recitals.

The Cathedral of St. Anastasia AGES 8 AND UP Standing next to St. Donat's is the Cathedral of St. Anastasia,

ZADAR

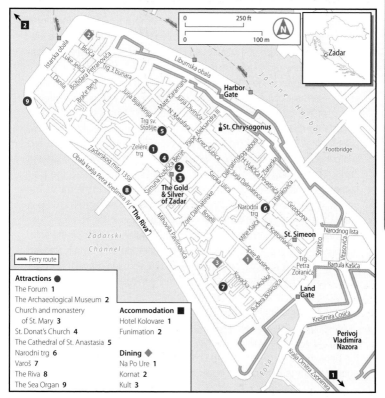

```
0          250 ft
0          100 m
```

Zadar

Attractions ●
The Forum **1**
The Archaeological Museum **2**
Church and monastery
  of St. Mary **3**
St. Donat's Church **4**
The Cathedral of St. Anastasia **5**
Narodni trg **6**
Varoš **7**
The Riva **8**
The Sea Organ **9**

Accommodation ■
Hotel Kolovare **1**
Funimation **2**

Dining ◆
Na Po Ure **1**
Kornat **2**
Kult **3**

Map labels (selection): Istarska obala, I. Danila, I. Brčica, Luke Jelića, Bozidara Petranovića, Trg 3 bunara, Braće Berša, Jurja Bijankinija, Zadarskog mira 1358, Obala kralja Petra Krešimira IV ("The Riva"), Šimuna Kožičića Benje, Mihovila Pavlinovića, Zore Dalmatinske, Borelli, Kovačka, Spire Brusine, Kovačka, Sokolska, Rudera Boškovića, Mate Karamana, N. Matafara, Jurja Divnića, Pape Aleksandra III, Pape Knez Šubića, Široka ulica, Dalmatinskog sabora, Ulica Jurja Hvatinića Zlatarica, I. Barakovića, Grigogona, Mihe Klaića, E. Kotromanić, Stratico, Vitasovića, Narodnog lista, Bartula Kašića, Trg Petra Zoranića, Krešimira Ćosića, Kralja Dmitra Zvonimira, Foša, Perivoj Vladimira Nazora

Libumska obala, Jazine Harbor, Harbor Gate, St. Chrysogonus, Footbridge, Zadarski Channel, Ferry route, The Gold & Silver of Zadar, Trg sv. Stošije, Zeleni trg, Narodni trg, St. Simeon, Land Gate

Zadar (inset map)

which dates back to the 12th century. If you've got the energy you can climb up the imposing bell tower for a small fee, where you can enjoy some spectacular views of the city and beyond to the Adriatic islands.

Narodni trg ALL AGES The central square of the city, Narodni trg (or People's Square) contains the main civic building, the clock-tower-dominated City Guardhouse (now used as an exhibition hall) and the City Loggia (where justice was dispensed, again now used for

exhibitions). You'll also find the Tourist Information on the corner where Mihe Klaica joins the square at the northeast corner. This square is the place to sit and have a drink and watch the world go by.

Varoš ALL AGES Just south of Narodni trg, the narrow winding lanes and alley of the old quarter – Varos – are worth an hour's exploration. Venture east of it, through the imposing Land Gate, and you're in an area dominated by the massive city walls, and a number of parks.

The Winged Lion Of St Mark

All along the Dalmatian coast you will come across carvings of a winged lion, holding a book – usually above the medieval gate to a city. This was the emblem of the Venetian Republic, which ruled the Croatian coast and many of the islands for centuries.

The legend as to how Venice ended up with a lion (rather than something more nautical) is an interesting one. In the 9th century, it is said, a group of merchants from Venice stole the remains of St. Mark the Apostle from his tomb in Alexandria. In order to smuggle their valuable booty out of Egypt, they hid it in a basket, covered it in vegetation, and laid pork across the top (to give the impression that this was a basket of pork). They knew that to Moslems pork is unclean, and so the port authority officials were highly unlikely to rummage about in the meat. The trick worked, they got aboard their ship, hid the corpse by rolling it up in one of the sails, then set off across the Mediterranean for Venice.

The legend goes on to explain that a huge storm overtook the ship, and it was on the point of foundering when a vision of St. Mark advised them to strike their sails or perish. They did so, were saved, and got safely home, where the Doge immediately announced that henceforth St. Mark – whose emblem was the winged lion – would be the patron saint of the Venetian Republic.

Whenever the Venetians took over a city, they would carve the winged lion on the walls. If the city were annexed peacefully, by treaty, the book in the lion's paws would be open, whereas if the city were conquered by force of arms, the book would be closed.

Narodni Trg, Zadar

The Riva ALL AGES The promenade along the southern edge Zadar's centre is extremely pleasant, with lots of benches, shady trees and nice views across to the island of Ugljan (see p.153). It also provides grandstand seats for spectacular sunsets. An information board on the Riva leaves no doubt as to its merits: 'The New Town Quay of Zadar is the most beautiful town quay worldwide. This superlative statement is definitely well founded as there are only a few such nice and pleasant coastal promenades in the world.' A further information board reminds us that the most famous, most iconic picture of Alfred Hitchcock was taken right here on the Riva by Croatian photographer Ante Brkan (the master of suspense was visiting the city in 1964). But the best reason to visit the Riva is that it can offer you one of the greatest experiences you'll ever come across, in Croatia or anywhere else. Let's hear it for the sea organ.

The Sea Organ ★ ★ ★ FIND

AGES 2 AND UP Zadar's famous sea organ is situated almost at the western end of the Riva, near the new cruiser port. There's nothing much to see. A shallow 70 metre-wide set of steps lead down to the water. Some slots are cut into the top step, with holes drilled down into the concrete. You might even wonder why so many people are just sitting around, looking contemplatively out to sea.

Then you hear it. From all around you come the most extraordinarily beautiful, otherworldly fluting harmonies. If the water's calm, wait until the wake of a boat starts to lap against the quay. The sounds get louder, the harmonies more convoluted. If you're lucky enough to be able to visit the organ during a storm, you'll be treated to great rumbling symphonies of sound.

The organ was designed by Nikola Bašić, and installed by a team of academics and craftsmen in 2005. Consisting of 35 pipes of varying diameters, lengths and tilts, the organ is tuned to play seven chords of five tones when activated by air being forced through them by the sea. It is a truly brilliant and original concept and quite magical.

Shopping with Children

Zadar, as you'd expect from the main city in Northern Dalmatia, is a good general shopping centre, with all the usual clothes and gift shops, jewellers, photography shops and so on. There's also a good selection of markets and malls – the flavour can be judged from the Sarag supermarket, which offers 'free delivery to your boat'. But there isn't any particular specialism that might appeal to children or families.

Sea Organ, Zadar

Family Entertainment

Zadar's great strength in entertainment and the arts centres around music and drama. The Croatian Playhouse hosts a variety of serious drama and classical music (Široka ulica 8 ℓ 023-314-586), whilst the Puppet Theatre of Zadar is a national institution, and will delight children and adults alike (Sokolska 1, ℓ 023-319-181). The Croatian Playhouse also leads the ever-popular Summer Theatre Festival, with performances by theatre groups from all over Croatia, in a variety of venues across the city. Most of these performances are in Croatian, but the Zadar Dreams festival of alternative drama and performance art in July and August, features a lot of English-language content. Look out too for the Zadar Feštica in bars and restaurants on Friday nights throughout July and August, with regional dishes and local bands.

Family-Friendly Accommodation

The only hotel in Zadar's Old Town has a few rooms above an accommodation agency (the Venera), and isn't really suitable for families. There is one hotel just outside the city centre, not far from the bus and railway stations. Beyond that, the main hotel area is Borik, about four kilometres to the northwest, which has good bus and boat links the city centre. Further north, there is a lot of accommodation in the area around Nin.

Hotel Kolovare ★★ A major renovation in 2004 has turned this hotel into the only real alternative for families wanting to stay in modern accommodation within walking distance of the centre of Zadar. It has a swimming pool, and the rooms are airy and modern. Ask for a room with a balcony overlooking the pool, with views of the Zadar Channel beyond. The hotel has double rooms and suites suitable for families, and you can book guided tours, excursions and panoramic air trips at reception. *Bože Perčiića 14, Kolovare. ℓ 023-211-017. Fax: 023-213-079. www.hotel-kolovare-zadar.htnet.hr. 237 rooms. July–Aug: from 1015 Kuna (£ 100) double. AE, DC, MC, V. Rates include breakfast. Half- and full-board available. Amenities: Restaurant, bar, pool, valet service. In room: A/C, TV, dataport, minibar, hair dryer, safe.*

Funimation ★★★ If all you want is to keep the children occupied while you chill out, then the group of hotels in Borik, run by Falkensteiner Hotels and Resorts, is the answer to your prayers. The hotels themselves – all three or four stars – are comfortable and have all the facilities you'd expect in a top-end resort hotel. In addition they offer a huge range of activities for children, under the umbrella name of 'Falky-Land': sport, water activities, games and entertainment, all put on by professional 'animators'. Professional childcare, too, can be provided, from 10am to 9pm, for any children above the age of two. As regards accommodation, there are several types of suites that are perfect for families, from the 'mini-suite', designed for parents with two young children, through family, family royal, corner and panorama suites catering for parents and up to three older children.

Majstora Radovana 7, Borik. 023-206-637. Fax 023-332-065. www. hoteliborik.hr. 258 rooms. From 1335 Kuna (£ 130) double; from 1610 Kuna (£ 158) suite. Rates include breakfast, lunch and dinner; babysitting; use of all sports facilities; and some instruction programmes. Hotel prices are actually given per person, and children aged 0–5 are free, 6–17 pay 50%. Check the website. Prices based on a 7-day minimum stay during the high season. AE, DC, MC, V. Amenities: Restaurant, bar, live entertainment, two pools, water centre, children's programmes. In room: A/C, TV, hairdryer, safe. The other hotels in the group – Adriana Select, Puntamika, Jadran and Donat – sometimes take bookings for less than a week.*

Family-Friendly Dining

Kornat ★★ CROATIAN Almost at the end of Liburnska Obala, and handy for the ferry port, Kornat offers pleasant views of the mouth of the harbour and even more tempting food. Vegetarian and 'low calorie' cuisine is on the menu as well as the full range of fish and meat dishes. The wine list is extensive but reasonably priced. To finish – if you're not watching your weight – try the chocolate cake.

Liburnska Obala 6 Zadar 23000 023-254-501. Reservations recommended. Main courses 45–160 Kuna (£ 4.40– 15). AE, DC, MC, V. Daily 11am–1am.*

Kult ★★ COFFEE Not dining, I know, but definitely a place to head for with the locals when the sightseeing is getting wearisome and the children are getting fractious. The outdoor seating is on a deck under mature trees, there's the tinkle of a cooling fountain, and – wonder of wonders – there are a couple of children's swings. They're the kind you might set up yourself in the garden, it's true, but it's so rare to see an effort being made, it can only be applauded.

Stomorica 6 at the junction of Stomorica and Svete Nediljice. 091-392-2595. No credit cards. Daily 7:30am–1am.*

Na Po Ure ★ CROATIAN A single narrow doorway squeezed between shops on a narrow Varos back street may make you think that you've come to the wrong place. But walk in – there's a narrow passage that opens out into a pleasantly intimate restaurant with a little rear patio. Classed as a tavern, and suitable for smaller families, the food is good basic Croatian cooking – try the octopus followed by the caramel pudding – with an impressive wine list.

8 Špire Brusine, Zadar 23000 023-312-044 No credit cards. Mon–Sat 9.30am to 1am.*

ŠIBENIK

Šibenik is an attractive, no-nonsense kind of a place, with all the medieval alleys and small squares you expect in Adriatic towns. It has an A-list cathedral, a castle with splendid views, a fair selection of hotels and restaurants (including a very child-friendly holiday complex which would be just the place for an extended stay if you were going to cover Northern and Central Dalmatia from the same base), a pleasant Riva along the Krka river, and boat trips out to a few attractive islands. It also has one of Croatia's loveliest and most accessible National Parks right on its doorstep. Although hard hit economically by the Patriotic War (see p.248), the town's population is youthful (there was a baby boom after the war), it has a pleasant, un-touristy feel, and there are enough things for children to do to make for a really nice family day out. And if you're there during the last week

of June and the first week of July, Šibenik hosts an International Children's Festival.

Šibenik would make an excellent base if you wanted to cover both Zadar and Split, together with their hinterlands, in the same holiday – the new motorway, a little inland from the coast, joins all three.

Essentials

Getting There

Šibenik is the only largish town on the coast between Zadar and Split, and is 72 km (45 miles) from the former, 82 km (50 miles) from the latter. The bus station is on the seafront at Draga 14. The railway station is south of the bus station at Milete 24. Neither is more than a 10-minute walk from the centre.

Šibenik

Visitor Information

The Tourist Information office is at Fausta Vrančića 18 (📞 022-212-075).

Getting Around

The centre of Šibenik is pedestrianised – it couldn't be anything else, since main streets are alleys, with even narrower cross streets tumbling down flights of steps and tunnelling through buildings. So you'll have to walk.

What To See And Do

Local buses into Šibenik drop off southeast of the bleak **Poljana maršala Tita square**. At the far end, to the left of the theatre, is **Zagrebačka**, the town's main street. It's actually more of an alley, and heads north past a succession of notable churches.

The **Church of the Ascension** **ADULTS** has a belfry that looks like a pair of pulpits. Nearby is **St. John's** **ADULTS**, which has a balustraded flight of steps leading up the outside of the building to a couple of doors and a balcony. The town centre's oldest church is **St. Chrysogonus's** **AGES 5 AND UP** a simple building that is now a venue for seasonal art exhibitions. Look next to the door, where there is a large bell that was salvaged from a ship that sank off Šibenik. The inscription on it says that it was made in Asia Minor in 1266.

Beyond St. Chrysogonus the alleys get steeper, and are often stepped. You can either bear left for Šibenik's main square, or climb steeply to the right, up to the castle. By bearing left, down a steep little alley that burrows through two buildings, you come to Kralja Tomislava, Šibenik's other main street/alley. Turning right onto it brings you to **St. Barbara's Church** **ADULTS**, which has a collection of church art. The building is a mish-mash of different styles, explained by its many restorations and reconstructions.

Just beyond St. Barbara's the town's main square – **Trg Republike Hrvatske** – is the setting for one of the Adriatic coasts most celebrated sights. With its characteristic white stone, sharp cupola and barrel roof, **St. Joseph's Cathedral** ★★ **AGES 5 AND UP** is one of the most recognisable buildings in Croatia.

The work of at least three different architects, and interrupted in its construction by fire, plague and lack of funds, St. Jacob's was completed in 1536 and is a blend of Gothic and Renaissance styles and a miracle of craftsmanship (the masonry fits together so closely that no mortar was necessary to build it). One of the key architects of the building was Juraj Dalmatinac (c1420–1473), a Croat who came up with the novel idea of using prefabricated stone slabs to build the cathedral – an unheard of idea at the time.

Children will enjoy the embarrassed-looking **Adam and Eve** that adorn one of the side doors and, in particular, the **carvings of faces** (over 70 of them) that decorate the outside of the building at the dome end. Slightly cartoonish, but clearly

ŠIBENIK

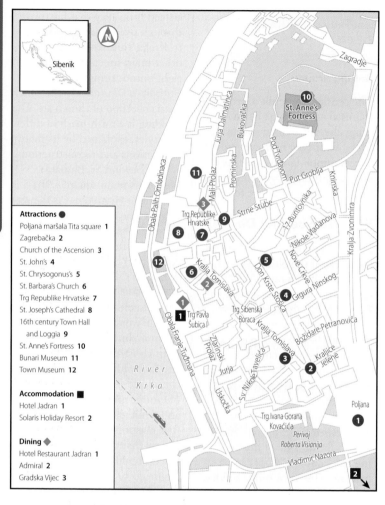

Attractions ●
Poljana maršala Tita square 1
Zagrebačka 2
Church of the Ascension 3
St. John's 4
St. Chrysogonus's 5
St. Barbara's Church 6
Trg Republike Hrvatske 7
St. Joseph's Cathedral 8
16th century Town Hall
  and Loggia 9
St. Anne's Fortress 10
Bunari Museum 11
Town Museum 12

Accommodation ■
Hotel Jadran 1
Solaris Holiday Resort 2

Dining ◆
Hotel Restaurant Jadran 1
Admiral 2
Gradska Vijec 3

representing real people, it is said that they were the architect's way of lampooning people who'd refused to contribute to the building's costs.

Opposite the Cathedral, on Trg Republike Hrvatske is the **16th century Town Hall and Loggia** AGES 8 AND UP — the arched arcade of the Loggia now houses a superior café and restaurant

(see Viječnica below). The square is often used for concerts and performances, and is frequently fitted out with temporary seating.

Just behind the Cathedral is the **Town Museum** AGES 8 AND UP (rather dull), and beyond the northern end of the square lies the **Bunari Museum** ★★★ AGES 5 AND UP , an interactive,

Šibenik was home to Faust Vrančić (1551–1617), an engineer and inventor who rivalled Leonardo da Vinci in the range of his designs – mills, bridges, clocks, a parachute and flood prevention schemes, to name but a few. He also wrote a dictionary.

multilingual look at the town's history with a pleasant café in the basement – a much better bet for youngsters.

If you walk down from the square onto the quayside, there are nice views of the yachts and cruisers that frequently call in, a not-half-bad children's playground and, a little further along, a crescent of café/bar tables that is *the* place to be for Šibenik's young crowd. All in all, a good place to keep the whole family happy.

Before leaving Šibenik, it is probably worth the effort, and braving a lot of 'do we have to?'s, to climb up the steep alleys and steps to **St. Anne's Fortress** **AGES 3 AND UP** . There's not much to see in the fortress itself, but the views of the town, the islands out to sea, other fortifications inland, and the elegant bridge that carries the motorway across the Krk river are terrific.

Carvings on the Cathedral, Šibenik

Family-Friendly Accommodation

Although there's only one hotel in the Šibenik's centre, the Solaris resort four kilometres south is a very good alternative for families.

Hotel Jadran As the only hotel in Šibenik, the Jadran has its own signposts in various parts of the town. It is situated on the Riva with views of the yachts moored across the road, and more or less next door to the Cathedral. The hotel is light on facilities – it hasn't exactly got to compete – but it's perfectly adequate. There's a tavern, a restaurant and coffee bar, with music on the terrace most evenings. A major drawback is the lack of air-conditioning. Highchairs, children's menus and children's portions are all available in the restaurant.

Obala Dr. Franje Tuđmana 52. Šibenik. 📞 *022-212-644. Fax 022-212-480. www.rivijera.hr. 57 rooms. July–Aug: from 680 Kuna (£ 65) double; from 827 Kuna (£ 80) suite, 1200 Kuna (£ 110) for studio apartment that sleeps four. Rates include breakfast. AE, DC, MC, V. Half- and full-board rates available. Amenities: Restaurant, terrace, bar. In room: Sat TV, mini bar.*

Solaris Holiday Resort ★ ★ ★
Just four kilometres southwest of Šibenik, the Solaris Holiday

Resort is an ideal base for families exploring northern or central Croatia (or indeed both) – it's only five minutes from the great Zagreb-Split motorway, so you can realistically range far and wide. Consisting of five resort hotels (the Ivan, Jure, Niko, Andrija and Jakov), it has a wealth of things for children and adults to do including swimming pools, an aqua park, the beach (concrete and pebbles), snack bars, wellness centres, a bowling alley, splendid play facilities and pleasant pathways through the trees. All sorts of sports are catered for and the hotels are so spacious that there's plenty of room for children to run around. There's also free parking. If you don't have a car, there's a bus every hour into Šibenik. A variety of excursions to nearby attractions are laid on, including one to Krka National Park (see p.147). The complex also has a spa. The Ivan and Niko were the most recently (2005) updated.

INSIDER TIP

If you're taking the bus from the Solaris Holiday Resort into Šibenik, be aware that the timetable is only approximate: the bus is likely to leave earlier than stated on the timetable.

Hotel Ivan

Hotelsko naselje Solaris bb, 22000 Šibenik. 022-361-001. *Fax 022-361-801.* **www.solaris.hr**. *335 rooms, 12 apts. Aug: from 820 Kuna (£ 80) double; 870 Kuna (£ 85) apt. AE, DC, MC, V. Rates include breakfast and are based on stays of four*

days or more. Free parking. Amenities: two restaurants, pizzeria, bar, two pools, two tennis courts, bowling alley, minigolf, ATM. In room: A/C, TV, minibar, hairdryer.

Hotel Niko

Hotelsko naselje Solaris bb, 22000 Šibenik. 022-361-001. *Fax 022-361-801.* **www.solaris.hr**. *218 rooms, two apts, all with shower only. Aug: 600 Kuna (£ 57) double; from 640 Kuna (£ 62) suite. All rooms have balconies. Rates include breakfast. Half- and full-board available. Rates based on stays of four days or longer. AE, DC, MC, V. Free parking. Amenities: Restaurant, bar, seawater pool. In room: A/C, TV, hairdryer.*

Family-Friendly Dining

Admiral ★★ PIZZERIA FIND A

good basic pizza joint, with air conditioning indoors and rough-hewn benches outside, just up from the Cathedral square. Nice staff, great attitude to children. If it's crowded, there's another good one (Pivnica Alpa) just across the alley.

Kralja Tomislava 15a Šibenik. Main courses: pizzas 28–40 Kuna (£ 2.50–4), other 45–60 Kuna (£ 4.50–6).

Gradska Vijećnica ★★

DALMATIAN Located in Šibenik's Town Hall (that's what its name means) and Loggia, and facing Trg Republike Hrvatske and the Cathedral, Gradska Vijećnica is nothing if not convenient. The interior is very pleasant with mahogany and mirrors inside, and pretty wrought-iron outdoor furniture under big parasols in the elegant square. The general ambience is one of relaxed elegance. The menu has some terrific fish courses, together with pastas and salads, and it's not too expensive.

Trg Republike Hrvatska 1. ☎ *022-213-605. Main courses 40–110 Kuna (£ 4– 10.50). AE, DC, MC, V. Daily 9am–1am.*

Hotel Restaurant Jadran

DALMATIAN The food here is much the same as in most Croatian coastal restaurants (and none the worse for that), but the chance to watch the world go by along the Riva and in the marina is a pleasure – there's always something for the children to watch going on. There's also live music most evenings.

Obala Dr. Franje Tudmana 52. ☎ *022-212-644. Fax 022-212-480. www.rivijera.hr. Main courses 40–90 Kuna (£ 3.80–8.50). AE, DC, MC, V. Traditional Croatian menu of meat and grilled fish. Daily 7am–11pm.*

Around Zadar & Šibenik

Krka National Park ★ ★ ★

MOMENT **ALL AGES** A mere 20-minute drive from Šibenik is one of Croatia's most popular day-trip destinations – the Krka National Park. It's a series of waterfalls and cascades between Knin and Skradin, created by deposits of limestone (called travertine) built up over millennia. The half hour boat trip from Skradin up to the Krka National Park's first set of waterfalls at Skradinski buk was a delight. We slid upriver, passing a succession of individuals fishing from boats, sitting placidly under parasols. Their reflections mixed with those of the rocky, reed-fringed banks and the distant waterfalls in a shimmering image of peace, quiet and contentment.

The most popular group of falls are the lower ones, Skradinski Buk, near the small town of Skradin. There are 17 cascades on an 800 metre (2,600 feet) stretch of water with a drop of 46 metres (150 feet). Access is by boat from the Skradin quayside.

Skradin itself is worth a quick potter if you have to wait for a boat. It has an old church, narrow streets and alleys, and some

Food Stall, Krka National Park

Waterfalls, Krka

pleasant cafés and restaurants. Parking at the quay is sometimes restricted, but there's plenty of room in the town car park, five minutes walk away.

Boats leave on the hour from 8am to 7pm, and return on the half hour. The boats do have an inside saloon, but try to get a seat on top. The trip is a pleasant half-hour's chug up-river, with lovely views back towards reed-fringed Skradin and of the steep banks sliding by. Local anglers dangle their lines from boats, fish jump, and dragonflies skim the water. You pay when you get off (adults: 50 Kuna (£ 4.60), children aged 7–14: 35 Kuna (£ 3.25), under 7 free).

The falls themselves are delightful. They tumble and roar down the hillside from travertine shelf to shelf, wreathed in a light haze of vapour, under a dense canopy of trees. Walkways and steps meander upwards, with stalls erected in the dappled sunlight selling nuts, dried fruit and bottles of coloured wines and liqueurs. There are café's and toilets both at the bottom and at the top of the falls, and viewing points and a belvedere (built for a visit to the falls by Emperor Franz Joseph I in 1875) to indicate the choicest views. Swimming is allowed in the bottom lake.

If you've time, you can continue to Lozovac, the second point of entry to the park. This will give you access to boats heading for the upper falls and Visovac Lake, with its much photographed Franciscan monastery.

Water Good Idea

As you might expect, past Croatians were not slow to harness all this raw natural power. The river was long lined with water mills (some are still on display), and the Krka Hydro Dam, generating direct current, was opened in 1895, making Šibenik the first town in the world to be lit in this way. A similar project in New York State can claim the first hydrodam of this type (by two days), but delays in laying transmission lines meant that the city of Buffalo trailed behind Šibenik in actually harnessing the power. A massive turbine from those days lies among the ruins, and there's a small modern hydroelectric scheme down by the river.

Nin ★★ MOMENT Lying in the sun like some once-famous celebrity, Nin, 18 km (11 miles) north of Zadar, is far more important than it looks. This little village, located on an island attached to the mainland by two bridges, has had an extremely chequered history. With some claims to being the cradle of Croatian nationhood – it calls

Town Gate, Nin

itself the oldest Croatian royal town – it is an important ecclesiastical centre, and to this day a renowned salt-producer. It is also one of the few places in Croatia with sandy beaches. All in all, Nin is a splendid place for a few days break with the family.

If you park outside the Tourist Office and stock up on some of its excellent literature about the town, you can then walk across the Donji most (lower bridge) and through the **Town Gate** AGES 5 AND UP erected by the Venetians in the 16th century. Notice the carvings of a bottle of wine and a loaf of bread – symbols of welcome – on the right of the gateway.

Walking down the main street, after a couple of cafés you come to the **Church of St. Anselm** AGES 5 AND UP. In the treasury next to the square stone bell tower you can introduce yourself to what's left of him: there are beautiful gold and silver reliquaries containing his shoulder-blade, his jawbones, his arm and his feet, and his skull, together with the remains of a number of other saints, known and unknown. There's also a small glass case containing what looks like an arm holding up a coin – this, it is claimed, is one of Judas's thirty pieces of silver.

Behind the church, there's another work by that man Ivan Meštrović (see p.72): a smaller copy of his statue of **Grgur Ninski**, which stands outside the Golden Gate in Split (see p.110). Grgur Ninski was, of course, the bishop of Nin in the 10th century, and petitioned the Pope to allow the liturgy in Croatian.

A few steps further brings you to the 9th century **Church of the Holy Cross** AGES 8 AND UP dubbed in 1887 'the smallest cathedral in Christianity' by British architect Thomas Graham Jackson (most famously responsible for Oxford's Bridge of Sighs). It's an extraordinary building – looking more Greek Orthodox than Roman Catholic, it is said that it is so positioned that the sunlight entering the church's narrow windows acts as a clock or, more

Church of the Holy Cross, Nin

likely, a calendar. Next to the church is a lovely restaurant (Konoba Branimir, see below) – a good time, perhaps, to stop for a drink or a bite to eat.

The **Archaeological Museum** AGES 8 AND UP has a variety of artefacts going back to the early days of the town. You can ask for a key here to get into the Church of the Holy Cross, though there's nothing inside. As you walk back across the bridge towards the Tourist Office, to your left you will see a little market made up of brand new stalls, and, moored next to it, a black boat. This is a reconstruction of an early (11th century) ship found sunk, possibly deliberately as a breakwater in Nin harbour.

Apart from its religious and historical artefacts, Nin also has its salt works **Solana Nin** AGES 8 AND UP, medicinal mud (a health centre is planned for 2007) and a **donkey farm** ALL AGES (ask about them all at the Tourist Office).

As you leave Nin, look out too for the 12th century **Church of St. Nicholas** AGES 8 AND UP perched on a mound just outside the town. It is said that seven kings of Croatia, after being crowned in Nin, would ride out to this church to pledge to defend the country.

Nearby (a five-minute drive or 20-minute walk) is the huge holiday village at **Zaton** ALL AGES a definite possibility as a base for all or part of your holiday (see below).

Church of St Nicholas, Nin

Family-Friendly Accommodation

Zaton Holiday Village ★★★

The huge apartment, mobile home and camping complex at Zaton is a real possibility as a base for exploring Zadar and the area around Nin to the north – it's 16 km (10 miles) from the first, and two kilometres from the second. In addition to a safe beach and a large swimming pool, it has a terrific range of facilities for youngsters – children's pool and club, teens' club, mini disco, sand pits, games, horse riding and competitions. For adults, there are shops, bars and restaurants, discos, a

supermarket, cultural programs, karaoke, beach games, a wide variety of sports (scuba diving, tennis, cycling) and a lot else besides. There's also easy Internet access and, should anyone come down with something, a doctor on site. The apartments (all recently renovated) are luxurious and have a full range of facilities. It's like living at home (or better!)

Zaton Holiday Village HR-23232 Nin. 📞 *023-280-280. Fax 023-280-310.* **www.zaton.hr.**

Rates depend entirely on whether you're in an apartment, mobile home or tent, what size you need, and when you want to go. The biggest, most luxurious, brand new apartments, at the height of the season, will set you back 1340 Kuna (£ 130) a day, but there are a lot that are cheaper than that – check out the website. There's a small charge for cots in high season, though otherwise they're free.

Family-Friendly Dining

Konoba Branmir ★★ FIND

CROATIAN Nin has several places to

Zaton Holiday Village

eat. One of the nicest is this restaurant overlooking the Church of the Holy Cross. Cool, heavy wooden beams dominate the interior, and the menu has a good range of Croatian food, with a number of vegetarian options available. The white fish 'baked under the lid' is especially good.

Višeslavov trg, 2 Nin. ☎ *023-264-866. Daily 8am to 1am.*

For Active Families

The proximity of rugged mountains and fast-flowing rivers means that there are many opportunities for adventure activities in the area, either by the day (consult the Tourist Office) or for the whole holiday. The Adventure Company, for example, (*www. adventurecompany.co.uk*) offers a package of activities in the Plitvice National Park for £ 699 (children £ 679, minimum age 5).

Tribunj

A pretty little fishing village on an island three kilometres off the coast road (E65) north-west of Šibenik, Tribunj is known for its swimming, seafood and gastronomic fishermen's nights. Becoming aware of the rapid disappearance of the once ubiquitous donkey, the people of the village formed the Association for the Protection of Donkeys, and set up a sanctuary on Logorun, the island that overlooks the town, to nurture and protect the survivors. Furthermore, once a year (on the first weekend in August) a donkey race is held in the village. It's all taken mock-seriously, the participants wear traditional dress, there are humorous commentaries over loud-speakers, and thousands of people attend for a good day out. It's ideal for children. For details, contact the Tourist Office (☎ *022-446-143*).

Vransko Jezero

One of Croatia's most important nature parks, Vransko Jezero, just inland off the coast road (E65) between Šibenik and Zadar, consists of a long, narrow, shallow lake (14 by 1½–3½ kilometres, never more than 4 metres deep). The lake is attached to the sea by an 18th century channel, which was intended to drain the lake, but has the opposite effect by allowing salt water into it at high tide. It received nature park status in 1999, in recognition of the more than a hundred species of bird recorded around the lake, with 50 or so regularly nesting. The park is still in the early stages of development, with paths being laid, information boards and signposts being erected, and it is already a powerful magnet for Croatian fishermen and bird-watchers. The easiest access to the lake is from the main road at Pakostane or from Prosika. You can get a flavour of the park from its website *www.vransko-jezero.hr*, but you'll need to speak Croatian to get full value.

THE ZADAR ARCHIPELAGO

Just off the coast from Zadar is a series of long, thin islands that can make a pleasant destination for a day out. The nearest island – just five kilometres west of Zadar – is Ugljn, which can be seen from Zadar's waterfront. There are 15 ferries a day from Zadar to Preko on the island. Attached to its southeastern end is Pašman, which, if anything, is even quieter than Ugljian. Other islands in the group include the wooded island of Silba (its name is probably a corruption of the Latin word 'silva' or wood), which has an upmarket feel that probably stretches back to its great days as a provider of sailing ships for the northern Adriatic, Dugi otok, is the longest island at 43 km, but is as thin as a piece of string (nowhere is it wider than four and a half kilometres), and beautiful with it. Also there is Iž, a low-key, nautical little strip of land. There is no particular reason to visit any of these islands – they are sparsely populated, with nothing much to see – yet a visit can involve a very pleasant sea trip, and, with none of the crowds you're likely to encounter on Croatia's more southerly islands, they have high potter-potential.

The Kornati National Park

★★★ **ALL AGES** Just southeast of Dugi otok lies the island of Kornat and its own archipelago of 140 islands, 89 of which were included in the Kornati National Park when it was set up in 1980. For the most part completely bare rock, with the occasional patch of shrubs, the islands were deforested in the 17th century to create sheep runs, only for the sheep to graze them bare. They now look like a scattering of *karst* (see p.21) jewels, made, as George Bernard Shaw described them, 'out of tears, stars and breath'. The Kornati Archipelago is famous for this barren landscape above the water, and the flourishing wildlife below, together with the majestic 'crowns' or cliffs that soar almost 200 metres (650 feet) out of the sea on some of the islands. You can take an excursion boat around the islands to enjoy the scenery and spot some of the island wildlife. The waters are perfect for snorkelling and, amazingly,

---

God Of Small Things

According to legend, when God created the world, he was left with a handful of white rocks. He hurled them into the Adriatic, saw how beautiful they were, and decided that they needed no further embellishment. The more prosaic scientific explanation is that the islands are the tops of hills drowned at the end of the Ice Age when the melting of glaciers raised the level of the surrounding sea.

Kornati Island National Park

there are 20 or so restaurants and taverns within the National Park. Since the archipelago actually belongs to Murter, this little island town, attached to the mainland by a bridge, is by far the best gateway into the National Park, and the main National Park Office is in the town (Butina 2, 22243 Murter ☎ *022-435-740 www.kornati.hr*). Several travel agencies in Murter arrange excursions – Atlas (*www.atlas.hr*), KornatTurist (*www.kornatturist.hr*) and Coronata (*www.coronata.hr*) – and each offers slightly different packages, usually involving the boat ride, the entrance fee to the Park, a meal and the services of a guide. A walk along the side of the harbour will take you past lots of boats offering alternative trips, usually involving a sightseeing cruise, a swim and a fish barbecue. Whoever you go with, the trip takes eight or nine hours. You can join excursions, too, in Primošten, Split, Šibenik or Vodice.

For those with a Robinson Crusoe complex, stays (and they are actually called 'Robinsons' locally) can be arranged in stone cottages or even lighthouses on the islands. You have to commit for at least a week, and need to book well in advance (again, contact the local travel agencies).

The National Park entrance fee is 50 Kuna (£ 4.60) if you buy the ticket outside the park, with children aged 7–14 paying half that, and children under 7 free.

6 Istria

ISTRIA

Koper
Bertoki
Obrov
Starod
Sapjane
Piran
Portorož
Lucija
Gračišče
Jelovice
Vele Mune
Savudrija
SLOVENIA
Brest
Sečovlje
Ružići
Umag
Buje
Šterna
Buzet
Roč
Istarske
Toplice
10
11
Kastav
Brtoniga
8
Oprtalj
12
Volosko
Opatija
Grožnjan
Livade
Hum
13
Lupoglav
Učka
Tunnel
Dajla
Motovun
9
Vranja
Ičići
Lovran
Novigrad
Karojiba
Boljun
Medveja
Višnjan
Cerovlje
Poreč
6
Nova Vas
Beram
Pazin
Mošćenička
Draga
Žbandaj
Baderna
Pićan
Brseč
Funtana
Flengi
Potpićan
Kršan
Brestova
Vrsar
5
Žminj
Plomin
Porozina
4
Kanfanar
Raša R.
Cres
Limski Chan.
Svetvinčenat
Labin
3
Rovinj
Golaš
14
Barban
15
Raša
16
Rabac
Bale
Štalije
Juršići
Krnica
Koromačno
Vodnjan
Marčana
Pt. Ubac
BRIJUNI N.P.
2
Fazan
Kavran
Valtura
Brijuni Arch.
1
Pula
Pt. Kumpar
ADRIATIC
Pomer
Medulin
Premantura
SEA
Pt. Kamenjak

Pula **1**
Brijuni Islands
  National Park **2**
Rovinj **3**
The Limski Kanal **4**
Vrsar **5**
Poreč **6**
Buje **7**
Grožnjan **8**
Motovun **9**
Buzet **10**
Roč **11**
Glagolitic Alley **12**
Hum **13**
Labin **14**
Raša **15**
Rabac **16**

0   5 mi
0   5 km

Istria is without doubt the most clearly defined of all Croatia's regions. Attached to the rest of Croatia by a narrow piece of land barely 24 km wide, it juts out into the northern Adriatic, and shares a border with Slovenia, which lies to the north. Mount Učka, almost a mile high, acts as a natural barrier between Istria and the rest of Croatia. It's easy to feel, as you approach the region on the motorway and drive out of the Učka Tunnel, that you are entering a different country.

More than any other part of Croatia's Adriatic coast, Istria is like Italy. There's no getting away from it. It doesn't look Balkan, or feel Balkan. The Romans called it 'Terra Magica'. Most of its towns and streets and roads have Italian as well as Croatian names. Many of its inhabitants – especially the older ones – speak Italian as fluently as they do Croatian. The regions many wonderful hill towns, most crowned by campaniles, look decidedly Italian. This is hardly surprising as it was, for a long time, under Italian control. Istria is even more strongly influenced by its connection with Venice and the Venetians than further south – you'll find the winged lion of Venice all over the place (see p.138). Venice is, after all, barely 100 km away, across the bay. And Italians flock here on holiday – it's just a short drive or an even shorter ferry ride from northern Italy – because it has all the convenience and familiarity of the best bits of home at half the price.

Yet in other ways, Istria is not just an Italian doppelganger. It is Italy seen through a Croatian lens, with a Slavic spin.

Istria is also a region of two – or even three – clearly defined and totally different areas. The west coast has one of the Mediterranean's prime holiday destinations, which has successfully managed to stop holiday sprawl spoiling its delightful coastal towns. Inland, within a kilometre or two of the coast, you're in a beautiful rural landscape, with breathtaking hill towns seemingly around every winding bend. And finally, along the peninsula's east coast, you have what was until recently Croatia's principal coal mining area. It's like no other mining area you'll have come across elsewhere – encapsulated by the sight of a pit's headgear, dormant at the foot of a delightful hill town that is poised above, on the far side, an attractive holiday seaside resort.

'Land of contrasts' has become a tired travel-writing cliché. But if ever a region earned that description, it's Istria. And if you do decide that this interesting, colourful, polyglot region is for you, getting there couldn't be simpler – the airport at Pula, Istria's biggest town and an excellent base for exploring the region, is becoming the destination-of-choice for a growing number of no-frills airlines flying from Britain's host of regional airports.

Istria has a delightful Mediterranean climate – summers that are comfortably warm rather than scorching as they can be further south, and pleasantly mild winters that escape the rigours of more land-locked areas further east. Spring and autumn can be particularly delightful times to visit – the weather's lovely, and the crowds haven't arrived, or have returned home.

TOP 10 FAMILY EXPERIENCES

❶ Sitting next to James Joyce at Uliks, bending the famous author's ear without fear of interruption, and watching the world go by.

❷ Exploring Pula's Amphitheatre, where gladiators once clashed, Christians were thrown to the lions, and stars such as Sting and Jose Carreras entertained their fans.

❸ Riding the little tourist train on Veli Brijun, the easiest

Pula's Amphitheatre

way of seeing the island's main sights.

❹ Watching the speeded-up film of a boat being built in the House of the Batana – explanation without the need for language.

❺ Climbing the observation tower above the Limski Canal, then buying wine, liqueurs or preserved fruits at one of the nearby stalls.

❻ Looking at the octopus and other sea creatures in aquarium aquariums at Poreč, Umag or Pula.

❼ Exploring the Baredine Cave – a guided tour of its five halls and all its weird and wonderful limestone formations takes about 40 minutes,

❽ Walking around on top of Motovun's fortifications, high above the surrounding countryside, and enjoying the view. Then shopping for locally produced artwork.

❾ Driving up the steep hill into the old town at Buzet, wheels spinning, then wandering its narrow twisted alleys.

❿ Taking pictures of all the monuments in Glagolitic Alley,

strung out along a rural road through countryside to die for.

ESSENTIALS

Getting There & Getting Around

By Air Pula Airport is flourishing as budget airlines and package companies increasingly use it as an entry into Istria and Croatia as a whole – the number of UK and Irish airports with links to Pula is on the increase. The airport is about five kilometres (three miles) from the city centre – there are no buses, and cabs cost around 90–100 Kuna (£ 8.50–9.60). It's currently a slow journey, as major work is going on to build a new motorway to the north.

By Car To enjoy Istria to the full, you really need a car. The area's motorway system (Pula–Rijeka and Pula–Trieste), though not dual carriageway, still gives fast access to both coasts and the interior. The pretty, winding roads are a pleasure to drive on.

By Ferry There's a regular catamaran service from Venice to Istrian islands and ports (*www.venezialines.com* ☎ *041-24-24-000*). Jadrolinija, Croatia's domestic ferry service doesn't appear to cover Istria.

By Bus There are bus services from Rijeka and Zagreb to Pula, and local services connect the main Istrian coastal towns. Inland towns usually have bus links with the coast, but they can be patchy. Consult Autotrans *www.autotrans.hr*.

By Train Although there are rail connections between Zagreb and Pula (7 hours) and Rijeka and Pula (2½ hours), as well as internal Istrian services (Croatian Railways *www.hznet.hr*), they are not really frequent enough to be viable for holidaying in the region.

VISITOR INFORMATION

The general website for Istria is *www.istria.com*. Pula's Tourist Office is right in the centre of town, on the Forum (Forum 3, summer daily 8am to midnight, winter Mon–Fri 9am to 7pm, ☎ *052-219-197, www.pulainfo.hr*).

Rovinj's Tourist Office is at Obala Pina Budičina 12, summer daily 8am to 9pm, winter Mon–Sat 8am to 3pm, ☎ *052-11-566, www.trzgovinj.hr*.

Poreč's tourist Office is located at Zagrebačka 9, summer Mon–Sat 8am to 10pm, Sun 9am to 1pm, 6pm to 10pm, winter Mon–Friday, 8am to 3pm, ☎ *0520451-293, www.istra.com/porec*.

ISTRIA ITINERARIES

If You Have 1 Day

Morning: explore Pula. Start at the fountain/relief map of Pula, then check out the Amphitheatre (see p.162), walk along the main street into town, having a quick look at the Cathedral (see p.164), the town hall, the Temple of Augustus (see p.165) and the Roman Forum (see p.165). Admire the Arch of the Sergians (see p.165), while sitting next to James Joyce at Uliks having a drink. Walk down to the market and have a thorough look around. Visit the Archaeological Museum (see p.166). Climb up to the Fortress (see p.166) and admire the view of the city and the ships being built just beyond it.

Afternoon: get on a boat at Pula harbour and take a look at the Brijuni Archipelago (see p.170) (though if you want to land on Veli Brijun and look at the sights, you'll need to drive to Fažana (about 20 minutes), setting aside time for a whole day's excursion.

Arch of the Sergians, Pula

If You Have 2 Days

Day 1 Spend Day 1 as above.

Day 2 Drive up the west coast to Rovinj (see p.171). Park at the big public carpark near Trg Valibora, walk past the town museum to Trg Marsala Tita. Pick up information at the Tourist Office, before climbing the main street Grisia, stopping to look at pictures in the many shops. At the top of Grisia, take a look inside St. Euphemia's Church (see p.173). Walk down the other side of the hill until you get to the street that's closest to the sea, turn left, and walk back towards Trg Marsala Tita, stopping at the House of the Batana (see p.173). Have a drink in Trg Marsala Tita then walk back to Trg Valibora. Before getting back to the car, pop into the Aquarium (see p.174). Continue north towards Poreč. Stop to look at the Limski Kanal (see p.174) from the observation tower on the left (you can't miss it). When you arrive in Poreč, follow the signs to 'Centar' until you see a new car park with a large map of the town. Park, and use the map for orientation. Walk along Nikole Tesle with the sea on your right, towards Zagrebačka, and pick up info at the Tourist Office. Cross the town square (Trg Slobode), and enter the Old Town past the Venetian Tower. Visit the Aquarium (see p.174), the District Museum (see p.177) and the Basilica of Euphrasius (see p.177). From Poreč, drive the eight kilometres (five miles) or so to the Baredine Cave (see p.178).

If You Have 3 Days

Days 1–2 Spend Days 1 and 2 as above.

Day 3 Take a tour of Inland Istria. Start by driving up the west coast motorway almost to the Slovenian border. Come off the motorway and head for Buje (see p.181). Call in at the Tourist Office on the crossroads, buy some truffles (see p.182) in Zigante. Then drive on to Grožnjan. Potter around the art shops, perhaps buy a picture. Press on to Motovun (see p.182). Have a drink at one of the cafés and enjoy the view. Take the path around the town's fortifications, starting at the far end of the square in front of the church. Buy truffles if you didn't buy any in Buje. Perhaps stay the night at the Hotel Kaštel (see p.184). Continue to Pazin (see p.184). Visit the museum in the castle, and take a look at the gorge that swallows up the Fojba river. Walk into town, spend some time in the park and let the children play on the swings. Drive to Roč (see p.185), either on the country roads or along the Pula–Rijeka motorway. Look around the village, visit the Tourist Office if it's open. Drive down Glagolitic Alley (see p.186), stopping to look at the monuments carved with Glagolitic script. At the end of the road, park next to the more modern church, then walk up into the tiny town of Hum (see p.186). Finally, drive on to Buzet. It's a steep drive up the hill into the Old Town. Park and let the children have a play in the little park while you recover from the climb into town, gird up your loins for the drive back down, and admire the view. Visit the new town, and perhaps buy truffles if you didn't get any in Buje or Motovun.

If You Have 4 Days or More

Days 1–3 Spend Days 1–3 as above.

Day 4 Explore the east coast (an ideal way to spend your last day, if you've got an early flight from Pula airport).

Drive along the east coast. As you pass Raša (see p.187), note the industrial elements included in the Mussolini-era design of its church. Drive into Labin (see p.187) and park. The main square – just outside the Old Town – is really pleasant, despite the cars. Climb up into the Old Town. Climb the campanile, if you've got a head for heights. What a view! Visit the Town Museum (see p.188), and take a look at the model coal mine. Return to Titov trg and have lunch. Then down to Rabac (see p.189) for a quiet afternoon and a swim.

PULA

Pula is a fascinating city with a history that stretches back to the 10th century BC when ancient Balkan tribesmen founded a settlement. Roman settlement began in the 1st century BC and Pula has one of Europe's largest surviving Roman amphitheatres. The amphitheatre is so well preserved that it is still used today, albeit not for torturing innocents (though Sting did perform there recently). Pula has a number of other splendid Roman monuments, as well as a thriving café society, and it's the only place in the world where you can sit at a pavement table and have a drink with the Irish writer James Joyce (see p.165). For those who love to shop, there is a thriving indoor and outdoor market that is thronged each morning and deserted each afternoon.

Exploring Pula is made more fun by its intriguing circular street plan – it's clustered around a hill with a castle in the middle (although hardly anybody ever goes up there). A busy port adds to the sense of life and ferries, cruise ships and excursion boats are constantly coming and going. In fact, this is one of the few places in Europe that still *builds* big ships (four or five a year, their huge hulls, festooned in cranes, dominating the skyline of the port, looking like blocks of flats under construction).

Oddly enough, Pula is not the regional capital – it's said the Yugoslav government plumped instead for Pazin, in the interior, as a slight to the more obvious, but also too Italianate, candidate.

Essentials

Getting There

Pula is at the tip of the Istrian peninsula, and is the region's largest city. It is 292 km (180 miles) from Zagreb, 110 km from (60 miles) from Rijeka and 711 km (440 miles) from Dubrovnik. The airport, endearingly rural with farmland between the runways, is a short way from the city centre. See 'Essentials – Getting There' at the beginning of this chapter for more information.

Visitor Information

See 'Essentials – Visitor Information' at the beginning of this chapter.

Getting Around

The centre of Pula is not very big, so it's easily walkable. The layout looks very much like a doughnut – the hole in the middle is the castle with the hill on it. There's not much up there, so not many people bother to go. The result is that all the streets of the city circle the base of the hill. Start walking at, say, the Arena, follow the main streets, and you end up back at the Arena. Which is great – you can see everything you want to, and you don't have to back track!

What To See & Do

All the sights of Pula are within easy walking distance of each other, so leave the car at the hotel, or park up and continue on foot. By far the best place to start a tour of Pula's attractions is the small park between the Amphitheatre and the city centre. At the opposite end of the park to the impressive war memorial is a fountain that consists of a metal model of the city. It's actually rather accurate and is a really excellent orientation aid. Use it in conjunction with the map on p.163 to plan your day's perambulations.

The Amphitheatre ★★★

MOMENT **ALL AGES** Nothing in the guide books or tourist literature, no photographs or description, had prepared me for how enormous Pula's ampitheatre is, or how beautiful. Its great ghostly floodlit mass reared skywards from the shrubs and trees of a little park, like some huge time capsule visiting the 21st century from the distant past. The 1st century BC amphitheatre is magnificent. It's the sixth biggest in the world, and its position – dominating the port and rising spectacularly from surrounding trees and gardens – would place it even higher up the 'most-impressive' league, especially at night when it is floodlit. Nobody is quite sure why this enormous structure (originally seating 22,000 spectators) was needed in a town with a population of around 5,000. Presumably it pulled in people from the surrounding countryside.

Built on land that slopes down to the harbour, the Amphitheatre's pale stone façade, three

PULA

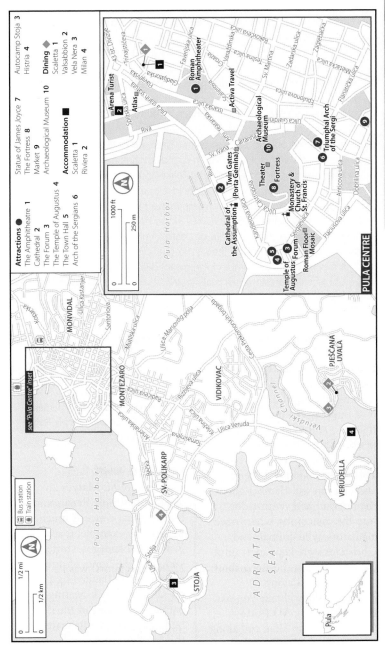

Attractions ●
The Amphitheatre **1**
Cathedral **2**
The Forum **3**
The Temple of Augustus **4**
The Town Hall **5**
Arch of the Sergians **6**
Statue of James Joyce **7**
The Fortress **8**
Market **9**
Archaeological Museum **10**

Accommodation ■
Scaletta **1**
Riviera **2**
Autocamp Stoja **3**
Histria **4**

Dining ◆
Scaletta **1**
Valsabbion **2**
Vela Nera **3**
Milan **4**

PULA CENTRE

Roman Amphitheater **1**
Arena Turist **2**
Atlas ■
Activa Travel
Cathedral of the Assumption **2**
Twin Gates (Porta Gemina) ✝
Temple of Augustus **4**
Forum **3**
Roman Floor Mosaic
Monastery & Church of St. Francis
Theater
Fortress **8**
Archaeological Museum **10**
Triumphal Arch of the Sergi **7**

MONVIDAL
MONTEZARO
VIDIKOVAC
SV. POLIKARP
STOJA
PJEŚĆANA UVALA
VERUDELLA

Pula Harbor
ADRIATIC SEA
Veruda Channel

Bus station
Train station

see "Pula Centre" Inset

Pula

Gladiators

Gladiators were professional fighting men (and possibly women), usually condemned prisoners, slaves or prisoners-of-war, but occasionally young men who volunteered, often as a last resort to pay off their debts. There were many different types of gladiator recognisable by their armament and armour. Gladiators were trained in gladiator schools, given the best food and medical attention, and rarely fought more than three times a year. They fought each other, usually one-to-one but sometimes in groups, in gladiatorial contests. Such public spectacles were often put on and paid for by the Emperor, or by rich citizens, to gain popularity with the mob. When a gladiator had been defeated, the sponsor, the Emperor, or even the audience as a whole decided whether he or she should die. Sponsors would be naturally inclined towards clemency – gladiators were very expensive to train. However, if they spared their gladiators too often, they would be accused of being tight-fisted. The signal indicating life or death involved the thumb, but we don't know exactly how – there's no real evidence that thumbs-up meant clemency, and thumbs-down meant death.

Gladiatorial contests were finally banned by Constantine I in 325AD.

tiers at the front, two at the rear, is remarkably complete. Unfortunately, the same can't be said for the inside – the local population scavenged most of it for their own buildings. But the amphitheatre is still used for public performances (the seating for a Jose Carreras concert was being assembled when I was there), and you can still clamber about the interior, and venture down into the catacombs, where once gladiators, wild animals and Christians were kept apart until their meeting in the arena above.

A short walk along Amfiteatarska will take you past the 2nd century AD **Porta Gemina** or Twin Gate and along Kandlerova to the Cathedral.

INSIDER TIP »

Check out future performances before you get to Pula's amphitheatre. People who have performed in there include Luciano Pavarotti, Sting, James Brown, Joe Cocker, Simply Red and Jamiroquai.

Cathedral ADULTS Pula's Cathedral of St. Mary is an apparently simple Renaissance building that conceals much – its altar, for example, is actually a Roman sarcophagus, stuffed, it's said, with the bones of numerous saints. It's flanked by a plain, no-nonsense clock-bearing campanile. This is one of the many buildings that owe its material to the Amphitheatre.

In the grounds of the Cathedral stands a simple stone with the word Vergarola engraved on it, with the date '18.08.1946' and the time '13 h'. This commemorates a disaster when a group of 28 huge deep-water mines stored by the Italians off Vergarola Beach near the city detonated – nobody quite knows why. It was a hot August afternoon, and the beach was packed. 70 people were killed, many of them children, and over 100 injured.

Nearby lies a jumble of Roman remains in front of a large block of flats – they were going to build a car park, but immediately stumbled across the remains of a Roman Villa, so all work has had to stop indefinitely. The Romans must be the bane of Pula's developers.

The Forum ADULTS The same problem arose just along the street. Plans were going ahead to repave the Forum – the city's main square – when the builders immediately hit Roman ruins. All work had to stop. An orange plastic mesh barrier was unrolled around it, to keep people out. So now the main square can't be used. Pula's Roman connection brings in lots of tourists, but sometimes the people of the city must get a little fed up with interference by their 2,000-year-old ancestors. Standing at one end of the Forum is **The Temple of Augustus** AGES 5 AND ABOVE, which dates from around the time of Christ. An excellent example of its type, it houses a rather good museum of some of the city's Roman finds.

The Town Hall AGES 5 AND ABOVE is beside the Temple of Augustus, and was once the Temple of Diana, until it was rebuilt in the 13th century, and further modified during the Renaissance. Look at the back of the building and you can clearly see the columns and pediment of the original temple. You'll find the city's main Tourist Office on the Forum as well. Continue to walk around, with the steps up towards the castle on your left, then along Sergijevaca. Nearby is the **Arch of the Sergians** AGES 5 AND ABOVE. Dating from the 1st century BC, the rather splendid arch was a bit of self-glorification by the Sergi family.

Statue of James Joyce ★★★ ALL AGES Close to the Arch of the Sergians can be found a statue of James Joyce, looking for all the world as if he is having a beer

Statue of James Joyce, Pula

at café-bar Uliks ('Ulysses' in Croatian). In October 1904, the 22-year-old Irish writer took up a post teaching English to Austro-Hungarian naval officers, and moved to the city with his bride-to-be, Nora Barnacle. The language school at which he taught is the yellow building – now Diesel – on the corner next to Uliks. There's also a display case of Joyce memorabilia inside the bar itself. So go ahead – sit the children next to the famous Irishman with a drink and get snapping. It's a family heirloom in the making.

Beyond the Arch of the Sergians Turning right at the Arch of the Sergians brings you to McDonald's (should you really need it), going straight brings you out at the market ALL AGES , a splendid two-story, cast-iron-and-glass edifice which, together with the open-air stalls that surround it, offers a wide variety of fruit, vegetables, cheese, olive oil and pastries. There are also numerous cafés and bars – try to arrive, or return, in the morning, or in the evening. Afternoons are dead. Turning left at the Arch of the Sergians brings you to Giardini ALL AGES , which is not gardens at all, but a succession of outdoor cafés and restaurants under mature lime trees, which is one of the city's most popular meeting places.

The Fortress AGES 5 AND ABOVE
Beyond Giardini, you get back to the Amphitheatre – having done a complete circuit of the

city. At any point on this route, you can climb up to the star-shaped Venetian fortress on the hill at the centre of town. There are impressive if drab fortifications, rather marred by 20th century additions, massed ranks of canons, informative context boards, and superb views across the city towards those huge ships-in-the-making.

Archaeological Museum
AGES 5 AND ABOVE Down from the Fortress, and past the remains of a Roman Amphitheatre, is the Archaeological Museum. With mainly Roman artefacts, it's got an old fashioned air – perhaps because it's set in an old secondary school – though the English labelling is very good. The grounds feature a small arena that is used for concerts in summer.

The Aquarium AGES 2 AND ABOVE
A couple of kilometres south of the town centre, on the Verudela Peninsula, is Pula Aquarium, set up in Fort Verudell during the summer of 2002. Small and friendly, it's a good introduction to the undersea life of the north Adriatic – a painless way of seeing starfish, crabs, sea-urchins and the like close up.

The Aquarium, Fort Verudella. 📞 091-568 2986.

Shopping with Children

Pula, as the biggest town in Istria, is undoubtedly the main destination for Istrians with money to spend. Shops seem to be in three distinct areas – the

Sergijevaca have a range of small,
independent souvenir, clothes
and craft outlets and a couple of
Internet cafés (try **www.enigma-
cafe.com**), whilst in the streets to
the east of Giardini it's all chain
stores. The area around the market contains food and flower
stalls and a variety of up-market
cafés. Dotted throughout are
restaurants.

Family Entertainment

For mainstream films the
Cinema Zagreb is centrally
located at Giardini 1 (☎ 052-212-
336), and there's an Arts cinema
and the Istrian National Theatre
at Laginjina 5 (☎ 052-222-380).
There are no beaches in the
town itself, but a string of them
around the Verudela Peninsula.
No sand, though – just the usual
shingle.

Across Istria, especially
during the summer, a range
of different festivals provides
family entertainment. Pula's
Film Festival takes place in the
Amphitheatre in July, and in
nearby Bale there's folk dancing
in regional costume in 'Bale
Night' on the first Saturday
in August. Vodnjan hosts a
craft and food fair on the first
Saturday of every month, and
on the second Sunday in August
head for Rovinj's famous open-
air arts fair, held on Grisiau, the
main street (or alley) – anybody
who registers can exhibit, so
works range from the highly
professional (and expensive) to
the frankly amateur.

There are even more festival
riches inland. Buje has a huge
wine festival (known as 'Grape
Days') during one weekend in
September, with much singing,
dancing and tippling. Famous
for its artists and musicians,
Grožnjan hosts open-air concerts
throughout July and August), a
jazz festival in late July, and a
variety of art exhibitions and
wine and truffle events. The
famous Motovun Film Festival
takes place in late July, and the
third Monday of every month
sees a craft and produce fair. In
keeping with its claim to be the
truffle capital of Istria, Buzet
cooks its huge truffle omelette
during Subotina (second
Saturday in September), and it
too has a craft and food fair (on
the third Thursday of the
month). Finally, the towns at
either end of Gagolitic Alley
make their own contribution:
Roč stages its international festival of accordion playing on the
second Sunday in May, whilst,
on the first or second Saturday
in June, Hum elects its mayor
with medieval traditions, food
and music.

Family-Friendly
Accommodation

The city of Pula itself isn't rich
in hotel beds, so if you're an
inveterate 'I like to stay in the
city centre' sort of a person,
you're pretty much stuck with a
very limited choice. Beyond
that, there's a whole complex of
hotels and campsites out on the
mass of headlands and bays

around three kilometres south and west of the city centre.

Autocamp Stoja ★★ Not a bad alternative to a hotel stay, and with lots to do for the youngsters, the Autocamp Stoja is just over three kilometres from Pula's centre. You can stay in your own tent (there are 670 pitches), or rent one of the mobile homes and enjoy your own terrace and Sat TV. Sports available include tennis, table tennis, basketball, volleyball and water sports. In addition, there are walking and jogging trails, and plenty of entertainment for the children. The site itself is pretty self-contained, with a bar, restaurant, mini-market, exchange office and excursion agency. You can't just have a couple of days, though – there's a minimum stay of seven nights at peak times, which must be Saturday to Saturday, or three nights off-peak.

52110 Pula. ☎ *052-387-144; 052-529-400. Fax 052-387-748. www.arena turist.hr. Camping – adults 30–52 Kuna (£ 3–5), children (5–10): 20–32 Kuna (£ 2–3), children 4 and under free. Mobile home with A/C from 210 to 790 Kuna (£ 20–75) depending on time of year. AE, DC, MC, V. Closed mid-Oct to mid-Mar.*

Histria ★★ Situated on a spur of the Verudela Peninsula, about four kilometres from Pula, the Histria is probably the best choice in the area for families with children. Rooms are large and comfortable, with all the necessary facilities, and there are lots of activities available, together with entertainment.

Verudela bb. ☎ *052-590-000. Fax 052-214-175. www.arenaturist.hr. 248 rooms. Aug: from 1130 Kuna (£ 110) double. Add 10% above the double-room price for suite. AE, DC, MC, V. Rates include breakfast. Amenities: Restaurant, café, bar, disco, casino, two pools, tennis courts, sauna, summer activity programs. In room: A/C, TV.*

Riviera The Riviera looks terrific on the outside – a stately, Habsburg-era pile, which could be a museum or an opera house. Don't expect luxury, though, when you walk inside – it's a survival from the early 20th century (1907), and its facilities seem to be almost as old, from the wheezing lift and ill-fitting windows, to the poor bathroom fittings and lack of air conditioning. Having said that, there's something attractive about its lofty reception, huge bar and dining room, and in particular the terrace-sized balcony on which you'll have breakfast. And the position – a hundred metres up from the harbour, just along from the railway station – couldn't be more convenient. There's nothing specific for children in the hotel, but they are likely to enjoy its antique spaciousness.

Spliska 1. ☎ *052-211-166. Fax 052-219-117. www.arenaturist.hr. 76 rooms. 610 Kuna (£ 60) double. Rates include breakfast. AE, DC, MC, V. Amenities: Restaurant. In room: TV.*

Scaletta ★★★ FIND The Scaletta is a lovely hotel – it looks a picture from the outside (though there's a fair bit of luggage-lugging involved in getting in), and the rooms, though now a little old-fashioned for some tastes (Ikea meets Hercule Poirot), do everything it says on the tin – the facilities are remarkably thorough for such a relatively small, family-run hotel. The breakfast room has a nautical theme – the youngsters will love all the model ships. Above all, though, the Scaletta has a perfect location – a mini-market next door for picnic stuff (and several little parks nearby in which to eat it), a chemist next door the other side in case of indigestion and other minor maladies, a nice little children's playground virtually across the road, Kompas Travel Agency and Europcar car rental offices in the same block as the restaurant, and the gob-smacking spectacle of the Roman Amphitheatre (a floodlit vision after dark) and the busy boat-interest of the port a five-minute toddler-stroll away. Its restaurant, too (see below), is one of the few I've come across in Croatia where they have children's toys available.

Flavijevska 26. ☎ 052-541-025. Fax 052-541-599. www.hotel-scaletta. com. 12 rooms (two singles, 10 doubles). 1 June–15 Sept: 750 Kuna (£ 73) double. Rest of year: 518 Kuna (£ 50) double. Rates include breakfast. AE, DC, MC, V. Amenities: Restaurant, wine cellar. In room: A/C, TV, minibar, hair dryer, safe.

Family-Friendly Dining

There are lots of good places to eat in Pula. For a first rate and unbiased summary and reviews of what's available, get your hands on a copy of 'Istragastro', produced by the Istria Regional Tourist Board. In particular, it gives restaurants (but not taverns) scores out of 100, although not all restaurants of quality are covered.

Milan ★★★ Out near the Naval Cemetery, the Milan excels not only in its food and wine list (700 wines to choose from), but also both in the quality of its service and in its overall ambience. It is used to children too, often providing family lunches and dinners for special occasions at which there are many children. The staff are happy to put tables together to accommodate as many people as are in the party.

Stoja 4, Pula. ☎ 052-300-200. Fax 052-210-500. www.milan1967.hr. Reservations recommended. Main courses 50–185 Kuna (£ 5–18). AE, DC, MC, V. Daily 11am–midnight.

Scaletta ★★ VALUE CROATIAN A warm, pine-beamed, bustling sort of place, the Scaletta restaurant is across the road from the hotel (see above). Much frequented by locals (always a good sign), the menu consists largely of variations on a theme of meat and fish – and they're happy to adapt both content and portion-size on request. The restaurant is big, semi-circular at one end, with tables to fit a variety of family sizes, and (a nice touch often missing in Croatian restaurants), a children's corner with lots of toys and games.

Flavijevska 26. ☎ 053-541-025. Fax 052-541-599. www.hotel-scaletta. com. Reservations recommended.

Entrees 60–220 Kuna (£ 5.50–21).
AE, DC, MC, V. Mon–Sat 10am–11pm.
Closed Sun.

Valsabbion ★★★
CREATIVE MEDITERRANEAN

Consistently voted one of
Croatia's best restaurants, weighed
down with awards, and much
visited by the great and the good
(including Sting, Naomi
Campbell, Placido Domingo,
and Vanessa Mae, to name but a
few), you can't go wrong with
the Valsabbion Hotel's restaurant. As long as you can afford it,
that is. Though the main courses
are reasonable, it's amazing how
it all mounts up. Nevertheless, it
makes a brilliant venue for a special occasion. The pasta and rice
in a cheese ring, fish fillet in
Mediterranean sauce, and black-
and-white mousse come highly
recommended.

Pjescana Uvala IX/26. 📞 *052-218-033.
Fax: 052-383-333.* **www.valsabbion.
net.** *Reservations required. Main
courses 90–120 Kuna (£ 8.50–11.50).
AE, DC, MC, V. Daily noon–midnight.*

Vela Nera ★★ **CREATIVE SEAFOOD**

Overlooking the marina at
Pješcana Uvala, some three
kilometres south of Pula's city
centre, Vela Nera is one of only
three restaurants in the region
to get 90/100 or above in
'Istragastro' (the other two are
Valsabbion and Milan). It has a
pleasant ambience, a matchless
location and delicious seafood
plus such treats as noodles with
truffles (see p.182). The tables
are big and round and can comfortably accommodate a family.

Pješcana Uvala bb. 📞 *052-219-209.
Fax 052-215-951.* **www.velanera.hr.**
*Reservations recommended. Main
courses 50–150 Kuna (£ 5–14). AE,
DC, MC, V. Daily 8am–midnight.*

The Brijuni Islands National Park ★★★ **ALL AGES**

Just to the
north of Pula lie the Brijuni
Islands. A trip to them makes a
really nice day out, either inde-
pendently (a half-hour drive to
Fažana, tickets from the National
Park office on the quayside, and a
four-hour round trip from there)
or on one of the many excursions
organised by travel agencies all
along the Istrian west coast.
Most hotels can offer excursions
too. They can be more expensive,
but they include a coach to
Fažana and sometimes lunch. If
you just want to look at them,
you can board a boat from Pula
Harbour, but they don't usually
land on the islands, or if they do
it's just for a picnic and a swim.

There are fourteen islands in
the Brijuni Archipelago. The
public are allowed onto only two
of them – Veli Brijun and Mali
Brijun.

The Brijuni Islands have a
fascinating history. In 1885 the
wealthy Austrian industrialist
Paul Kupelwieser, having taken
his family on a picnic to the
uninhabited islands, decided that
they had potential. He bought
them, cleared them of mosqui-
toes and scrub, and built a nine-
hole golf course, luxury villas
and hotels to create a very up-
market health resort. It attracted
the cream of European society
including Franz Ferdinand, heir

Brijuni

to the Austro-Hungarian Empire, Kaiser Wilhelm II and the writer Thomas Mann. Then came World War 1, and the resultant upheaval destroyed the moneyed, leisured German and Austro-Hungarian upper classes upon which the islands depended. They went into steep decline.

After World War 2, Tito (see p.226) came to power and, in 1947, commandeered the islands as a presidential retreat. The Bijela Vila (White Villa) on Veli Brijun became his summer bolthole, at which he entertained a new mon-eyed and leisured class, this time celebrities such as Sophia Loren, Elizabeth Taylor and Richard Burton, and various world lead-ers. In 1983, three years after Tito's death, the islands were given National Park status, and the two main ones were opened to the public.

Visits to Veli Brijun usually include a guided tour (English available) of the island on a little train, which takes in the small safari park created to look after animals given to Tito during his time in power. The park also contains deer descended from herds introduced by Kupelwieser, the golf course (now 18 holes) and an exhibition on 'Tito on Brijuni'. It is possible to stay in one of Kupelwieser's hotels, but they are very expensive – perhaps to keep out the riff-raff.

ROVINJ

Just 41 km (25 miles) by main road up the coast from Pula, Rovinj is a beautiful jumble of old houses clustered around its imposing campanile – one of the highest in Istria – on what was, until the mid-18th century, an island. Since then, as the settle-ment spread onto the mainland, Rovinj has, through luck or judgement, kept most recent development away from the Old Town. The result is a delightfully mellow gaggle of pastel houses interspersed with the occasional tree, where you can explore meandering lanes, rummage through lots of little shops, or visit the odd museum, catching glimpses between the houses of a sparkling sea. There is also the opportunity of swimming in that sea, though don't expect miles of golden sand.

What is really appealing about Rovinj is its human scale, and the fact that it's not pre-served in aspic. It is a modern town with its share of industry (it is the biggest manufacturer of cigarettes in Croatia), and there's no doubting that many of the

Rovinj

trees that peek out here and there among the houses, the boats in the harbour – it's no wonder that its image is so heavily used to promote Croatian tourism. I will never forget my first glimpse of Rovinj – it was as if a great painting had suddenly come to life.

Essentials

Getting There

See 'Essentials – Getting There' at the beginning of this chapter.

Visitor Information

See 'Essentials – Visitor Information' at the beginning of this chapter.

Getting Around

Like Pula, the centre of Rovinj is not very big, so it's easy to get around on foot. There's a fair amount of climbing, too, since the must-see Church of St. Euphemia stands on a hill in the centre of the Old Town. There's plenty of parking on either side of the 'mainland', north and south of the Old Town.

What To See & Do

Trg Marsala Tita, the Balbi Arch and Grisia ALL AGES More about ambience than any particular attraction, Rovinj is a delight to explore. The main square – Trg Marsala Tita – sits right on the harbour on the south side of the peninsula, and is lined with cafés that often have live music. The square also

vessels that crowd its harbour are working *batanes,* the local flat-bottomed fishing boat. Other vessels in the harbour include private yachts, excursion boats, a variety of water taxis, and the occasional cruise ship.

Rovinj is famous for art and artists – think St. Ives in Cornwall but with more clement weather – and there's no better place to pick up original paintings at reasonable prices. If you're in Rovinj early in August, you can enjoy the town's annual Art festival with open-air displays of painting all along its main street (usually held on the second Sunday of the month). Anybody can display their work in the show as long as they register at the town museum.

Croatia's Adriatic coast boasts a succession of beautiful towns and cities, but if I had to name the best of the best, I would have to choose Rovinj. The pastel walls of the old houses that plunge straight into the sea and pile up the hill, the church and campanile of St. Euphemia at the summit, the dark foliage of the

Rovinj

contains the Town Museum (Trg Maršala Tita 11, 052-816-720) – rather staid paintings and sculpture, but look out for interesting temporary exhibitions (closed Mondays). Through the ornately baroque 17th century Balbi Arch, you can climb the town's main street, Grisia, which is narrow, steep and stepped, and lined with little shops selling paintings and craft objects.

St. Euphemia's Church

AGES 3 AND ABOVE At the top of the hill Grisia opens out onto the imposing Church of St. Euphemia and its signature campanile – you can climb to the top for incredible views, but it's not recommended for the very young or the faint of heart. St. Euphemia was an early Christian martyr from near Constantinople, who was tortured and thrown to the lions during the reign of Diocletian, that scourge of the Christian faith (see box on p.107). The story goes that, to prevent her remains being disturbed by the iconoclasts, in 800AD her sarcophagus left Constantinople and floated ashore in Rovinj, a miracle indeed, since it must weigh a ton – it's on display in the church. A statue of the saint also tops the campanile, and the name Euphemia is still a popular one for Istrian girls.

St. Euphemia was martyred on 16th September 304AD, a day that is still commemorated with a week of festivities and events all over the town. It's well worth attending if you're around.

The House of the Batana

★★★ **AGES 5 AND ABOVE** Just along the Riva from the Tourist Office, this beautiful little museum is dedicated entirely to the *batana*, the local flat-bottomed fishing boat. Although exhibits are labelled only in Croatian, a lot of the displays are self-explanatory (a speeded up film of a *batana* being built, for example), and there's an excellent free leaflet in English explaining all the display panels. The building itself is 17th century, and strongly associated with fishing and the sea – it was home to sailors, craftsmen involved in the fishing industry, a sailors' tavern, and the local dock workers. Displays include information on how the boats were built, their structure, fishing nets and how they were used, as well as other aspects of life associated with fishing. Among the more unusual revelations are details about the *spácio* (wine bar), and

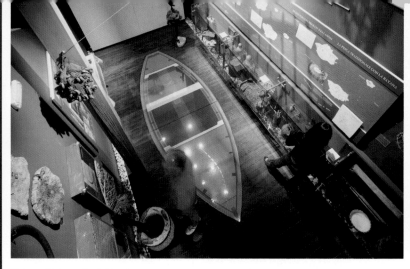

House of Batana, Rovinj

the *bitináda*, which was a type of music in which the human voice had to mimic the accompanying musical instruments so that the fishermen could keep their hands free to mend nets and such like.

Obala/Riva P. Budicin 2. ☎ 052-805-266. batana@rv-batana.htnet.hr. Open daily from June–September 10am–3pm and 5pm–10pm. Otherwise 10am–1pm and 3pm–5pm (closed Mondays, and in January and February). Adults 10 Kuna (95p). Children (up to age 10), students and pensioners free.

Trg Valibora ★★★ ALL AGES

Rovinj's other main square, Trg Valibora, is on the north side of the town, just a couple of hundred metres from Trg Marsala Tita. It is a good place for families to head for and has a small open-air market – selling everything from sandals to sunglasses to souvenirs – public toilets, and a well-equipped playground. Beyond it is the town's main car park – you pick up a ticket as you enter, then take it to the kiosk before you leave to pay the tariff.

The Aquarium AGES 2 AND ABOVE

Before leaving Rovinj, it's probably worth a quick look at the Aquarium, just along from the car park in the Centre for Marine Research, to see some of the local marine life at close quarters (Obala G. Paliage 5 ☎ 052-804-712).

The Limski Kanal

AGES 3 AND ABOVE The briefest look at the signs next to excursion boats in Rovinj's harbour will tell you that their most popular destination is the Limski Kanal, a 12 km long fjord about 16 km north of Rovinj, which once marked the border with Poreč ('Limski' is from the same Latin root as 'limit'). Once the habitat of pirates who preyed on Venetian coastal shipping, it has spawned legends involving notorious privateer Captain Morgan, said to have holed-up here with some of his men. The name of the nearby village of Mrgani seems to lend credence to the story.

The Kanal is worth a visit, if not by boat, then by car. There's a viewing point on the road to Poreč, with a platform that carries an ominous sign warning that you climb it 'at your own responsibility'. The Poreč water is a beautiful emerald green/blue, contrasting with the foliage of the trees that cover its banks. The water is dotted with boats as well as the many floats that carry the ropes on which oysters and mussels are encouraged to grow. Indeed, the Limski Kanal is famous for its shellfish, and draws many local people from Rovinj and Poreč to its numerous restaurants.

Vrsar AGES 3 AND ABOVE Just north of the entrance to the Limski Kanal, the pretty village of Vrsar is dreamily situated on its hilltop. Once the seat of bishops, it was visited several times by Venice's famous 17th century wide-boy Casanova. He wasn't attracted by the presence of one of Europe's largest naturist colonies at nearby Koversada, though, because that wasn't established until 1960 (see box).

Family-Friendly Accommodation

In common with most of Croatia's coastal towns, Rovinj is short of hotel accommodation in the city centre.

Hotel Katarina ★★★ FIND The Hotel Katarina has got to be one of the best bets for families with children in the whole of Europe. The reason? It's on an island, just off Rovinj, the prettiest town in Istria, and the island contains a children's club, playground, nature park, pool complex with children's pool, aqua sports centre, garden and beaches, together with walking and jogging paths, mini golf, floodlit sand tennis, beach and pool bars, pizza parlour, ballroom and restaurant. It's even got its own vineyard. And because it's an island, with no bridge or causeway, it is totally traffic free! When you get to the Dolphin Jetty in Rovinj, your luggage will be picked up for delivery to your room, and you can then take the hotel boat with your hand luggage.

HR-52210 Rovinj. ☎ 052-804-100. Fax: 052-804-111. www.hotelinsel-katarina.com. 745 Kuna (£ 70) per person for a family two-bedroom apartment (and up to 2 children under 12 go free). Amenities: children's club, playground, nature park, pool complex with children's pool, aqua sports centre, garden, vineyard, and beaches, together with walking and jogging paths, mini golf, floodlit sand tennis, beach and pool bars, pizza parlour, ballroom and restaurant. In room: hair dryer, Sat TV, safe, minibar, balcony/terrace with sea view.

Villa Angelo d'Oro ★★★ It seems impossible that the Villa Angelo d'Oro has room to house a hotel. It's a tall old town house – in fact, a bishop's palace – on the main street (actually more of an alley) that skirts the northern side of the Old Town. Despite seeming small, it manages to contain not only 25 luxurious rooms but also a bar, restaurant, library (with balcony), sauna, Jacuzzi and solarium. For families, there are two suites, and extra beds and/or cots can be fitted in double rooms. The restaurant is happy to provide small portions for, or divide portions between, children. Babysitting can be arranged. Although you can't park at the hotel, staff will meet you and carry your luggage back to the hotel.

Via Svalba 38–42. 📞 *052-840-502.* ***www.rovinj.at.*** *25 rooms. 905 Kuna (£ 90) double, 2167 Kuna (£ 200) suite that will sleep 2–4 people. 50% discount for children aged 3–11. Children under 3 free. Rates include breakfast. Half-board available on request. AE, DC, MC, V. Limited free parking 15 minutes from hotel. Amenities: Restaurant, terrace dining, wine cellar, Jacuzzi, solarium, library. In room: A/C, TV, minibar, hair dryer.*

Family-Friendly Dining

Angelo d'Oro ★★★ ISTRIAN

The quality of the hotel (see above) is reflected in its restaurant, which features good food in beautiful surroundings. In the summer you can dine in the hotel garden, in the winter in the 'golden angel' dining room. The restaurant also has a fine wine cellar. The tables aren't overly crowded together so there's room for the children to move around, and, although there's no children's menu as such, the staff are only too pleased to divide portions, or adapt courses to smaller appetites.

Via Svalba 38–42. 📞 *052-840-502.* ***www.rovinj.at.*** *Reservations recommended. Main courses 90–165 Kuna (£ 8.50–15). AE, DC, MC. Daily 7pm–midnight.*

Konoba Veli Joz ★ ISTRIAN The restaurant is cluttered with sailing-related paraphernalia, which means the children have got something to look at and talk about. The food is excellent, and though the fish dishes are on the pricy side, there's plenty of alternatives if things are tight. Try the cod in bianco, noodles with cream, scampi with mushrooms or oven-baked lamb with potatoes.

Svetog Kržia 1. 📞 *052-816-337. Main courses 30–120 Kuna (£ 3–11.50). AE, DC, MC, V. Daily 11am–1am.*

POREČ

Poreč is 56 km (35 miles) north of Pula, and is by far Croatia's biggest holiday resort. The large number of people who flock to the huge hotel complexes north and south of the town are a significant factor when deciding whether to visit – it really does get chock-a-block (the 17,000 permanent inhabitants are joined by over 50,000 holidaymakers in summer).

Having said that, it is a pleasant place, especially off-peak, with the UNESCO-listed Basilica of Euphrasius, a number of beautiful Gothic and Romanesque houses, a well-preserved 15th century Venetian tower, and a few jumbled Roman remains – even more jumbled, apparently, since World War 2, when RAF bombs aimed at Italian ships in the harbour went astray and hit the town.

Essentials

Getting There

See 'Essentials – Getting There' at the beginning of this chapter.

Visitor Information

See 'Essentials – Visitor Information' at the beginning of this chapter.

Getting Around

The centre of Poreč is pedestrianised. There's a big new car park on the northwest approach, from which the 10-minute walk into the centre is very pleasant.

What To See & Do

The Basilica of Euphrasius

AGES 3 AND ABOVE Yet another UNESCO World Heritage Site, added to the list in 1997, the Basilica of Euphrasius and its associated buildings (the Baptistry and the Bishop's Palace) are a rich feast of early Christian and Byzantine church architecture, painting and mosaics, with liberal decorative use of mother-of-pearl. Even if the detail is lost on members of the party who have little interest in ecclesiastical history, the atmosphere of eastern piety is almost manifest. And there's a great view across Poreč from the campanile.

Poreč

The rest of Poreč is a combination of Roman and Venetian. Two Venetian towers adorn the entrance to the old part of the town, and the main street – Dekumanska, or Decumanus – is named for the fact that 10 Roman soldiers abreast could march down its length. Just off this street is the **Aquarium** ★★ AGES 2 AND ABOVE, a fairly small and intimate but nicely organised display where a variety of Adriatic sea life can be seen, including moray eels, rays, dogfish, octopus and red scorpionfish. There's also a café and a small gift shop.

The District Museum

AGES 5 AND ABOVE Set in a Baroque palace once owned by the Sinčić family, Istria's oldest museum contains a selection of Roman artefacts, which provide some interesting insights into life in Roman times including an illustration of the local olive harvest.

Beyond the District Museum, look out for the impressive **Romanesque House** AGES 11 AND ABOVE, and the remains of the **Temples of Mars and of Neptune** AGES 8 AND ABOVE. Right at the tip of the peninsula on which Poreč is built are two reminders of more recent history – buildings that were used to house refugees during the Patriotic War (see p.248). They are now boarded up, presumably awaiting renovation.

The Baredine Cave ★★

ALL AGES A popular day out from Poreč is the Baredine Cave, about eight kilometres (five miles) northeast of the town. The cave has spectacular stalactites and stalagmites, and a wide variety of limestone formations – rippling curtains and natural sculptures that have, sometimes fancifully, been compared to the Virgin Mary, the Leaning Tower of Pisa (or pizza, as the information leaflet has it), and a snowman holding a torch. While in the

Basilica of Euphrasius, Poreč

cave look out for Milka, a 13th century milkmaid of legend who was thrown into the cave by the mother of her well-born lover Gabriel. According to the story, she became petrified and is now on an underground journey to be reunited with the lovelorn Gabriel, who entered a different cave while hunting for her, and met the same fate.

There are six main chambers and an underground lake, and the guided tour that comes with the entrance fee lasts about 40 minutes.

Family-Friendly Accommodation

Although Poreč is a big player in Croatia's tourist industry, the really big resort hotels have been kept outside the town – to the north in Pical, and at Plava Laguna and Zelena Laguna to the south. Nevertheless, there are several attractive hotels within the town's central area.

Diamant ★★ A kilometre from the centre of town, the Diamant prides itself on being a sports and fitness hotel. So its beauty, health, fitness and wellness facilities and programmes are second to none. It also goes out of its way to keep youngsters happy: there's a children's swimming pool, a children's playground and, from May to October, a children's entertainment programme. Older children and teenagers can, of course, make use of the sports facilities. You can order double rooms with extra beds, or several rooms together in a group. The restaurant operates a buffet system, so children can choose exactly what they want.

Brulo. ☎ *052-400-000. Fax: 052-451-206. www.riviera.hr. 244 rooms. End of July to mid-Aug: from 1100 Kuna (£ 105) double. Rates include breakfast and are per person daily based on a stay of four or more days. 20% surcharge for stays of three days or fewer. AE, DC, MC, V. Amenities: two restaurants, bar, Internet café, juice bar, two pools, hot tub, whirlpool, children's program, excursions, massage, solarium. In room: A/C, TV, minibar, hair dryer.*

Hotel Fortuna ★★ Another hotel-on-an-island, the Fortuna sits in parkland on the island of St. Nikola, a 10-minute boat ride from Poreč. Open from April to October, the hotel can offer double rooms, and double rooms with an extra bed, so it should be possible to tailor the rooms booked to the needs of the family. There's a children's swimming pool, a beach 50 metres from the hotel, and full sports and children's programmes throughout the holiday season. Meals are buffet-style – always a plus when you've got children.

Valamar d.o.o., Miramarska 24, Zagreb, Croatia. ☎ *052-465-100. Fax: 052-451-440. 187 rooms. 500 Kuna (£ 46) pp double, half board. Children under 3, sleeping with parents, free. Children up to age 6, free if sharing with two full-rate adults, 50% otherwise. Children 7–13 sharing with two full-rate adults, 50%, otherwise 30%. Cots and extra beds on request. Amenities: supervised parking, free ferry to and from Poreč, lift, restaurant, bar, children's playground, sport and*

children's entertainment programmes, sports centre, tennis courts. In room: Sat TV, all rooms with shower, most with baths as well, hair dryer.

Family-Friendly Dining

Poreč goes in a lot for the old staples – pizza, pasta, fish and meat. They no doubt know their customers.

Old Pub Cotton Club ★ ITALIAN You might ignore this restaurant on the grounds that it's just for tourists. It's not. Yes, you can get UK and Irish beers (including Guinness), but the food – an inventive mix of Italian favourites like tortellini, tagliatelle, pastas and pizzas – is excellent. And poised as it is at the entrance to the Old Town, on a newly-paved square (Trg Slobode), you couldn't ask for a better vantage point from which to watch the world go by than sitting under its maroon awnings. The ice cream is delicious, and there's often live music at weekends.

Trg Slobode 5. ☎ *052-453-293. Fax 052-432-074. Main courses 40–110 Kuna (£ 4–10.50). No credit cards. Daily 9am–1am.*

Restaurant Villa Filipini ★★★ ISTRIAN Well-reckoned by locals, this little restaurant, attached to the Filipini Hotel, has an attractive simplicity indoors and a rustic feel on the terrace. There's lots of room, a lovely ambience, and the food on offer depends on what's good locally at the time. The ravioli, fuži (a kind of pasta) and the polenta are all home made.

Filipini 1B. 📞 *052-463-200.* **www.
istra.com/filipini.** *Main courses
40–150 Kuna (£ 4–14). AE, DC, MC,
V. Daily midday to midnight.*

Ulixes ★ ISTRIAN Tender-hearted
children will love the cats that
come begging at your table.
Rustic implements adorn the
walls of the restaurant's interior.
Outside, there's a terrace and a
walled garden. The menu is
mostly seafood based, although
the meat dishes can be a little
hit-and-miss.

Decumanus 2. 📞 *052-451-132.*
www.istra.com/ulixes. *Main
courses 40–110 Kuna (£ 4–10.50).
DC, MC, V. Daily noon–midnight.*

INLAND ISTRIA

In total contrast to the busy and
touristy coast, venturing inland
reveals a rural mosaic of forest
and field, swinging up to heights
invariably topped by campanile-
dominated hilltop towns. Over
the years the region has become
depopulated, first by an exodus
after World War 2 of Italians
reluctant to accept rule by communist Yugoslavia, then by the
countryside's youth flocking to
work in the burgeoning coastal
tourist industry. And, as has
happened in many other attractive areas in Europe, the empty
houses have begun to be filled by
the prosperous in search of a
rural bolthole. Although this second-home market has driven up
property prices and earned the
region the reputation of being
the Croatian Tuscany, the

government is trying to combat
it by offering incentives to
attract artists, musicians and
writers into the area. Its success
in some villages is spectacular.

Although it might be thought
that there's nothing to attract
families with children to the area,
this would be a mistake. The
tightly-packed alleys and lanes of
the numerous hill towns, the
peaceful views, the little shops
selling pictures, sculptures and
wood carvings, the various art
festivals, and the opportunities
for horse riding and other physical pursuits make it a desirable
alternative, or at least adjunct, to
the more obviously child-friendly
coast. And when you factor in
the (usually truffle-related) cuisine along with a number of natural and man-made attractions
the area begins to look distinctly
appealing. Although Istria's interior maybe too quiet to base an
entire family holiday, it would
make for an excellent day – or
even couple of days – tour in the
car. You do need a car, though –
trying to do it by less than reliable public transport would be a
nightmare.

Essentials

Getting There

Once you're in Istria, there's no
substitute for a car to make the
most of it. So if you haven't got
one already, rent one for the day.

Visitor Information

Each inland town – even the
small ones – has its own Tourist

Office. In addition, the Istria County Tourist Association – Poreč at Pionirska 1 (✆ *052-452-797*; fax: *052-452-796*; *tzzi-po@pu.hinet.hr*) and Pula at Forum 3 (✆ *052-215-799*; fax: *052-215-722*; *www.istra.com*) – produces a lot of really good pamphlets and maps.

Getting Around

These are tiny towns – the only way to explore them is on foot.

INSIDER TIP »
Wear rubber soles – some of the streets are very steep, and the stone is often worn as smooth as ice.

What To See & Do

Istria's inland roads vary from the excellent to the execrable. And it's not just a matter of main roads being good and side roads bad – they can go from one to the other and back again in the space of a few hundred metres. But it doesn't matter, since any tour of the area will, almost by definition, be leisurely. I'm assuming a start in the north, with a meandering potter southwards; if you're staying in the south, you can get to the north in no time on the motorway, which has now been extended to the Slovenian border.

Buje ALL AGES You can see Buje from the motorway, and it looks delightful – a hill town with, not one, but two campaniles. The town is surrounded by vineyards and olive groves, and has beautiful views back towards the coast.

When you get there it might seem a little untidy – there's a lot of building work going on – yet it is with a sense of relief that you enter a normal town, thronged with local people, with that elusive off-the-beaten-track feel. Find a place to park and have a look around.

It's probably best to call in at the Tourist Office first – it's on the crossroads as you enter the town. Turn right and you'll see a supermarket, so this is a good time to stock up for a picnic and in-car supplies. Then walk back to the crossroads and go straight on up into the town. Look out for the memorial commemorating Tito's visit in 1954. Outside the public library there's a powerful war memorial, a statue of two soldiers carrying a fallen comrade. Further up there's a truffle shop (one of the Zigante chain (*www.zigantetartufi.com*), and a museum, just before the two churches and the maze of alleys between them. There are plenty of cafés to choose from – try the 'Film' café-bar on the main street, 'Kavana City Caffe' (with a really nice terrace), or 'Fantasy' next to Konzum. If it's time to eat, the Konoba Pod Voltom, down an alley that burrows through the museum, has great views from its own terrace. And if you're in Buje during the third weekend in September, enjoy the music, eating and drinking that accompanies the local wine festival.

Grožnjan ALL AGES On a side road between Buje and Motvun

The World's Biggest Truffle

Parts of Istria – specifically the area around Oprtalj, Livade and Buget – are famous for their truffles, which grow in relative abundance. A delicacy since Roman times and the preserve of the rich ever since, the truffle – a rather ugly fungus that grows just under the forest floor among the roots of oak trees – provokes an orgy of hunting from September to early November each year. Several thousand hunters with trained dogs fan out into the autumnal Istrian woods in search of this most unlikely of delicacies. Truffle-hunters are regarded by some as shady characters: chancers and *geezers* as it were.

In truffle-hunting country, you'll soon come across the name Zigante. In 1999 Giancarlo Zigante, found the largest truffle in the world. Officially accredited by the Guinness Book of Records, it was the size of a melon and weighed 1310 kg. Zigante had it commemoratively cast in bronze, ate the original with a hundred guests, then opened a truffle-based restaurant in Livade. Since then his empire of shops, all selling truffles and truffle-related products, has (sorry about this) mushroomed.

Look out for the Truffle King's emporia in Pula, Buzet, Motovum, Buje, Groznjan and Livade, as well as in America, Japan and Germany.

Look out, too, in September, for a variety of 'Truffle Days' in the region's towns and villages, which feature tastings, live music and ample opportunities for alcoholic intemperance – most famously Buzetska Subotini (Buzet Saturday), and truffle-hunts organised through Restaurant Zigante or Activa Travel in Pula.

is the little hill town of Grožnjan, one of those likely targets of second-home seekers that's saved by artists and musicians being offered empty property as studios. There's a regular summer school for young musicians, and a series of outdoor classical and jazz concerts in July and August, organised as part of the Grožnjan Musical Summer (*www.tz-groznjan.hr*). Local artists exhibit their work in the municipal gallery and in around 20 private establishments. Numerous workshops, displays and exhibitions can be found around town.

Motovun ★★★ ALL AGES

Motovun, probably Istria's most celebrated hill town, is another that has taken on artists in considerable numbers including Krsto Hegedušić, one of the leaders of the Croatian naïve movement, who settled here in the 1960s. Several studios and craft shops open during the summer, and you might catch glimpses of people at work.

Motovun was a largely Italian town. Formula 1 racing driver Mario Andretti was born here. One wonders if it was the steep, tortuous approach road that

Truffle Shop, Motovun

gave him his taste for fast, skilful driving.

When you get to the church below the town, turn around and park (15 Kuna (£ 1.40), paid to the ticket seller) – only locals' vehicles are allowed beyond the barrier into the town itself. Then walk up the steep flagged street to the first of the town's two 13th century gates, which has a display of Roman reliefs. The second gate – about a hundred metres further on – opens into the town square on one side, and the delightful Kaštel Hotel on the other.

The Renaissance church of St Stephen, in the town square, has a fine crenellated campanile, which gives the Motovun its distinctive silhouette when seen from a distance. The stone well in the square was once used to draw the town's water supply from a huge cistern below. Outside the hotel, restaurant tables have been placed in the deep shade beneath a massive chestnut tree.

If you cross the square in front of the church, you can start a walk around the town battlements that offers terrific views of the lower town, the patchwork of fields and vineyards and woodland and the hills that stretch off to the horizon in all directions. Stop for a drink or something to eat at one of the restaurants (Caffe Bar Motovun has wonderful views from the terrace), buy some truffles at the inevitable Zigante shop (nearby Livade has the original Zigante restaurant), and perhaps invest in a painting or wood-carving.

If you decided to divide your tour of Istria's interior into several days, Motovun, and the Kaštel Hotel, would make an ideal overnight stop (see below). And if you're into art house movies, and you're around in early August, why not check out the very accessible, five-day-long Motovun Film Festival (*www. motovunfilmfestival.com*).

INSIDER TIP >>

Why not break the tour in Motovun, and stay at the Hotel Kaštel.

Hotel Kaštel ★★★ FIND

Perched in its eyrie in the centre of Motovun, this hotel makes a lovely stop over on a tour of inland Istria. It has pretty, eccentrically-shaped rooms, a beautiful restaurant and bar, and tables out in the square under mature chestnut trees. There are terrific views from the terrace, and the hotel even has its own art gallery. It's a remarkably child-friendly place with two suites ideally suited for families, or even better, an apartment with kitchen just across the square that can accommodate up to six people. Also, there are triple rooms to which a cot could be added.

HR-52424 Motovun, Trg Andrea Antico 7. 📞 *052-681-607. Fax 052-681-652.* **www.hotel-kastel-motovun.hr***. 28 rooms, two suites and one apartment. 275–400 Kuna (£ 28–40) pp double, depending on type of room, breakfast included. Amenities: restaurant, dining room, art gallery, great views in all directions. In room: Sat TV, Internet connection.*

Pazin ★★ ALL AGES

Pazin is a pleasant town that sits virtually at the centre of Istria. Its centrality was one of the reasons the communist government chose it to be the regional capital after World War 2. Another reason is that it never fell to the Venetians, and was considered more Yugoslav than the region's largest town – cosmopolitan, Italian-influenced Pula (see p.161).

A visit to Pazin provides an opportunity to see a couple of well-known sights, and also to chill out, have something to eat in one of the many restaurants and cafés, and let younger children have a play in one of the town centre's parks. The best place to park is near the Pazin's imposing (and deafening) bell tower.

Around 50 metres down Prolaz Vincenta od Kastva is the Tourist Office (**www.tzpazin.hr**), and beyond it, a short way along Velog Jože and Prilaz Kaštelu is the formidable medieval castle whose very existence explains the Venetian's lack of success. The castle contains the rather good Ethnographic Museum of Istria and the Pazin Museum.

From the terrace in front of the castle you get the best view of another of Pazin's attractions – the awesome gorge into which the river Fojba disappears, to resurface kilometres away towards the coast. It's said that Dante used this chasm in 'The Inferno' when describing the gateway to hell, and Jules Verne certainly did in his 1885 novel *Matthias Sandorf*, where the eponymous hero escapes execution by climbing down a lightening conductor and jumping into the river where he keeps afloat by hanging onto a log until he emerges into the Limski Kanal (see p.174).

Although Verne never visited Pazin (the mayor provided him with pictures), there is now a Jules Verne Club in the town, established in 1997, which celebrates Jules Verne Day each year to commemorate the date (26th

June, 1867) when Matthias Sandorf made his daring escape.

Buzet ★ ALL AGES About 32km (20 miles) north of Pazin, Buzet is Istria's second largest settlement and famous for its truffles. Each year, on the second weekend in September, truffle days are kicked off by the cooking of an enormous omelette (locally, *fritaja*) made up of 2,000 eggs and 10 kg of truffles, cooked in a pan that measures several metres across. Live music and dance adds to the merriment.

Most of the population live in the rather pedestrian new town, where there's not much else to do but buy truffles or truffle-related products, or sample *biska,* the local mistletoe-flavoured liqueur. The old town – Grad Buzet – perched on a hilltop is worth a visit, if only for the experience of driving up to it. After a steep, winding hill, expecting to be forced to park up any minute and walk the rest, you find yourself driving through a narrow town gate and squeezing the car up incredibly narrow alleys. The only thing that makes it possible is the one-way system.

You can park in the town, though there's nothing much to see, apart from pretty medieval alleys, the church and campanile, and the compulsory wonderful views. If you drive as far as you can go, there's a small children's playground next to the town battlements (again with lovely views). The drive down is even hairier than the drive up – steep, and with those hard, slippery

cobbles that make you glad that tyres are made of rubber.

Roč ★★ ALL AGES Some 10km (6½ miles) from Buzet, just to the left off the main road to the motorway, is the tiny, and very pretty, village of Roč, which has diminutive 16th century defensive walls and a lovely town gate with some Roman tombstones.

Other than its bijou charm, Roč has two claims to fame. First, it was a 15th century centre of Glagolitic literature. The first book to be printed in Croatia came from here, a 1483 Glagolitic prayer book. Second, Roč is famous for its folk music, particularly the music of the buttons-only accordion peculiar to this part of Istria and northeastern Italy. Almost everybody in the village is involved in music in some way. The local folk music society (called Istarski željezničar) is made up of brass bands, choirs, and an accordion band and walking round the village you'll come across statues of

Statues of Musical Instruments, Roč

a double bass, a violin, a clarinet and, of course, an accordion. On the second of May there is a big accordion festival here.

Glagolitic Alley ★★★ MOMENT

ALL AGES Across the main road from the turning up to Roč stands a strange, mushroom-shaped stone, covered in what looks like runic writing. This is the *Pillar of the Chakavian Parliament*, and it marks the start of a series of monuments that appear every kilometre or so along both sides of the seven kilometre stretch of country road between Roč and Hum.

They are not, as might be thought, ancient standing stones, but a piece of art commemorating Glagolitic, the 9th century script invented by monks Cyril and Methodius (see box).

The actual installation was established in 1977, and is the result of cooperation between writer Zvane Črnja, academic Dr Josip Bratulić and sculptor Želimir Janeš. Other sculptures include the *Table of Cyril and Methodius*, *The Rise of Istrian Razvod*, *The Wall of Croatian Protestants and Heretics*, *The Resting Place of Gregory of Nin*, *The Resting Place of Zakan Juri* and the *Monument to Resistance and Freedom*. The final monument is the actual copper gates that mark the entrance to Hum.

Apart from the monuments (and you can buy a guide to their meaning in the little shop in Hum), the road itself is a delightful meander through classic Istrian countryside, past farms with neatly stacked firewood and little haystacks built in a local style.

I sat on a step near the church in Hum, the 'smallest town in the world'. I'd started at Roč, tiny, fortified, and dotted with statues of musical instruments. I'd arrive in Hum after a five mile drive along the meandering country lane that connects the two villages, past peaceful farms and fuel stores of chopped wood and traditional Istrian haystacks. I'd stopped at each of the ten monuments to Gagolitic script, built since 1977, that have given the road the name Gagolitic Alley. The sun beat down and the birds sang. Could there be any better way to spend an afternoon?

Hum ★★ ALL AGES
Hum's inhabitants claim that they live in the smallest town in the world, and you can see their point. It is blessed with everything a town should have including medieval walls, an entry gate, an impressive church with lofty campanile, a shop and attractive houses. What it seems to lack is any great number of people. At the last count the population was 22.

The East Coast

A visit to Istria wouldn't be complete without a drive along the east coast to take a look at what was, until the late 1990s, Croatia's main coal-producing area. Passing Barban (known now only for its annual Tilting at the Ring Festival – the vestigial remains of medieval jousts,

Glagolitic Script

Glagolitic script is something that you're unlikely to have come across before, yet you'll find examples of it in many parts of Croatia. Looking like a cross between the runic alphabet and something from Harry Potter, its origins go back to the 9th century AD, when two monks – Cyril and Methodius – were charged by the Byzantine Emperor to convert the Slavs to Christianity. Finding that neither Latin nor Greek easily represented the sounds of the Slav tongue, they invented their own script, containing 38 letters, which was widely adopted in the Slav speaking world. It survived the spread of the Roman Catholic faith, and became increasingly used in the secular world of government and politics. It gained strength during the Reformation, when Protestants, wanting religious books to be written in Croatian rather than Latin, adopted it, and the Roman Catholic Church, deciding that discretion was the better part of valour, followed suit. Increasingly, Glagolitic script was coming to be identified with Croatian and Slav Nationalism. And this, it turned out, was to lead to its downfall. The link with Croatian nationalism wasn't lost on Croatia's foreign rulers – Austria in the north, Venice along the coast – who began to attack its use. Despite an attempt to revive it in the late 19th century, Glagolitic finally died out. But it is close to the heart of the new nation of Croatia, and you'll see it celebrated in many places.

where lance-carrying horseback riders try to spear a ring), you arrive at the southern edge of the coalfield at Raša.

Raša ALL AGES Built by the Italians during the time of Mussolini's rule, Raša is notable for St. Barbara's Church, in which the campanile resembles pit headgear, and the church roof itself looks like the inverted wagons used to haul the coal. No need to stop – the church stands right beside the main road.

Labin ★★ ALL AGES A further five kilometres along the main road brings you to Labin. Anybody who knows Britain's coalfields will think: 'This doesn't look like any pit village I know'. Labin is yet another gorgeous hill town off the Istrian production line. A wooded hill gives way to impressive fortifications, while a cluster of houses rise to an elegant campanile.

The mining itself, of course, was done down in the valley – it makes sense to get as close as you can to the seam before starting to dig. Labin has its share of industrial sprawl, and its last remaining traditional headgear stands forlorn at the foot of the hill. Now rusty and unkempt, it has the word 'Tito' in letters of steel on its tower flanked by crossed hammers to one side, and the hammer and sickle to the other.

Rural Relaxation In Croatia

Croatia, like many countries in Europe, has suffered in recent times from rural depopulation. Farming areas find it difficult to hang onto the young people, who can't wait to leave for the big cities in search of jobs and entertainment. As the older generations die out without being replaced by the young, houses stand empty, fields return to the wild, shops go out of business and traditional crafts and festivals disappear. A whole way of life can wither and die within a generation.

Like many other countries in Europe, Croatia has come to the conclusion that one way of saving the lifestyles and traditions of its rural areas is to encourage the growth of 'agri-tourism'. This involves renovating attractive old buildings to create atmospheric small hotels, persuading farms to supplement their incomes by providing visitors with food and accommodation (and even the chance to help on the farm), reinvigorating small restaurants that offer regional cooking, reviving rural crafts and craft fairs, and promoting traditional festivals. This is all carried out with environmental protection in mind, using sustainable resources to promote high-quality, low-density tourism.

The result is that visitors – from elsewhere in Croatia as well as abroad – are replacing the depleted rural youth. Tourists take up the empty accommodation, buy regional food and the output of local crafts, and act as a shot in the arm for declining traditions and festivals. Local people get to keep their way of life, and visitors get to experience a holiday-with-a-difference that gives them an insight into Croatian life and

Close up, Labin's old town isn't quite as lovely as it looks from a distance. Many of its houses are empty and have been boarded up, as people fled the decline of the coalfield and the subsidence caused by the mining. Yet Labin is on the mend. Since the pits closed, it has bent over backwards to entice people back to the town. Cheap studio space is on offer to artists and craftsmen, museums and churches are made much of, and pastel shades have brightened up the exterior of many of its buildings.

The starting point for an exploration of Labin is Titov trg, the pleasant town square lined by cafés, the Tourist Office, and the shady 16th century town loggia, which is spoilt only by the cars that rattle past and force themselves into every inch of parking space available.

Once you've climbed up out of the square past the 16th–17th century bastion and through the town gate, the lanes and steps of the Old Town are traffic free. A formidable bank of 14 tourist information signs point the way to the sights. The **Town Museum** ★★★, housed in the Battiala-Lazzarini Palace, is worth a look – in addition to the usual culture. Instead of destroying local traditions, tourism can preserve them. It's win-win all the way.

For those who decide to go in for it, 'agri-tourism' has a lot to offer. Accommodation, though rarely luxurious, is of high quality – local tourist boards vet it strictly, and only the best is accepted. Prices are low: 100–150 Kuna (£ 9–14) per person per night. Accommodation is often in traditional buildings that are full of character. Food may be on offer, but much accommodation is self-catering.

This kind of holiday is particularly suitable for families with young children. Venues are well away from the busier arrears – so there'll be lots of peace and quiet, but it does mean that you'll need a car. There are usually lots of farm animals to be seen on site – you may even be able to persuade the owner to let the children help with feeding, milking and so on – and it is quite common for visitors to help out with farm activities (though it's totally voluntary!). Attitudes to children are invariably very positive – these are local communities that cherish children and family life in general. And language needn't be a problem – tourist boards can usually tell you what languages are spoken in each venue, so you can look out for ones that speak English. Agri-tourism (or, sometimes, 'agro-tourism') is very much a growth area in Istria, particularly in so-called 'green Istria' – the rural interior. Contact:

www.istra.hr/en/agritourism
www.istra.com/agroturizam
www.histrica.com/istria/green/agritourism.html

collection of Roman artefacts and local costumes, it also has a recreation of a coal-mine. Nearby is the 17th century **St. Stephen's Church**, and the 11th–16th century **Church of the Blessed Virgin Mary's Birth**. Continuing upwards will bring you out on the remains of the fortress – the **Fortica** – which has great views towards Rabac, the coast and the island of Cres beyond.

Returning by a different route will bring you to the **campanile**, now used as a viewing platform (summer, 9am–12 noon, 1pm–7pm, Adults 5 Kuna (45p), children 2 Kuna (18p). Not suitable for children under eight, or those who don't like heights). A number of different routes, all involving steps, will bring you the Uzkok Gate, which commemorates the feared Uzkok pirates being cowed into submission by local tactics that involved iron cutlery and ox blood. Don't ask!

Rabac ALL AGES The industrial working-class theme is continued in Rabac, on the coast below Labin – you can see it clearly from Labin's Fortica. It was originally built by the Italians as a worker's holiday development, though there's not much left of

Labin

that now – it's all modern apartment blocks and hotels. You can walk to Rabac from Labin in about 40 minutes. An increasing number of UK package companies are beginning to use Rabac, partly because of its proximity to Pula airport, and there are plenty of bars and restaurants, and a not-bad beach (shingle, as usual).

For Active Families

Although the opportunities for family activity holidays are fewer in Istria than in the more rugged parts of Dalmatia, it is still possible to find adventure if you know where to look. The Istrian Tourist Board produces an excellent series of little pamphlets on a variety of outdoor activities, with price information and contact details. This includes details on paragliding, trekking, potholing, fishing, diving, sailing, horseriding, even beekeeping. Go to *www.istra.hr/en/activities* for further details. Alternatively try *www.responsibletravel.com* for package holidays that provide adventure elements in Istria.

Island Hopping

In this book Croatia's many islands are treated simply as possible excursions from the main centres on the mainland. It is also possible, of course, to organise a complete holiday that involves visiting a number of islands instead of a mainland/island package. Organising either option is simplicity itself – just get the Jadrolinija booklet of timetables (☎ *051-666-111*) or even better, log on to *www.jadrolinija.hr*. When you've decided which islands you'd like to visit, simply consult the timetables and work out your itinerary. It's a doddle!

7 Zagreb

'Where?' your friends may ask, **when you tell them you've been to Zagreb.** Yet if you want a family holiday with a difference, the Croatian capital has a lot to offer.

Zagreb is a substantial European city with a population approaching one million. Yet it is little known in the rest of Europe. The swirling stag-night and hen-party pack haven't yet (thank heavens) turned their attention away from Dublin, Barcelona, Prague and Budapest.

A thriving business and cultural centre, Zagreb has influences that range from the (Austro-Hungarian) staid to the (Mediterranean) laid back. It's a heady combination of impressive civic buildings, museums, theatres, formal gardens and venerable historical edifices with a vibrant café and restaurant society, and plenty of bars, nightclubs, sport and all-out shopping. It has a flourishing university and the large numbers of students add to the city's vigour.

In fact, it has all you need for a family holiday – parks and pavement cafés, buses, bars and boating lakes, hotels and history, statues, swimming and ski slopes, fountains, football fever, even a funicular railway. A lot of guidebooks doubt its family appeal – don't believe them.

Outside the centre, in one direction there's Maksimir Park (see p.222), which includes the park itself, a zoo, and Dinamo Zagreb's impressive football stadium. In the other direction the recently constructed Jarun Lake provides opportunities for a wide variety of water sports and has cafés and bars, and, in the summer, discos. Even better, there's Bundek (see p.221), a brand new attraction that has a large beach and one of the biggest and most imaginative play areas I've ever seen.

Behind the city, to the north, you can ascend the 1,000-metre-plus (3,300 feet) Mount Medvednica (see p.222) and its highest peak Sljeme (on foot, or by cable car), as well as enjoy country walks, terrific views, and, in winter, skiing. Beyond Medvednica, north and west of the mountain, the lanes and villages and hilltop castles of the Zagorje region (Austria to a tee), stretch to the border with Slovenia.

ESSENTIALS

Getting There

By air Pleso International Airport ☎ 01-626-52-22 (*www.zagreb-airport.hr*) lies 15 km to the southeast of the city centre, off the main road to Velika Gorica. It handles flights to and from most major European cities, and is also the hub for internal flights (operated by Croatia Airlines) to Pula, Rijeka, Zadar, Split and Dubrovnik, as well as Bol (Brac summer only).

A bus service (☎+358 (0)1-615-79-92) operates daily from the airport and terminates at Zagreb's main bus station. Tickets costs 25 Kuna (£ 2.30), and the journey takes half an hour. Between 7am and 8pm the buses are fairly frequent, most on the hour and half hour. Between 8pm and 7am the shuttle service is coordinated with flights.

A taxi to or from the airport will set you back 150–250 Kuna (£ 14–23), depending on the time of day.

By Car Zagreb is the hub for Croatia's motorway system and is very easy to get to by car. However, once there, driving in the city can be something of a nightmare – street signs, where they exist, are small and hard to see, navigating can be complicated by roadworks, one-way systems and pedestrianised zones, and parking can be difficult. So, if your hotel has free parking, best leave the car there and use public transport (see p.196).

By Bus Zagreb has a growing number of international coach connections to other European cities, together with internal services to all Croatian cities. In conjunction with local services, this means that you can get to Zagreb by bus from almost anywhere in Europe.

By Train Zagreb railway station is a rather splendid (and recently restored) 19th century relic of the golden age of steam. It lies south of the city centre, a 15-minute walk, facing Trg Kralja Tomislava. The Orient Express used to stop here – you get a glimpse of it in the Bond film *From Russia with Love*. It has a

pleasant restaurant and terrace, exchange facilities, cash machines and an information centre.

VISITOR INFORMATION

The main **Zagreb Tourist Information Centre** is at Trg Bana Jelačića 11 ☎ *01-481-40-51*: ***www.zagreb-touristinfo.hr*** . Its opening hours are 8.30am–8pm Monday–Friday, 9am–5pm Saturday, 10am–2pm Sundays and holidays. It provides a wide selection of pamphlets to the city's attractions, a free seasonal 'Welcome to Zagreb' magazine which contains a useful Calendar of forthcoming events and an excellent monthly 'Events and Performances' booklet that tells you absolutely everything that's happening, in Zagreb.

In addition, you can pick up Zagreb Cards here. These cost 90 Kuna (£ 8.60), and offer unlimited city travel (trams, buses, the funicular, even the

Tram

Sjleme cable car) for an adult and one child, a 50% discount at most museums and galleries (including the zoo), and assorted discounts at many theatres and concert halls, car rental agencies, car parks, restaurants, shops and sightseeing buses. The card must be signed and dated and is then valid for 72 hours.

A second Tourist Information Centre is at Trg Nikole Subica Zrinskog 14 (☎ 01-492-16-45), while the Zagreb County Tourist Association, at Preradoviceva 42 (☎ 01/487-36-35; *www.tzzz.hr*), has lots of stuff about excursions from Zagreb into its hinterland. Hours are 8am–4pm Monday–Friday.

There are lots of travel agencies in the city that can book flights, packages, and hotels. Atlas Travel (☎ 01-481-39-33) at Zrinjevac 17 is the largest in the country and is also Croatia's American Express agent. Another big player is Generalturist at Praska 5 (☎ 01-480-55-55; *www.generalturist. com*).

For flights to the rest of Croatia or the rest of Europe, contact Croatia Airlines. Their main office is at Trg Nikole Subica Zrinskog 17 (☎ 01-481-96-33). It's open 8am–7pm Monday to Friday and 8am–3pm Saturday.

City Layout

Zagreb lies on the southern slopes of Mount Medvednica, between the foothills and the River Sava. The centre is compact, and consists of Gornji Grad, medieval 'upper town' and Donji Grad, the 19th century 'lower town'. South of the river is Novi (New) Zagreb, which dates from the 1960s. Away from the centre are three principal recreations, all of which are popular with the city's residents. Jarun (see p.219) is a huge sports complex built around an artificial lake in the southwest suburbs. Bundek (see p.221) is a brand new and smaller equivalent in Novi Zagreb, while Maksimir Park (see p.222) some three kilometres east of the city centre, has woods, formal gardens, a zoo and Dinamo Zagreb's football stadium, which is also used by the Croatian national side. Nearby Mount Medvednica has lots of pleasant walks and picnic grounds in the summer, as well as a ski resort complete with lifts and snow-blowing machines in the winter.

On arrival in Zagreb, a good way of getting to know the city is to sign up for one of the tours. Two-hour walking tours of the Old Town set off from the Tourist Information Centre at 4pm (Mondays and Wednesdays) and 10am (Tuesdays and Thursdays), while three-hour walking and bus tours of the Gornji Grad leave the Hotel Arcotel Allegra, Branimirova 29 (near the railway station) at 4pm (Fridays) and 10am (Saturdays and Sundays). They cost 95 Kuna (£ 9) and 145 Kuna (£ 13.50) respectively, and can be booked at *www.event.hr*.

The Tourist Information Centre in Trg Bana Jelačića provides a lot of good tourist literature about the city. Look out particularly for the single coloured sheet that has a map of the centre on one side, and a map of the tram system and of the whole city and its environs on the other.

The Neighbourhoods in Brief

The crucial reference point for finding your way around Zagreb is its central square, **Trg Bana Jelačića**. Almost everything worth seeing is within easy reach of here. It is a wide open space, thronged with cafés and shops. While in the square look out the clock on stilts, an impressively florid equestrian statue of the 19th century Ban of Croatia, Josip Jelačić (after whom the square was named), much Art

Statue of Ban Josip Jelačić, Trg Bana Jelačića

Noveau architecture, and the intersection of seven tram routes. This is also (at the eastern end) where you'll find the city's main Tourist Information Centre.

Just north of the square is **Dolac**, the city's open-air market. The market is on two tiers. The lower tier has a large number of food stalls selling a variety of meat, fruit, vegetables, cheese, oil, olives and, on Fridays, fish. On the upper tier you can buy gifts including toys, lace and embroidery. There can't be many capital cities where such a market survives. Around the edges are cheap-and-cheerful cafés and restaurants.

To the north, above the square and the market, lies **Gronji Grad** or 'Upper Town', which consists of two ancient enemies, **Gradec** and **Kaptol**, once separated by a brook (Potoc) that has become, since it was filled in 1898, the stunningly pretty street of **Tkalciceva**. With the twin-spired Cathedral bracketed by the Archbishop's Palace, Kaptol is the capital's religious heart. You can still see a fair number of priests and nuns going about their business on the streets. Gradec and Kaptol – one secular, the other religious – never got on: at the southern end of Tkalciceva, between the two settlements, lies the Blood Bridge (Krvavi most), the scene of many a mortal engagement. Gradec (commonly called Grič), immediately to the west is the oldest part of the city, and consists of narrow lanes, little squares, churches, many of Zagreb's best museums and Baroque palaces, together with a group of civic buildings and the remains of Zagreb's impressive fortifications.

To the west of Trg Bana Jelačića stretches Zagreb's lengthy main shopping street Ilica, while away to the south lies the Donji Grad or 'Lower Town'. Where the Gronji Grad is characterised by quaint, winding alleys, Donji Grad is stately and linear. Designed and built largely in the late 19th century along Habsburg lines, its architect Milan Lenuci was aiming for an impressive formality. Here, then, you will find the big architectural set pieces – the Archaeological Museum, the Academy of Arts and Science, the Art Pavilion, the Ethnographic Museum, the Modern Gallery, the Museum of Arts and Crafts, the Mimara Museum, the National Theatre. The impressive 19th century railway station is in good company. Here, also, you'll find a series of rectangular gardens and parks, arranged in a not-quite-completed U shape known as Lenuci's Horseshoe. One of these green spaces, the Botanical Gardens, is a haven of peace and calm in the heart of the city.

Further south still, across the River Sava, lies Novi Zagreb or 'New Zagreb', a vast area of housing projects and motorways which, while no doubt pleasant enough as a dormitory area for many of the city's population, needn't detain family holiday-makers a great deal. Watch this space, though – Novi Zagreb is just beginning to develop its own style and facilities, and the new recreation complex at Bundek is a good example.

Getting Around

By Public Transport Zagreb's integrated urban transport system consists of modern electric trams, which cover the central zone, and buses that run out to the suburbs. The system operates 24/7, though with reduced services and confusingly modified routes at night. Pick up a London-tube-type map at the Tourist Office that shows the tram routes and its connections with the buses.

The system is fast, reliable and efficient. You can buy tickets at Tisak news kiosks, ZET kiosks and post offices for 7 Kuna (65p), or you can pay 9 Kuna (85p) on board. If you're caught without a ticket, expect a 150 Kuna (£ 14) on-the-spot fine, or more if you haven't got the cash on you and have to pay later. There are also one-day tickets, or (a real bargain) the Zagreb Card, available from Tourist Offices and most hotels (see p.193). If you've got a Zagreb Card, you don't need to show it unless asked by an inspector.

The only problem with using the transport system is knowing if the tram or bus is coming or going! Have a street map as well as the tram/bus map with you, check out the final destination, which should be shown on the front of the vehicle, and work it out. Or, simply say the name of your destination to the driver or another passenger, point to it on the map, and look questioningly. Operators rarely speak English.

By Car Unless you're travelling outside the city, it's not worth using the car. If you have to drive, there are no particular problems, though watch out for drivers who dodge into the tram lane then dodge back out again if they encounter a tram. Also remember that if you're in a rented car, other drivers have no way of knowing that you're a guest in their country, so they're likely to be as rude to you as they would be to a local driver!

By Taxi Zagreb taxis are expensive, even for short hops. There's a flat charge of 25 Kuna (£ 2.35) a trip, plus a charge based on the distance the travelled. There's also a 20% out-of-hours surcharge. But if you're feeling flush, call ☏ 01-668-25-05, or look for a cab-rank (try Trg maršala Tita or the bottom end of Bakačeva, between Trg Bana Jelačića and Kaptol). Negotiate a price before you get in.

Planning Your Outings

One of the great things about Zagreb is the wide variety of things to see and do. This means that you can plan a balanced itinerary that will take into account everybody's interests, preferences, stamina and attention spans. Another great thing about Zagreb is that the actual centre of the city is relatively small, and everything worth seeing is within walking distance, even if you're pushing a buggy.

A word of warning: In Zagreb it seems to be accepted that cyclists habitually ride on the pavements so watch out for them.

Should you or the children start to get tired, the tram system is simplicity itself to use, especially once you've got used to the general layout of the city centre, and especially if you've got Zagreb Cards (see p.193) covering all family members, because you don't have to have them punched or show them to the driver.

Remember the days when people gave up their seats to pregnant women, mums with toddlers or the elderly? They still exist in Zagreb! If in doubt as to where to get off, local people are always happy to help, and youngsters invariably speak

English – they study it at school. Finally, if the weather's really hot, look out for the new breed of trams – they've got air conditioning.

Zagreb has absolutely loads of cafés and restaurants, and you're rarely more than a few metres from a park. So it's easy enough to break up any longer walk into sections. And discrete breastfeeding is perfectly OK. A little something to keep you going is never far away either, because around almost every street corner there seems to be a Konzum supermarket, small food shop or street market, and putting together an impromptu picnic becomes a really viable option.

The capital has a range of places to go for a whole day out and all are accessible by tram or car. Jarun Lake (see p.219), Bundek (see p.221), Maksimir Park (see p.222) and Mount Medvednica (see p.222) are all ideal for a restful day's excursion, active or laid back as you prefer.

Finally, Zagreb is surrounded by some truly beautiful countryside with a lot of interesting things to see. One of the best excursions is to the Croatian Zagorje, which is so rural that it's difficult to believe that you're only half an hour's drive from the city centre. Whether you approach it from the top of Mount Medvednica, or from the motorway to Slovenia, it's a brilliant day (or more) out.

ZAGREB ITINERARIES

If You Have 1 Day

If you have only one day take yourself to Trg Bana Jelačića (see p.203), the central square, and have a look round. Here you can see the trams rattling along, examine the statue of the man after whom the square is named and trail your fingers in the fountain. Then climb up through 'Harmica' to Dolac, Zagreb's market (see p.204) and possibly buy a *burek* (a type of pasty) at the little shop to the left of the steps as you climb. Do a quick tour to the Cathedral (see p.205) to have a look at the tomb and lifelike effigy of Archbishop Alojzije Stepinac, then back to the square, and along Zagreb's main shopping street Ilica. Call in at Vincek Slastičarnica, Zagreb's best ice-cream parlour. Catch the funicular up to Gradec (see p.207). If you've got time, let the children go up and down a few times. If you get things right, you'll hear the noon gun fire from the Burglar's Tower. Warn the children – it's deafening. The more energetic can climb the tower, while the rest of the family can sit about on shaded, arty and very pleasant Strossmayerovo šetalište; a street following the top of an escarpment overlooking the city with great views. Have lunch. If you want posh, go down the steps to

Pod Grič kim Topom, if you want cheap go back down on the funicular (or down the steps) to Vallis Aurea. Both are good.

Now it's time to drag the children around Golec's lanes and squares and, more specifically, the Naïve Art Museum (see p.212) and the Natural History Museum (see p.212). On through the Stone Gate (tell them the story of Dora (see p.207), let them see the eccentric shrine inside the gate, and point out the gas lights), and down to Tkalčićeva, where the children can play in the little playground as you go down (if they're young enough). Stop at Restoran Ivica I Marica for a drink or a cake. No e-numbers here, although the children are hardly likely to be hyper-active by now. Finally, head back to Trg Bana Jelačića. In a few hours, you've captured the essence of Zagreb!

If You Have 2 Days

Day 1 Spend Day 1 as above.

Day 2 Start at the Zagreb School Museum (see p.217), which should remind the children how lucky they are to be on holiday. Have a calming wander through the Botanical Gardens (see p.215) before moving on to the Technology Museum (see p.218) – they'll love the planes and boats and trains, and especially the coal mine.

Time now for a total chill-out swim and run around. Head out to Jarun (see p.219) or Bundek (see p.221), and let them wear

themselves out, and perhaps even make a few little Croatian friends. To top off the day perhaps take them to see a film at CineStar near the station.

If You Have 3 Days

Days 1–2 Spend Days 1 and 2 as above.

Day 3 It's now time to take in the outer reaches of the city and beyond. Stop off at Maksimir Park (see p.222), wander around, use the two playgrounds, enjoy the zoo, and take a look at Dinamo Zagreb's football ground (to tell fellow football enthusiasts back home). Drive to the Mirogoj Cemetery (see p.221), and enjoy the peace and quiet. Climb the steep road (or catch the cable car) to the top of Mount Medvednica (see p.222). Have lunch up there, or a picnic, or if it's still early, a drink. Then swoop down the other side and explore the Croatian Zagorje (see p.223), where there is so much to see and plenty of cafés and restaurants to stop at.

If You Have 4 Days or More

If you've got more than three days, do the above but take it easy. Intersperse the sightseeing with walks in the parks and Botanical Gardens, picnics and afternoon or evening visits to the cinema. Perhaps you could visit Hard Rock Café or one of the other many places you can hear live music.

FAST FACTS: ZAGREB

(See also 'Fast Facts' in Chapter 2 (p.49).)

American Express American Express services are available through Atlas Travel Agency at Zrinjevac 17, 10000 Zagreb (☎ 0 01-487-39-33). There is also an American Express office at Lastovska 23 (☎ 0 01-612-44-22).

ATM/Cash Machines & Currency Exchange the centre of the city has lots of cash machines where you can withdraw cash using American Express, Diners Club, MasterCard, Cirrus and Visa. Money can be exchanged in all the usual places (see 'Money' on p.24).

Business Hours see 'Fast Facts: Croatia' on p.49.

Dentists'& Doctors a dental emergency service (at Perkovèeva 3 (☎ 0 01-482-8488) is always open and you can get treatment without appointment. For medical emergencies, try the Emergency Center at Dratkovieeva 19 near the Sheraton – open day and night. Doctors from KB Dubrava at Avenija Gojka Šušca 6 (☎ 01-290-24-44) will make house calls to most parts of the city.

Embassies & Consulates see 'Fast Facts: Croatia' on p.50.

Emergencies see 'Fast Facts: Croatia' on p.50.

Internet Access Ch@rlie's near the Hotel Dubrovnik at Ljudevita Gaja 4a (☎ 01-488-02-33) – pick up your e-mails for 10 Kuna (just under £ 1) per hour while you sip an espresso. Hours are 8am to 10pm daily. Sublink Cybercafe is close to Trg Jelačića at Nikole Tesla 12 (☎ 01-481-13-29). For 14 Kuna per hour (£ 1.30) you can e-mail, print, copy or scan to your heart's content.

Mail the Central Post Office is at Jurišićeva 13 near the Jadran Hotel (☎ 01-481-10-90). Hours are 7am to 9pm Monday to Friday, 8am to 4pm Saturday. Mail delivery to foreign countries is unreliable, though – it may take weeks or even more for mail to get to the UK or Ireland, and it has been known for it to disappear completely.

Newspapers & Magazines finding English language newspapers in Zagreb isn't easy. For magazines and books, a usually reliable source is Algoritam at Gajeva 1 (☎ 01-481-86-72), on the ground floor of the Hotel Dubrovnik. Hours are 8am to 9pm Monday to Friday, 8am to 3pm Saturday. Closed Sunday.

Pharmacies there are several 24-hour pharmacies in Zagreb. Two are at Trg Jelačića (☎ 01-481-61-54) and at Ilica 301 (☎ 01-375-03-21).

Safety Zagreb is a relatively safe city. It's OK to use public transport at night, and to walk along busy streets. There does seem to have been an increase in thefts from (and of) cars and, as in any modern city, it's probably best to avoid deserted streets late at night.

Taxis dial ☎ 970 if you're in Zagreb, or ☎ 01-661-02-00 if you're elsewhere.

Telephones see 'Fast Facts: Croatia' page on p.49.

WHAT TO SEE & DO

Zagreb is more suitable for holidays with children than almost any capital city I can think of. The whole of the centre is 'walkable', though using the city's public transport, particularly its trams, funicular railway and cable car, is part of the fun. It's true that in summer it can get very hot, but there are excellent cafés and restaurants at which to take refreshment, most of which offer the choice of shady outside tables or indoor air conditioning. In addition there are so many pools, parks and play areas within reach that it's possible to plan a succession of days out in which the hot and tiring are balanced against the cool and relaxing. There's plenty for youngsters to do and teenagers will be kept happy by the flourishing music and arts scene. Should parents wish for the occasional night out alone, most hotels can call on the services of professional babysitters.

Children's Top 10 Attractions

Technical Museum packed full of planes, fire-engines, submarines, space vehicles and lots of other technological gear, and with an excellent reconstruction of a coal mine taking up the whole of the basement. See p.218.

Technical Museum

201

Zagreb Zoo nicely laid out under the trees in Maksimir park, next to Dynamo Zagreb's football stadium, with all the animals you'd expect in a top-class zoo, together with a good selection of indigenous creatures, from beavers to bears. See p.222.

Jarun/Bundek the city's top recreational areas, with swimming, picnic area, cafés and restaurants, a variety of sports, and, in Bundek, a vast, brand new children's playground. See p.219.

Museum of Naïve Art contains the world's best collection of Croatian Naïve art – colour, simplicity and humour. See p.212.

Natural History Museum all creatures great and small, including an enormous stuffed basking shark. See p.212.

Museum of Zagreb with lots of models of the city and artefacts illustrating its history. See p.213.

Croatian School Museum initially uninviting, but bound to provoke much discussion of school experiences then and now. See p.217.

Maksimir Park Zagreb's answer to London's Hyde Park has acres of meadows, paths, trees, pavilions and monuments. See p.222.

Mount Medvednica towering over the city to the north, with nature trails, ski lifts and a cable car. See p.222.

Kumrovec's 40 or so preserved and renovated houses from the late 19th and early 20th century, including the one that Tito was born in. See p.225.

Ties & Cravats

The tie, and its fat friend the cravat, both have their origins in the florid silk scarves sported by Croatian soldiers-of-fortune during in the Thirty Years War (which started in 1618, no prizes for guessing when it ended).

After some of these mercenaries appeared at the French court, French courtiers began dressing in the scarves and referred to the style as dressing 'à la Croate' from which the French word 'cravate' soon derived. The craze swept across Europe and 200 years later, laced-up Victorians refined them into the ultra-respectable 'tie' without which you couldn't get into any place of work, restaurant or golf club. The tie also became a sort of tribal badge, signifying your membership of a school, regiment, club or county cricket team for instance.

Ties sometimes appear on statues in Zagreb, and just around the corner from Trg Bana Jelačića is a branch of Croatia's leading tie company (*www.croata.hr*).

ZAGREB

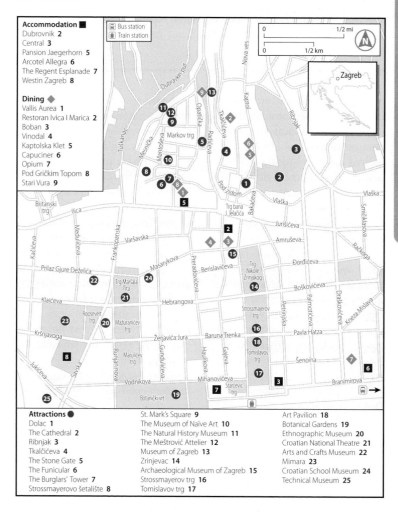

Accommodation ■
Dubrovnik **2**
Central **3**
Pansion Jaegerhorn **5**
Arcotel Allegra **6**
The Regent Esplanade **7**
Westin Zagreb **8**

Dining ◆
Vallis Aurea **1**
Restoran Ivica I Marica **2**
Boban **3**
Vinodal **4**
Kaptolska Klet **5**
Capuciner **6**
Opium **7**
Pod Gričkim Topom **8**
Stari Vura **9**

🚌 Bus station
🚆 Train station

0   1/2 mi
0   1/2 km

Zagreb

Attractions ●
Dolac **1**
The Cathedral **2**
Ribnjak **3**
Tkalčićeva **4**
The Stone Gate **5**
The Funicular **6**
The Burglars' Tower **7**
Strossmayerovo šetalište **8**

St. Mark's Square **9**
The Museum of Naïve Art **10**
The Natural History Museum **11**
The Meštrović Attelier **12**
Museum of Zagreb **13**
Zrinjevac **14**
Archaeological Museum of Zagreb **15**
Strossmayer trg **16**
Tomislavov trg **17**

Art Pavilion **18**
Botanical Gardens **19**
Ethnographic Museum **20**
Croatian National Theatre **21**
Arts and Crafts Museum **22**
Mimara **23**
Croatian School Museum **24**
Technical Museum **25**

Trg Bana Jelačića

Standing on the dividing line between Zagreb's upper and lower towns, the hub of some of the city's main shopping, café and restaurant streets, and the biggest intersection of its tram routes, stately Trg Bana Jelačića is without doubt the nearest thing the capital has to a central square.

The square is dominated by a huge equestrian statue of Josip Jelačić, who in the 19th century ruled Croatia as 'Ban' or viceroy for the Habsburg empire, and won something of a reputation as a patriot by negotiating a degree of autonomy. When the communists took over after World War 2 they were suspicious of anything that smacked

Famous Brandy

The type of cherry brandy made in Zagreb has had many celebrity fans, including Napoleon Bonaparte, Queen Victoria, Tsar Nicholas II, King George V and Alfred Hitchcock.

of Croatian nationalism, and first boarded the statue up then dismantled it. A local museum curator saved it from being melted down by storing the parts in the basement of what is now the Croatian Academy of Arts and Sciences.

The square was given its present name when Croatia broke away from Yugoslavia in 1990 and the statue was re-erected. The statue's drawn sabre originally faced towards the old enemy Austria-Hungary. When the statue was again in place the sword was facing Serbia – local folklore insists that this was no accident.

Dolac ★★ ALL AGES North of the square, through an arcade called 'Harmica' (the old name for the square, and a reference to the tax of 1/30th levied by Austro-Hungary in the old imperial days), a flight of steps leads up to Dolac, the city's main indoor and outdoor market. Half way up the steps and off to the left is a terrace of awning-shaded café tables, small shops, travel agencies and so on. Look out for the 'Burek' shop – the Croatian equivalent of a fish and chip shop. The burek is a sort of flaky pasty, usually filled

with cheese or meat – it's said that one burek, eaten for elevenses, will see you through to your evening meal.

The market proper, created in 1930 by the demolition of a warren of small houses and alleys, is a colourful affair, with, largely, fruit and veg on the upper level, cheese, olive products and so on, on the lower level, with fish in its own little ghetto. You'll also come across artificial flowers, oil lamps, baskets, plants and a great deal more, all under the rosy light cast by the bright red parasols attached to the stalls.

Mon–Fri 6am–2pm; Sat 6am–3pm; Sun 6am–noon.

Gornji Grad (Upper Town)

Kaptol

Beyond Dolac is the first of the two towns that are the original settlements around which Croatia's capital formed, and which make up Gornji Grad. Kaptol is dominated by the Cathedral of the Assumption of the Virgin Mary and the 18th century Archbishop's Palace. Even today it is much visited by clergy, monks, nuns and pilgrims, and is the ecclesiastic heart of the city.

The Cathedral of the Assumption of the Virgin Mary ★ AGES 5 AND UP

The Cathedral (almost permanently covered in scaffolding, it seems) has had a troubled history. It was originally built in the 13th century, but was destroyed by Tartars. It was later restored and extended with new buildings and towers and in 1512 its fortifications helped to repel the Ottomans. Another tower was added in the 17th century to take bells and to serve as a lookout tower. The Cathedral was almost completely wiped out by the great earthquake of 1880. What remains is almost totally 19th century, and is partly the work of the architect Hermann Bollé, who has greatly influenced the way modern Zagreb looks – some say for better, some say for worse.

After the earthquake in 1880 Bollé decided to rebuild the Cathedral in a style that he felt would reflect the importance and dignity of Zagreb. For this, he demolished the ancient walls and the central tower (though other towers remain as part of the Archbishop's Palace) and gave the new building vaulting twin towers and a neo-Gothic interior. A vainglorious column with a golden statue of the Virgin Mary at the top and the statues of four angels around the base is the work of architect Antun Fernkorn.

There's much of interest inside the Cathedral. The main altar, along with several other pieces, was designed by Zagreb's design school. Behind the altar is the tomb and lifelike effigy of **Archbishop Alojzije Stepinac**, Croatia's modern version of Thomas à Becket. Stepinac is a hero to many ordinary Croatians because, as leader of the Croatian church during World War 2, he resisted pressure from Tito after the war to renounce the Pope as head of the church (see box). Stepinac's popularity continues unabated to this day, and his grave and memorial are

Hermann Bollé (1845–1926)

Wherever you go in Zagreb you come across the work of Hermann Bollé. A German who came to work on the rebuilding of the Cathedral after the great earthquake of 1880, Bollé married locally and stayed in Croatia for the rest of his life. Most of what you see in the Cathedral is his doing, for good or ill, the fountain and meteorological column in Trg Nikole Šubića are also his work, as are the Museum of Art and Craft, the restoration of St. Mark's Church, St. Cyril and St. Methodius, St. Catherine's Church, the entrance gate to Golden Hall and a number of projects elsewhere in and outside the city – he even designed the mayor's chain! Bollé laid out the Mirogoj Cemetery in 1876, and was himself laid out there on his death.

Alojzije Stepinac

It is sometimes easy to forget that Croatia is a devoutly Roman Catholic country. The church plays a much larger part in everyday Croatian life than in the UK, and its churches are far fuller on Sundays and feast days than they are in the UK (though perhaps not in the Republic of Ireland). Furthermore, the church has in the past been much more active in Croatian politics.

The clash of politics and religion is no more clearly exemplified than in the life of Archbishop Alojzije Stepinac (1898–1960). Becoming Archbishop of Zagreb in 1937 (at the age of 39), he supported the Nazi-created Independent State of Croatia (NDH) in 1941 on the grounds that it would promote Croatian nationalism against the twin ogres of communism and freemasonry. He even initially misinterpreted some of the regime's atrocities as the work of unauthorised individuals.

When it became clear that this was not the case, he began to criticise the regime, and used his own position to save opponents of the NDH from death. When the war ended, his virulent opposition to the new Communist government earned him a 16-year prison sentence (for refusing to sever the links between the Croatian church and Rome). He actually served five years in jail, but then spent the rest of his life under virtual house arrest in his home in the Zagorje. Left-leaning Croatians tend to think of Stepinac as a quisling, whereas devout Roman Catholics regard him as a martyr.

always surrounded by votive offerings and candles. There's also a relief by Meštrović (see p.72) of Stepinac being blessed by Christ, and an enormous Glagolitic inscription on one of the walls (see p.187).

Kaptol 31, 10000 Zagreb. ☎ 01-481-47-27. Free admission. Mon–Sat 10am–5pm; Sun 1–5pm. Masses are at 7, 8, and 9am weekdays; and at 7, 8, 9, 10, and 11:30am Sun.

Behind the Cathedral is Ribnjak, a shady garden once reserved for priests, and now (courtesy of the Communist government, who tore down the railings in 1947) open to all. It is a nice place to take a break and catch your breath. Up a flight of steps behind and beyond the Cathedral is Šalata, a sports complex with a public swimming pool – you can't miss it if you head for the floodlights.

Tkalčićeva ALL AGES A stroll up Kaptol Street past the Komedija Theatre and then through a small park brings you to Opatovina Street. On one side it is lined with stalls selling clothing and basketwork, on the other there is a good selection of restaurants. A short climb down some steps, and you're in Tkalčićeva, one of the prettiest and most fashionable streets in

Zagreb. Its origin as a stream that separated Zagreb's two districts is immediately obvious – you have steps up to Kaptol on one side, steps up to Gradec on the other. Tkalčićeva is now a pleasant mixture of boutiques and art galleries. Newly-opened cafés and bars attract lots of young people on summer evenings. Children will love Tvica I Marica, a confectioners and restaurant with a Hansel and Gretel theme (see below). From here it is a brisk 10-minute walk south to Trg Bana Jelačića (see p.203).

Gradec

Kaptol's great rival over the centuries was the town that topped the hill to the west – Gradec. If Kaptol is the religious centre of Zagreb, then Gradec represents its political heart. There are two ways to approach it from Trg Bana Jelačića, via the Stone Gate or on the funicular railway. Both are equally interesting. And whichever way you choose to enter Gradec, why not use the other to leave?

The Stone Gate ★ ★ ★

AGES 4 AND UP If you walk back up Tkalčićeva from Trg Bana Jelačića, past the Krvavi most, the 'Bloody Bridge' that frequently marked the disputed border between the two towns, you will eventually come to a flight of stone steps on the left. These can be found just past a nice little playground and a statue of St. George, who

appears to have chosen to slay a catfish instead of dragon. Above you now is **Kamenita Vrata** (Stone Gate), the only one of Gradec's four 13th century gates to survive. There are several things to look out for around the Stone Gate.

The first things to notice are the gas lamps. Zagreb still has 217 gas lamps, and the city employs two men whose full time job is to light them and put them out (see box below). Inside the gatehouse is the Chapel of the Miraculous Lady of the Stone Gate. This is a shrine to a picture that miraculously survived a great fire in 1731. The picture itself is there, surrounded by votive offerings, candles and plaques, some dating back to before World War 2. Across the gateway there are several pews at which people can sit and contemplate. This is a very strange gateway indeed!

In a niche to the left as you come out of the Stone Gate is another oddity – a statue of

Stone Gate and St. George

Dora, the heroine of an 18th century novel about a 16th century fictional daughter of a goldsmith who lived next to the Stone Gate and who (as in many Croatian folk-tales) loved a lord while herself being loved by a fellow commoner. The whole thing, needless to say, ended in tears. Dressed in figure-hugging clothes, teenage boys might well find Dora rather tasty. She carries a key and a small wooden chest, to symbolise Zagreb's security – I'm not sure why.

Just beyond the Stone Gate is what is said to be the second oldest pharmacy in Croatia. It dates back to the 14th century and was once run by Dante's grandson Nicolo Alighieri. It's still in business today, though it wasn't always on this site.

Funicular railway

> **INSIDER TIP** »
> While walking along Ilica look out for Vincek Slastičarnica. This is Zagreb's best known ice-cream parlour. It can get very crowded but is definitely worth investing in some delicious homemade ice-cream.

All the above are put on by 'Event', www.event.hr. Cost is from 87 Kuna (£ 8.50) to 350 Kuna (£ 34). Price includes costumes, programme kit, drinks and prize for the winning team.

The Funicular ★ ★ ★ ALL AGES

From Trg Bana Jelačića, if you walk west along the main shopping street Ilica, avoiding the numerous trams that clatter along at a heck of a lick, then, after couple of hundred metres

turn right, you'll see ahead of you a neat little funicular, or cabled, railway (daily 6.30am–9pm, every 10 minutes or so, three Kuna (28p) or use your Zagreb Card).

The railway was built in 1889 and was at first driven by steam, before going electric in 1937. It takes a couple of minutes to go up or down, and children love it.

The Burglars' Tower (Kula lotršćak) ★ ★ ★ AGES 5 AND UP

Situated just at the top of the funicular railway, this is a remnant of Gradac's fortifications. At one time an evening bell was rung from here to signal that the city gates were closing (what, to warn burglars to leave? Seems a bit daft to me). It now has two attractions that will certainly appeal to all children bar the youngest. First, you can enter the tower (May to October, 11am to 8pm (except Mondays) five Kuna

Zagreb In Costume

The gas lamps of Zagreb provide one of several costumed entertainments that children might enjoy. Groups of adults and children are allocated to each of the two city lamplighters, and a competition is held as to which man and group can light the most lamps.

Other costumed entertainments include: 'Find the Witch in the Grič', (witches, spells and potions), a historical treasure hunt, city tours with costumed guides, and musical soirees in elegant Zagreb homes.

(46p)), and climb to the top. This requires a lot of huffing and puffing, but you are rewarded by some great views. Second, if you arrange to be outside the tower at noon, you'll see (and especially hear) the firing of a cannon, a practice begun in 1877 to synchronise the city's bell ringers. Some locals also claim that the ringing of the bell celebrates a 15th century victory over the Ottomans. There's a very loud bang (warn the children, and put your hands over babies ears),

Burglars' Tower

a substantial puff of smoke, before a shower of smouldering bits of paper descends from the sky. Great fun!

Strossmayerovo Šetalitše 9. ☎ *01-485-17-68. Admission 10 Kuna (95p). Tues–Sun 11am–8pm for climbing. Closed Mon.*

Strossmayerovo šetalište

★★ **ALL AGES** This beautiful tree-shaded promenade stretches along the escarpment either side of the Burglars' Tower, affording some terrific views across the city. It seems to be becoming a gathering place for the artistic – film students make short films of drama students acting, performance artists practice, paper sculptures hang from buildings, musical notes dangle from branches. A metal statue of Antun Gustav Matoš sits on a metal bench – it's called 'Statue of Matoš resting on a bench'! Well supplied with real public benches, and enjoying wonderful views, it's a brilliant place to stop and have a picnic. North of Strossmayerovo šetalište stretch the narrow streets and little squares, museums and art galleries of Gradec.

St. Mark's Square (Markov trg) AGES 7 AND UP

This is Gradec's central square, and is surrounded by modest and understated parliamentary and government buildings. It doesn't look very much like the seat of Croatia's government, though the presence, in this otherwise sleepy little square, of so many armed policemen is a bit of a giveaway.

In the centre of the square stands St. Mark's Church. The church is going through yet another renovation, as indeed is the whole square, which was repaved in 2006. St. Mark's was badly damaged by the 1880 earthquake, and it was Bollé who again who led the renovation (see p.205). Bollé decided on a roof tiled colourfully in a spectacular Germanic fashion – you can see the coats-of-arms of united Croatia on the left (the red-and-white check familiar from their football strip represents the Kingdom of Croatia, and the three lions and the marten represent the Kingdom of Dalmatia and the Kingdom of Slavonia respectively), and the city of Zagreb on the right.

St. Mark's Church

If you look at the building on the corner of St. Mark's Square and Čirilometodska, you can see the relief of a bearded figure, with his name engraved underneath – Matija Gubec. Gubec was the leader of a peasant uprising in 1573, who, having allegedly been elected 'king' by his followers, came to a particularly horrible end in St. Mark's Square by suffering 'coronation' with a crown of red-hot iron.

The Marten

The humble marten is a commonly used image in Croatia – it's on Slavonia's coat of arms, it was adopted as Croatia's national animal, and it gave its name to the currency – the Croatian for marten is 'kuna'. Why, you might ask, is this? The answer is pretty straightforward – the trade in kuna was once one of Croatia's staples. Everybody knew the value of a kuna pelt. So people started to value everything in terms of its equivalent in kuna pelts, and even to exchange things they wanted to sell for kuna pelts, which they could save, or exchange later for something else. In other words, kuna pelts became money.

The Croatian Naïve Art Movement

Among the works of respected academy-trained artists that went on display at an exhibition in Zagreb's Art Pavilion on 13th September 1931, twelve were paintings by a 16-year old called Ivan Generalić and three by a 21-year old called Franjo Mraz. Nobody fully realised it at the time, but the Croatian Naïve movement was on its way.

The two young artists were from poor peasant families in the same village – Hlebine – near the Hungarian border. Both had left school early, and neither had any formal art training. But their work had great potential. It was spotted by painter Krsto Hegedušić who was visiting his father's birthplace in 1930 on a working holiday.

Having settled in Paris, Hegedušić was aware of the 'new realist' tendencies in modern art, a reaction against the abstract and the avant-garde. He'd certainly seen paintings by Rousseau, and was becoming convinced that, for both artistic and political reasons, there was a need for art in Croatia to slough off academic theorising, to end its monopolisation by the middle classes, and to return to the simplicities of rural life. A member of the Zemlja Artists' group, he believed that art should be political, that it should be used to draw attention to the oppression of the working class.

Hegedušić was electrified by the honesty and originality of the two young painters' work, and immediately decided to promote their development. He steered them away from traditional and religious subjects towards scenes from everyday life, and advised them on artistic techniques (whilst being careful not to taint their originality). Hegedušić was George Martin to the two young artist's Lennon and McCartney.

During the 1930s the duo went from strength to strength. Ivan Generalić, in particular, soon moved away from politically committed subjects to lyrical scenes of peasant life. Other giants of the movement started to exhibit – Mirko Virius, for example, who started at the late age of 47, and sculptor Petar Smajić.

Immediately after World War 2, Ivan Generalić, once the pupil, now became the teacher as he started to teach some of his young neighbours in Hlebine. Franjo Filipović and Dragan Gaži are his two best-known pupils.

Naïve art was now beginning to move in slightly different directions. From the 1950s Generalić become less realistic and more symbolic and allegorical. Emerik Feješ painted city scenes and buildings in a colourful, highly mannered way. Ivan Rabuzin, painter of beautifully stylised landscapes, moved into theatre design. Josip Generalić, son of Ivan, carried the movement into the second generation.

Critical acclaim (especially from Mića Bašičević), the foundation of the Peasant Art Gallery in Zagreb (in which Bašičević was involved) and exhibitions across Europe and the New World sealed the movement's success.

Gingerbread Hearts

Love tokens often define an area and a group of people. In Wales, swains gave their sweethearts intricately-carved wooden spoons, on transportation ships convicts engraved copper coins with messages for the wives or girl friends they'd left behind.

In the Zagorje region of northern Croatia, the token-of-choice is the so-called gingerbread heart – they're not ginger flavoured at all, but are heavily laced with pepper and honey – an oblique way of saying 'I fancy you'.

These days you can see them everywhere. The 'licitar' has come to represent the region. Brightly decorated, baked rock-hard, varying from the tiny to the gigantic, they are nowadays seen more as a souvenir than as a type of food. Indeed, if you insist on attempting to eat one, check your dental insurance first!

The Museum of Naïve Art ★★

AGES 5 AND UP Just south of St. Mark's Square, the Museum of Naïve Art houses paintings and sculptures from a very specifically Croatian branch of the so-called Naïve movement. These paintings, many of which are by self-taught artists from the Croatian countryside, have particularly strong roots in Zagreb, the Zagorje and eastern Croatia. Starting in the 1930s with beautiful representations of peasant life, the collection is still evolving today, with colourful cityscapes and narratives of the everyday.

Children will love the exhibitions in this museum – there's something about the simple, almost child-like style and the vibrant colours that speaks to them. There's even a sense of humour: I defy anybody to look at Martin Mehkek's *My Neighbour, Cross-Eyed Steve*, or Ivan Generalić's *Unicorn Horse* without smiling. And the point

of the Naïve movement – that you don't have to spend a lifetime studying in academies to create valid art – is an important one if children's imaginations are to be freed. The staff run a lot of workshops with Croatian schoolchildren based on the exhibits.

Ćirilometodska 3. ☎ 01-485-19-11. www.hmnu.org. Admission 10 Kuna (95p) adults, 5 Kuna (48p) children and retirees. Tues–Fri 10am–6pm; Sat–Sun 10am–1pm.

The Natural History Museum

★★★ AGES 3 AND UP Northwest of St. Mark's Square is the rather old-fashioned Natural History Museum. While no match for its South Kensington counterpart in London, there is still a lot to enjoy, with excellent geological displays (alas with no English captions), a large collection of stuffed birds (with English names), and an extensive display of fish, including some well-stuffed smaller sharks and a huge but rather tired looking basking shark, caught in the 1950s, which is beginning to show its age.

Demetrova 1. 📞 *01-485-17-00.* ***www. hpm.hr.*** *Admission 10 Kuna (95p). Tues–Fri 10am–5pm; Sat–Sun 10am–1pm.*

The Meštrović Attelier

AGES 5 AND UP Due north of the Square is the delightful house of sculptor Ivan Meštrović (see p.72), who lived here between 1924 and his escape to the USA in 1942. Full of lovely examples of his work including a small study for the huge statue of Grkgr Ninski, which visitors to Split will have seen outside the Golden Gate (see p.110), and the smaller one which visitors to northern Dalmatia will have seen at Nin (see p.148). In all, the 17th century building houses some 300 sculptures, which were Meštrović's gifts to the capital. It might not hold children's interest for long, but they'll enjoy a quick look around.

Mletačka 8. 📞 *01-485-11-23.* ***www. mdc.hr/mestrovic.*** *20 Kuna (£ 1.90) adults, 10 Kuna (95p) children and seniors. Tues–Sat 10am–6pm; Sun 10am–2pm.*

The Museum of Zagreb

AGES 4 AND UP Useful either as an introduction to the city on arrival, or as a summary before departure, the Museum of Zagreb has some excellent models and displays explaining the development of the city, wherever possible incorporating unusual artefacts such as old bicycles (including what we would call a penny-farthing and a boneshaker), cartoons, statues and carvings rescued during renovations, and items dating from the Patriotic War (see p.248). In the basement of the museum there is an excellent restaurant, Scara Vura (see below).

Opatička 20. 📞 *01-485-13-64.* ***www.mdc.hr/mgz.*** *Admission 20 Kuna (£ 1.90) adults; 10 Kuna (95p) children, students, seniors, persons with disabilities, military; free for children under 7. Tues–Fri 10am–6pm; Sat–Sun 10am–1pm.*

Ivan Meštrović Foundation

Donji Grad (Lower Town)

Lenuci's Horseshoe

While the streets of Gonji Grad are narrow and medieval, those of Donji Grad are broad and straight in the Victorian manner, a formal grid of stately buildings and rectangular parks. Famously, the parks were designed to create a U-shaped succession of green spaces, known as Lenuci's Horseshoe after the city engineer who planned it. What a boon these are to families with children! It means that you can, with the odd interruption, walk almost all the way from the city centre to the railway station and back, and only walk on asphalt as you cross the roads. Few of Donji Grad's great buildings are of specific to families, but there is still much to see.

Zrinjevac ★ ALL AGES The first
of the open spaces on the eastern arm of the horseshoe is Zrinjevac, which opened in 1863. Being the closest one to the centre, it has become the city's 'promenade' of choice. It is a fine park, complete with mature plane trees (imported from Italy), shady fountains (designed inevitably by Bollé), and a bandstand (in which there are concerts, from spring to autumn, every Saturday from 11am to 1pm).

Archaeological Museum of
Zagreb AGES 4 AND UP Situated in
an imposing mansion on the western side of Zrinjevac, the Archaeological Museum contains beautifully displayed collections of ancient artefacts. There's a whole room devoted to the Zagreb mummy. The body is in a glass display cabinet, and the bindings (upon which is the longest continuous Etruscan text in the world) are framed on the chamber's wall. In another room there are impressive collections of Egyptian and Roman artefacts.

Trg Nikole Šubića Zrinskog 19. ☎ *01-487-31-01. www.amz.hr. Admission 20 Kuna (£ 1.90) adults, 10 Kuna (95p) children and retirees, 30 Kuna (£ 2.80) family. Tues–Fri 10am–5pm; Sat–Sun 10am–1pm.*

> **INSIDER TIP** ≫
>
> There's a very pleasant café and lapidarium in the museum courtyard at the back of the museum.

Strossmayerov Trg ALL AGES
The next square, Strossmayerov Trg, is notable mainly for the Academy of Arts and Sciences, and particularly for the

Statue of Strossmayer

The Botanical Gardens

Meštrović statue of Bishop Juraj Strossmayer, a 19th century Croatian patriot who founded the Academy in 1866. There was once a public toilet in the park, but it was moved, leading local wags to say that the Strossmayer statue is pointing to its new position as if to say 'It's over there!'

Tomislavov Trg ALL AGES The final square, Tomislavov Trg, contains the impressive Art Pavilion – check its website (*www.umjetnicki-paviljon.hr*) to see if there's anything of interest on. Even if there isn't, the building itself is worth a look. It served as the Croatian Pavilion in the Hungarian Millennial Exhibition of 1896, and was actually moved from Budapest to its present site once the exhibition was over. There's also a rather nice restaurant on the ground floor (Mon to Sat 11am to 7pm, Sunday 10am to 1pm, 20 Kuna (£ 1.90), children 10 Kuna (95p).)

Beyond the Arts Pavilion is a huge equestrian statue of Tomislav, a 10th century Croatian king. Beyond that is the impressive rail station, once used as a stopping-off point on the route of the Orient Express. It features in at least one James Bond film.

Below the station is a shopping mall – the Importanne Centar. Accessible via escalator across the road from the western wing of the station building, it is useful if you want to do a bit of shopping, or just duck down there for a drink and a snack.

The Botanical Gardens ★★ ALL AGES A short walk west brings you to the Botanical Gardens, which are open to the public except in the depths of winter. It is a good place to have a picnic. With winding paths, splendid mature trees, dense shrubbery and bridge-spanned ponds, you could almost be in the country. Keen gardeners might also add to their knowledge of plants as all the trees and shrubs are clearly labelled.

Trb Marka Marulića. 01-484-40-20. Free admission. 9am–6pm. Closed Mon.

The Western Arm of the Horseshoe

The western arm of Lenuci's Horseshoe continues north of the Botanical Gardens, each square containing its stately building – the imposing former University Library (the books have now been moved to a modern building), the Ethnographic Museum (see below) and the splendid Croatian National Theatre. In front of the National Theatre is yet another Meštrović statue (see p.72), the well-reckoned (no pun intended) *Well of Life*.

Just west of the parks are the Arts and Crafts Museum (worthy, but not of much interest to children) and, allegedly Croatia's Louvre, the Mimara ADULTS, the authenticity of whose fine art collection has been in doubt.

Indeed, even the authenticity of Mimara himself, who donated the collection to the nation, has been under question – some claim that he was a chancer who stole another man's identity on a World War 1 battlefield. Certainly, nobody knows where his wealth came from.

Children are likely to be more interested in the massed skate-boarders who rattle up and down the flagstones at the front of the museum – they're often there, and seem to be viewed with remarkable tolerance, not only by local people, but by the authorities. As for the contents of the museum, unless the children are interested in art history, there's nothing much for them there. There are three other museums, though, that are more likely to be of interest.

The Ethnographic Museum

★ ★ ALL AGES The only purpose-built museum in the capital (when it opened in 1903 it housed collections on Applied Arts and Trade), the Ethnographic Museum has

If It's Really Hot In Zagreb

It can sometimes get really hot in Zagreb during the summer. In July and August the average temperature is 25°C and it can often be much hotter than this. If it does get very hot, it is best to take action. To cool down you might go swimming at Šalata (see p.206) in the city centre, or get out to Jarun (see p.219) or Bundek (see p.221). Another way to keep cool is to use only the modern trams, as they've got air conditioning. Try to eat inside restaurants rather than outside, as they, too, are usually air-conditioned. Stop at cafés for refreshment as often as you can (or can afford), and always carry a bottle of water around with you.

Croatia's Great Inventors

Born in Lika, Croatia, Nikola Tesla (1856–1943) could be the template for the popular idea of a mad scientist. He talked of splitting the earth in two, and of developing a death-ray that could destroy battalions of enemy soldiers from hundreds of miles away. His bread-and-butter work, though, was of far more use to humans. He pioneered radio technology, and, even more importantly, alternating current – the type of electricity that powers heavy industry, domestic appliances and everything else, everywhere! Tesla moved to the United States in 1884 where he carried out pioneering work on such things as wireless communication, robotics, computer science and nuclear physics. Despite all his achievements, Tesla has never got the attention he deserved and he died, alone and penniless, in a New York hotel room.

If Nikola Tesla was the world's favourite mad scientist, then Eduard Penkala (1871–1922) was the archetypal mad inventor. His greatest contributions to modern life were in the field of writing implements. In 1906 he patented the first propelling pencil, then a series of other writing devices including prototype ball-point and fountain pens, which made Zagreb, during and after World War 1, the world capital for the manufacture of writing implements. Penkala had other interests, however. He became Croatia's first aviator in 1909 and developed a two-seater aircraft and a hovercraft. By the time of his untimely death from pneumonia at the age of 50, he had worked on hundreds of inventions, and had lodged over 70 patents. Among his many other inventions were a rotating toothbrush, railway-carriage brakes, the world's first hot-water bottle and a recipe for washing detergent. Look out for displays at Zagreb's excellent Technical Museum.

excellent displays of costume from all over Croatia, together with wickerwork, pottery, musical instruments, and artefacts gathered from around the world by Croatian explorers. The museum also hosts imaginative temporary exhibitions – when I was there, it was of shoes.

Mazuranicev trg 14. 📞 *014-558-544.* **www.srce.hr/etno.** *Tues–Thurs 10am to 6pm, Fri–Sun 10am to 1pm. 10 Kuna (95p); children and concessions 5 Kuna (48p).*

The Croatian School Museum
★★★ AGES 3 AND UP On Trg Maršala Tita stands the Croatian School Museum, housed in the Croatian Teachers Hall along with the offices of various teachers' unions. Despite a very uninviting entrance, press on to the museum upstairs. It contains tableaux showing 19th and early 20th century teaching methods, wall charts and other display materials, educational equipment and photographs of schools in

Schools In Croatia

Children in Croatia go to school in shifts – a morning shift from 8am to 2pm, and an afternoon shift from 2pm to 8pm. One week a child will attend school in the morning, the next week in the afternoon. This means that, every other weekend, when they're changing from the morning to the afternoon shift, they have a three-day weekend, finishing at 2pm on Friday, and restarting at 2pm on Monday! The down side is, of course, that on the other weekend they finish at 8pm on Friday and restart at 8am on Monday. Another perk for Croatian schoolchildren is that their holidays are longer. Croatian schools close for the summer on the nearest Friday to 15th June, and return on the first Monday in September, giving Croatian school children around 10–11 weeks of summer holiday!

the past. Children might enjoy comparing then with now, and older people will be amazed at how similar methods of education in Croatia and the UK once were.

Tues to Fri 10am to 5pm, Sat and Sun 10am to 1pm. Adults 20 Kuna (£ 1.90), children 10 Kuna (95p).

The Technical Museum ★ ★ ★
FIND AGES 3 AND UP The staff at Zagreb's Technical Museum acknowledge that Britain leads the world in technical and industrial preservation and restoration. So it might be thought that UK families will have been spoilt by the excellence of our own technical museums, and won't find much of interest in Zagreb's. Far from it. This museum has superb collections of agricultural implements, power units, railway engines, trams, cars, an Italian miniature submarine, planes and their engines, a small armoured vehicle, fire appliances, and exhibits relating to

space exploration, including a small planetarium. Best of all is a wonderful 350 metre long recreation of a coal mine which goes all the way around the basement of the museum.

Tribute is also paid in the museum to the giants of Croatian scientific and technical history, most notably Nikola Tesla and Slavoljub Penkala (see box). The museum is a reasonable walk from the city centre, so you might want to catch a No. 9, 12, 13 or14 bus or the No. 17 tram.

Savaska cesta 18. ☎ 01-43-54-46. Fax: 01-42-84-31. www.mdc.hr/ tehnicki. Adults 15 Kuna (£ 1.45) children 10 Kuna (95p), planetarium 15 Kuna (£ 1.45) Open Tues to Fri 9am to 5pm, Sat and Sun 9am to 1pm.

Top 10 Family Experiences

❶ **Ride on** a tram/funicular/ cable car, Zagreb's three exciting non-standard means of transport.

② **Wander** around Dolac, market eating a burek bought at the shop on the flight of steps up from Trg Bana Jelačića.

③ **Swim/canoe/roller blade** etc with natives of the city in the wide open spaces at Jarun.

④ **Play** in Bundek's wonderful children's playground – it has probably the biggest range of equipment of any play area in Europe.

⑤ **Climb** the 13th century Burglar's Tower and hear the gun go off at noon – it has done so every day since 1877.

⑥ **Sit on** the lap of the metal man sitting on the metal bench – the statue of Antun Gustav Matoš – on the Strossmayerovo šetalište, then have a picnic.

⑦ **Watch the animals** being fed at the zoo, then have a good long walk around Maksimir Park.

Bundek's Playground

⑧ **Pose for a picture** next to Tito – either in Klanjek, or in Kumrovec, outside the house in which he was born.

⑨ **Feed the deer** at the Grešna Gorica restaurant, near Veliki Tabor, admire the peacocks, and have an al fresco feast whilst looking across the valley at the castle.

⑩ **Take part in a gas-lighting competition** in Gornji Grad, or find the Witch in the Grič, or go on a treasure hunt, or take part in a musical soirée (see box, p.209).

Away From The City Centre

Despite Zagreb's many attractions, it is perhaps inevitable that Croatia's capital will begin to pall and the children begin to yearn for new amusements. Should that happen, help is at hand away from the city centre where you will find plenty of open spaces for the children to burn off some excess energy.

Jarun ★ ★ ★ **ALL AGES** A sports and leisure complex created around an off-shoot of the River Sava for the World University Games of 1987, Jarun is the place where the residents of Zagreb go to let their hair down. These days it is looking a little tired but there's still so much to do here that it's hard to know were to start. You can sail, row, jog, paddle canoes, swim, picnic, have barbecues, fish, cycle, rollerblade, play table tennis,

GREATER ZAGREB

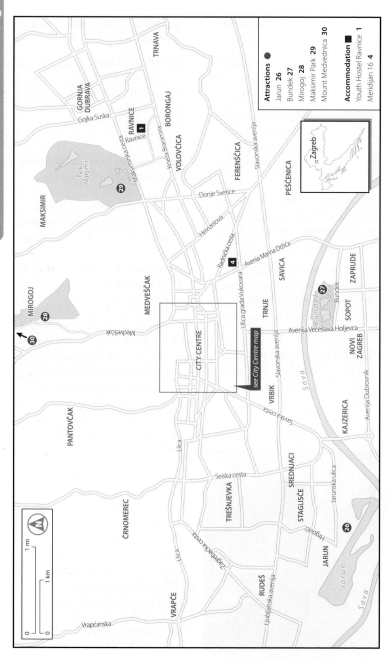

Attractions ●
Jarun **26**
Bundek **27**
Mirogoj **28**
Maksimir Park **29**
Mount Medvednica **30**

Accommodation ■
Youth Hostel Ravnice **1**
Meridijan 16 **4**

Zagreb

see City Centre map

0 — 1 mi
0 — 1 km

football, basketball and mini-golf. Equipment can be hired for a variety of sports and there's a gravel beach. The whole area is dotted with gazebos, picnic tables, children's play equipment, outdoor table tennis tables, as well as cafés and restaurants. In summer, bars and discos are open late into the night. Jarun is four kilometres southwest of the city centre. It is just 20 minutes on the No. 17 tram, or you can drive and park at the entrance. You can take your car in (3 Kuna (28p)), but it hardly seems worth it. There's no charge for people to enter.

Bundek ★ ★ ★ ALL AGES If Jarun is beginning to show its age, Bundek certainly isn't. Situated in Novi Zagreb, the concrete 1960s suburb to the south of the River Sava, Bundek was the gravel pit created in the construction of all those tower blocks. Having become dangerous (Bundek was actually the name of a small boy drowned there), the city transformed it into a terrific facility for the people of Zagreb. It opened in June 2006 and has already become popular with local people. Bundek consists of similar facilities to Jarun but all are brand new. There's a swimming lake with diving platform, a gravel beach, and lots of landscaped gardens. More importantly for parents, there's a huge state-of-the-art children's playground that contains some of best equipment I've ever seen. Take the 'Nove Zagreb' bus from Zagreb's bus station, and get off at the first stop after crossing the river.

Mirogoj ★ ALL AGES Zagreb's magnificent cemetery is one of the most beautiful in Europe. It is just 2.4km northeast of the city centre, and is another of Bollé's projects (see p.205) – indeed, he's buried here. The cemetery features two stunning arcades that stretch both sides of the entrance, which are lined with grand family tombs and shrines. The cemetery is also notable for the equal status given to all religions and you will see the Catholic cross, the Orthodox cross, the Star of David, and the Crescent of Islam side by side. The most famous modern tomb is the black polished slab that marks the last resting place of Croatia's first President Franjo Tuđman. A guide to the cemetery is available from the Zagreb Tourist Board.

Mirogoj bb, about 2.4km (11/2 miles) northeast of the city centre. Daily 8am–8pm.

Mirogoj Cemetery Arcades

Maksimir Park ★ ★ ★ ALL AGES

This large open space of grass and woodland has developed from a small public garden that was donated to the city in 1774, and is three kilometres from Trg Bana Jelačića on a No. 11 or 12 tram. The landscaped grounds are dotted with five lakes and a number of follies including a belvedere and a Swiss-style chalet. There is plenty of room to roam, a café for refreshments, children's playgrounds, and a nicely designed and impressively stocked city zoo. Opposite the entrance to the park stands the forbidding concrete bulk of the Maksimir Stadium, home to Dinamo Zagreb and the Croatian National football team.

Maksimirirski Perivoj bb. ☎ 01-230-21-98. Zoo: www.zoo.hr. Admission 20 Kuna (£ 1.90) ages 7 and up, 10 Kuna (95p) below age 7, and free for everyone on Mon. Daily summer 9am–8pm, winter 9am–4pm.

Mount Medvednica ★ ★

ALL AGES Not many capital cities can have such impressive open country so close to the centre as Zagreb has in Medvednica (Bear Mountain). The road zigzags upwards through dense forest, getting to its highest point, where you can park near a group of chalet style restaurants and continue upwards on foot through pretty meadows. You feel as if you're a long way from civilisation, yet the drive from central Zagreb takes less than half an hour. Alternatively, you can catch a No. 14 tram from Trg Bana Jelačića to the terminus, then a No. 15 to Dolje, whence a 10-minute walk will bring you to the lower cable-car station (8am to 8pm, 17 Kuna (£ 1.50) return). From there it's 20 minutes to the summit of Sljeme, the highest peak of the Mount Medvednica massif.

The whole mountain is a recreational area for the city. In summer the slopes are dotted with hikers and families enjoying picnics, or people visiting the Hotel Tomislavov or the Pansion Medvednica. There are cliffs used for rock climbing, caves, mountain-bike paths, children's educational trails and the medieval fortress of Medvedgrad. In winter, of course, everybody digs out their skis and sledges and heads for the slopes. Two of Zagreb's champion skiers, Janica and Ivica Kostelić, honed their skills here and the facilities, which include ski lifts and snow blowing machines, are so good that Zagreb is the only capital city ever to host a World Championship skiing event.

DID YOU KNOW? ⟩⟩ Filling the Cemetery ⟨⟨

Zagreb's spectacular Mirogoj Cemetery is so short of space that, when it is thought that one of the families with a tomb in the cemetery has died out, after a waiting period of 15 years, the remains (or as my Croatian informant called them, 'leftovers') are removed to a common burial place, and the plot is then reassigned.

Cable car: ☎ *01-458-03-94.* **www. zet.hr.** *11 Kuna (£ 1) one way; 17 Kuna (£ 1.50) return. Daily 8am–8pm. Leaves on the hour daily.*

For Active Families

Most of the sporting and recreational activities in Zagreb occur in facilities in the city (especially Jarun and Bundek), but for hiking (and skiing in the winter) the obvious destination is Mount Medvednica. It has a host of trails and lodges, ski lifts and, of course, the cable car. Its outdoor feel makes it difficult to believe that you're only 20 minute's drive from the centre of the city.

Out Of The City

From the top of Mount Medvednika, you get wonderful views of Zagreb's hinterland – the Croatian Zagorje, a hilly swathe of beautiful countryside, farmland, villages, castles and churches that stretches northwards from the capital to the border with Slovenia. For trips out of the city you're likely to need a car.

Gornja Stubica – The Museum of Peasant Uprisings

AGES 5 AND UP After driving down the north side of Mount Medvednica, the first village you come to is Stubičke Toplice. Turn right, and head towards Donja Stubica. Keep going – the signs make it seem as if the museum is imminent, but it isn't. Drive past a public swimming pool and a garage on the left. Eventually, you'll come to the village of Gornja Subica and its Museum of Peasant Uprisings.

Housed in the Orsić Palace, the museum tells the story of a famous revolt in Croatia's history when, in 1573, Roman Catholic peasants, led by Matija Gubec, tried to overthrow their Protestant Habsburg landlords. After a fierce battle, Gubec was captured and taken to Zagreb where he was tortured and executed by being forced to wear a red-hot crown of iron. As well as detailing the facts of the rebellion, the museum aims to paint a portrait of life at the time. Exhibits include items relating to traditional crafts and day-to-day village life as well as displays on such practices as wine making (visitors have the opportunity to drink some of the end produce in the beautifully cool barrel-vaulted cellars).

Outside the museum, just up the hill, there is a delightfully rustic tavern (Birtija Pod Lipom, a good place to stop for refreshment) and a picturesque church. Between the tavern and the church is an ancient tree – this is the Gubec lime tree, under which Matija Gubec and his followers met to launch their peasants' revolt.

The museum hosts a festival in June, with lots of workshops and displays and opportunities to try archery, dancing, housebuilding, fighting and tilting. The museum's website is at **www.mdc.hr/msb**, and has an English-language version.

Samci 63–64, Gornja Stubica. ☎ *049-587-880. Fax: 049-587-882. msb@kr. htnet.hr. Admission 20 Kuna (£ 1.90). Apr–Sept daily 9am–7pm; Oct–Mar daily 9am–5pm.*

Gornja Stubica 1
Klanjec 2
Kumrovec 3
Veliki Tabor 4
Krapina 5
Tragošćan 6

Klanjec ★★★ AGES 3 AND UP Up against the Slovenian border in western Zagorje is Kanjec, a pretty village with a nice church and a pleasant terrace under the trees, surrounded by vineyards on steep hillsides. The main reason for stopping is to visit the Antun Augustinčić Gallery, a modern brick and tile building housing works by Augustinčić, a locally-born, 20th century sculptor. Inside are busts of famous people (including one of Tito and his last wife), an enormous eight metre high plaster replica of a horseman designed for the UN building in New York, and a powerful statue of a coal miner created for the International Labour Office in Geneva.

Outside is a beautiful sculpture garden. The copy of the Brussels Manekin Pis (a little boy having a wee) is bound to raise a giggle from the children. The other statues, including one of Tito looking pensive in full uniform and a greatcoat, and another of a lone horse, are all very accessible. Under the statue entitled *Carrying the Wounded* lie the remains of the sculptor and his wife.

If you continue on towards Kumrovec (see below), notice a tall column next to a Croatian flag standing at the side of the road. This is a memorial to Antun Mihanović, who is mainly remembered for writing the words to the Croatian national anthem in 1835.

Trg A. Mihanovica 10, 49290 Klanjec. 04-955-0343. www.mdc.hr/ augustincic. Admission 20 Kuna (£ 1.90), children 10 Kuna (95p), April–Sept daily 9am to 5pm; Oct–March (except Monday) 9am to 3pm.

Kumrovec ★ ★ ★ AGES 3 AND UP

The village of Kumrovec is about 10 km (6 miles) from Klanjec and has an excellent 'Old Village Museum'. There's a big car park on the right as you enter the village, and an even bigger one across the road. The museum shop sells refreshments, and is also where you buy your tickets.

The museum consists of 30 vernacular buildings – preserved or restored, not brought here from elsewhere – which give an insight into the way people lived in the village at the end of the 19th and beginning of the 20th century. Each building illustrates a different aspect of life, from the work of the cooper and the weaver, to a typical village wedding and the house of a young married couple. Among the buildings is the childhood home of Josip Broz, better known as Tito (see box). There's a statue of him, standing pensive in full uniform and a greatcoat (surely the one you've just seen in Klanjec?) outside the cottage, with exhibits illustrating his life inside.

Be careful as you walk around, though. Not all the houses are part of the museum – some still have people living in them!

Staro Selo. 049-553-107. www. mdc.hr/kumrovec. Admission 20 Kuna (£ 1.90). Apr–Sept daily 9am–7pm; Oct–Mar daily 9am–4pm.

Museum of Country Life, Kumrovec

Tito

The man known to the world as 'Tito' was born on 7th May 1892 in the small Croatian village of Kumrovec, which at the time was a part of the Austro-Hungarian monarchy. Nothing in his early years foreshadowed his destiny as Yugoslavia's most famous 20th century figure. Known simply as Josip Broz, he was the seventh son of a peasant couple, his father a Croat, his mother a Slovene. Josip himself was apprenticed to the local blacksmith before being called up into the Austrian army. He fought on the Eastern Front during World War 1, and was captured by the Russians in 1915. If there was a decisive event in Tito's life, this was it. While a prisoner of war in Russia, he was inspired by the ideals of the Bolshevik Revolution, joined the Red Army, and became embroiled in the Russian Civil War. He finally returned home to Yugoslavia in 1920, speaking, it is said, with a Russian accent.

During the 1920s Tito rose slowly through the ranks of the Yugoslav Communist Party and in 1934 he joined the Central Committee. It was at this time that he adopted the nickname 'Tito'. No-one is quite sure why. The official version was that he chose the name to honour the 18th century Croat writer Tito Brezovački: less respectful sources say that he simply wanted a short, sharp *nom de guerre* like his heroes Lenin and Stalin. In 1937 Tito became General Secretary of the Yugoslav Communist Party, and he still held this position when the Nazis invaded Yugoslavia four years later.

A short while after the invasion Tito issued a call to arms and began to form a Partisan army. Despite heavy retaliation, Tito and his fellow Partisans proved to be highly successful in fighting the Germans, tying up increasing numbers of troops. Churchill was impressed by Tito's abilities and in 1943 Allied help and support was switched from the Serbian Chetniks to the Partisans, virtually ensuring that Tito would take over Yugoslavia when the war ended. In 1945 Tito did indeed become leader of Yugoslavia and, though a communist, began forging links with the West, eventually helping the country to enter a period of unprecedented prosperity. He remained leader until he died in 1980. No fewer than 128 world leaders attended his funeral.

Despite certain reservations Croats have about Tito (he was strongly anti-Catholic and not at all keen on Croatia's demands for self government), he is still honoured. A statue stands outside the cottage where he was born in Kumrovec. Other places in Croatia associated with the great man are similarly honoured. For example, you can still visit Tito's Cave on Vis (see p.130), where he holed up to devise strategies for Partisan resistance to the Nazis. And many streets and squares across Croatia named after Tito during his lifetime have retained his name long after his death.

Veliki Tabor ⭐ AGES 3 AND ABOVE

Some 15km (10 miles) north of Kumrovec along the border with Slovenia is what is probably the most typical of the Zagorje castles. The castle is up a very steep cobbled road, and dominates the vineyards, pastures and woodland that surround it. To British eyes, used to the rigid architecture of the Normans, it is an absolute delight and looks more like a fortified manor house than a castle capable of garrisoning troops.

Compared to its lovely exterior, inside the castle is a bit of a comedown. Like so many buildings in Croatia, late Medieval Veliki Tabor is being renovated slowly, as money allows. Displays of weapons, weaving implements, wine-making paraphernalia and a few old carriages disappoint, though models of the castle give a good idea of what it was originally like. The castle also has the inevitable sad tale of love and death, involving the bricking into the walls of beautiful village girl Veronika by the castle's owner Count Herman II, to put an end to her liaison with his son. Youngsters will inevitably get a delighted shiver up the spine, especially as a skull, found in the walls during renovations in 1982, is now on display. The nearby spot where, it is said, the lovers used to meet is now called the Hill of Sin.

Near Desinioc. 📞 *049-343-963.* **www. veliki-tabor.hr.** *Admission 20 Kuna (£ 1.90). Apr–Sept daily 9am–6pm; Oct–Mar daily 9am–5pm.*

INSIDER TIP ≫

Located on a hill opposite, with wonderful views of the castle, the **Grešna Gorica Restaurant** ⭐⭐⭐ **ALL AGES** is a must for families. The restaurant is on a working farm. With rustic tables and benches spread under the trees, wooden play equipment, and deer, chickens and peacocks to feed, it's a delightful spot for family dining.

The castle, Veliki Tabor

Krapina ★ AGES 3 AND ABOVE . The town of Krapina, some 32km (20 miles) from Veliki Tabor, was made famous for all time in 1899 when the Neanderthal remains of 'Krapina Man' were discovered here. There's a pleasant wooded hill dotted with modern sculptures, a nice little museum tracing the evolution of man, and a walk up through the trees to the cave (more a bit of an overhang) where the remains were found. Life-sized statues of a Neanderthal family now mark the spot, and there's a reconstruction of a bear whose bones are in the museum.

Just around the hillside, a brand new concrete and glass museum is being built into the slope (there's a model of it in the existing museum), and when it opens (probably in May 2007), the site will have display facilities in keeping with the importance of the site.

Entry to the museum is 10 Kuna (95p). Daily 9am–5pm Monday–Friday in summer, 8am–3pm in winter.

Tragošćan ALL AGES The final sight to see in the Croatian Zagorje is the famous, imposing, but alas mostly fake castle at Tragošćan. It's actually one of those 19th century 'reconstructions' of a 13th century original, where the builders have followed an idea of what medieval castles *should* look like rather than what they actually did look like. Still, it's an imposing edifice in a terrific setting, and the image of its crenellated battlements and crisp white walls, perched on a steep hill, which is reflected in the ornamental lake, is one of the most famous in the area. It's also a pleasant place to spend some time, with woodland walks, a café and a boating lake (boats are available for hire April to September, 9am to 6pm, October to March, 9am to 3pm, 20 Kuna (£ 1.90)). You can join the motorway near Krapina from where it is only half an hour and an 18 Kuna (£ 1.60) toll back in the centre of Zagreb.

☏ *042-796-422. www.trakoscan. net. Admission 20 Kuna (£ 1.90) adults, 10 Kuna (95p) children. May–Sept daily 9am–6pm;Oct–Apr daily 9am–3pm.*

Shopping with Children

Zagreb has all the shopping opportunities you'd expect in one of Europe's capital cities. There's a good variety of shops on the streets which radiate out from the city's main square Trg Bana Jelačića – in particular, Ilica, Radićeva and Opatovina, together with streets that run from Ilica – especially Frankopanska. Here are all the chain stores, small independent shops, high fashion outlets, food and wine emporia and souvenir shops you could wish for. There are numerous bookshops – the one with the best selection of English language books and magazines is Algoritam, at Gajeva ulica 1 ☏ *01-481-86-72*. The number of shopping malls in Zagreb is increasing – try the Importanne Centar at Starčevićev trg 1 (*www.importanne.hr*), Centar

Kaptol, Nova Ves 11 (*www. centarkaptol.hr*) or the Branimir Centar on Branimirova 29 (*www.branimircentar.hr*). On Opatovina there are stalls selling good quality clothes and bags, and you'll get a huge choice of ties and cravats at Croata, Prolaz Oktogon, Ilica 5 (*www.croata.hr*). For toys go to Turbo Limač at Ljudevita Gaja 9a ☏ *01-481-15-48*, or the little arcade leading up to the Pansion Jaegerhorn (see below) off Ilica, or in the Branimir Centar.

Family Entertainment

The greatest source of theatre, ballet and opera in Zagreb is the Croatian National Theatre at Trg maršala Tita 15, ☏ *01-482-85-32, www.hnk.hr*), but there's a whole host of other specialist venues – Gavella City Drama Theatre (☏ *01-484-85-52, www.gavella.hr*), Komedija Municipal Theatre (☏ *01-481-45-66, www.komedija. hr*), Kerempuh Satirical Theatre (☏ *01-483-33-47, www.kazaliste kerempuh.hr*), ITD Theatre (☏ *01-459-35-10, www.sczg.hr*) and the Exit Theatre (☏ *01-370-41-20, www.teatarexit.hr*). Particularly suitable for children are the Zagreb Theatre of the Young (☏ *01-487-25-54, www. zekaern.hr*), the Dubrava Children's Theatre (☏ *01-291-04-87, www.ns-bubrava.hr*), the Zagreb Puppet Theatre (☏ *01-487-84-45, www.zkv.hr*) and the Small Stage Theatre (☏ *01-468-33-52 www.mala-scena.hr*). But performances are often in Croatian, so there's no

alternative to phoning or checking their websites before deciding whether to buy tickets.

The nearest cinema to the city centre is the 12-screen cinestar in the Branimir Centar (☏ *01-468-66-02, www.blitz-cinestar.hr*) – films are usually in English, with Croatian subtitles.

Zagreb is rich in festivals, the most important of which are:

Test! (middle of March) – a festival of student drama (*www. test.hr*)

Thirsty Ear (March/April) – alternative rock festival run (together with several other festivals) by the KSET students club (*www.kset.org*)

Music Biennale (April) – contemporary classical music held in odd-numbered years (☏ *01-482-53-60*)

Contemporary Dance Week (late May/early June) – modern dance from around the world (*www.danceweekfestival.com*)

Eurokaz Theatre Festival (end of June/beginning of July) – intellectual avant-garde drama. (*www.eurokaz.hr*)

International Folklore Festival (last weekend in July) – performances of ethnic music and dance all over the city (*www. msf.hr*)

Zagreb Baroque Festival (mid-July to mid-August) – classical music (*www.zabaf.hr*)

International Festival of Puppet Theatre (end of August) – puppet shows for children and adults from all over the region. (*http://public. srce.hr/pif-festival*)

World Theatre Festival (mid-September) – festival of A-list names in theatre (*www.zagreb theatrefestival.hr*)

Zagreb Film Festival (October) – documentaries and art films from all over the world (*www.zagrebfilmfestival.com*)

Nebo (October or November) – festival of Croatian and world music (*www.nebo festzagreb.com*)

Earwing No Jazz Festival (November) – a mixture of jazz, far-out rock and classical avant-garde (*www.kset.org*)

FAMILY-FRIENDLY ACCOMMODATION

As a general rule, top-end hotels in Zagreb are concentrated in the city centre, while those whose charges are more moderate are scattered in a ring around its outer edges. There's very little budget accommodation. As in much of the rest of Croatia, there's not much attempt to cater specifically for children, and detailed enquiry about facilities for children tends to elicit blank looks – particularly as most places regard themselves as hotels for businessmen, not tourists. However, whether facilities for children and families are made explicit in the hotel's literature or not, they will usually bend over backwards to fulfil any requests you may have. And the more expensive the hotel, the more likely they are to take such requests in their stride. So the

advice here is clear – don't be afraid to ask.

Note that most hotels in Zagreb increase their prices during the city's spring and autumn Fairs by up to 20%. Note also that quite a few offer a 'Daily Rest' rate, where you can rent a room from (say) 10am to 6pm, usually for 50% of the normal rate. I think this is to give you a base for shopping, though it might be open to misinterpretation!

An alternative to hotels is the range of private accommodation on offer in the capital. There are full contact details of agencies offering this service in the booklet 'Private and Confidential – private accommodation, rooms, apartments and villas' available from the Tourist Board.

EXPENSIVE

Arcotel Allegra ★ ★ ★ One of a chain of hotels in Germany, Austria and the Czech Republic, the Arcotel Allegra is comfortable (as you'd expect at these prices) and, although principally a business hotel can adapt easily to families. Cots and extra beds for children are available free of charge, and junior suites (ideal for families) are available at weekends for normal room rates. Close to the bus and railway stations, and handily placed at the southern edge of the Donji Grad, the Arcotel Allegra's trump card is its position right next to the Branimir Centre, a mall that contains a toy shop, a 12-screen multiplex (with lots of

The Regent Esplanade Hotel, Zagreb

English language films and cartoons – look out for 'Original Version', or you'll end up watching a dubbed one), a bookshop with numerous English-language books for both adults and children, and the highly rated Opium restaurant (see below). There's also a casino, for those who enjoy a flutter.

Branimirova 29, 10000 Zagreb. 📞 *01-469-60-00. Fax 01-469-60-96.* *www.arcotel.at/allegra.htm. 151 rooms. From 1085 Kuna (£ 105) double; from 2320 Kuna (£ 220) suite. Rates do not include breakfast. AE, DC, MC, V. Parking garage 4 Kuna (£ 3.80) per day.* **Amenities:** *Restaurant, bar, sauna, room service, free lobby Internet (one terminal). In room: A/C, TV/DVD player, minibar, hair dryer, safe, valet service.*

The Regent Esplanade ★ ★ ★

If the family includes any train spotters, this is the hotel for you. Built in 1925 specifically for passengers of the Orient Express, and situated close to the railway station, the corridors are adorned with photographs from the great age of transcontinental steam. Ask for the cheque-book-sized booklet about all the famous actors, film stars, musicians and politicians who have stayed at the hotel. The décor is beautiful: a total vision of 1920s Art Deco, tastefully renovated in 2004 to provide every luxury known to humanity. And though it can be regarded as more of a business than a holiday hotel, it considers meeting your every need and request as a matter of professional honour. There are numerous adjoining rooms and suites, pull-out beds and cots are available, and bathrooms are of unimaginable luxury. The hotel also has three of the most famous café/bar/restaurants in the city. All in all, a wonderful hotel. Grab the chance if you can afford it.

Mihanovićeva 1, 10000 Zagreb. 📞 *01-456-66-66. Fax: 01–456-66 020.* *www.theregentzagreb.com. 209 rooms. From 1080 Kuna (£ 103)* double; from 2200 Kuna (£ 210) suite. AE, DC, MC, V. No pets. **Amenities:** two restaurants, terrace dining w/live music, bar, casino, sauna, salon, club floor, concierge, room service, non-smoking rooms, valet service, two rooms for those w/limited mobility. In room: A/C, TV w/pay movies, free wireless connection/dataport, mini-bar, hair dryer, safe, trouser press.

Westin Zagreb ★★★ A great slab of a hotel, the Westin Zagreb could hardly be better placed for access to the centre of the city – it's just off the western arm of Lenuci's Horseshoe, right next to the Mimara Museum. There's a tram stop directly outside. You can walk to Trg Bana Jelačića (see p.203) in 10 minutes. The accommodation is luxurious, the facilities excellent and this is one of the few hotels in Zagreb that offers explicit support for families with children. Through its 'Westin Kids Club' the hotel provides, on request, cots, a 'baby kit' of bottle warmer, nappies and wipes, babysitting, children's menus in the restaurant and a variety of other services, furnishings and amenities geared to children of all ages.

Kršnjavoga 1, 10000 Zagreb. ☎ 01-489-20-00. Fax 01-489-20-02. www. westin.com/Zagreb. 377 rooms. From 1050 Kuna (£ 100) double; from 1885 Kuna (£ 180) suite. Rates do not include breakfast. AE, DC, MC, V. Pets welcome with advance registration. **Amenities:** two restaurants, café, bar, business centre, nonsmoking rooms, valet service, laundry service, 24 hour room service, heated indoor pool, solarium, massage, fitness centre, sauna, beauty salon, ample car parking (110 Kuna,

£ 10.50) per day). In room: A/C, TV, minibar, coffeemaker, hair dryer, safe, iron/ironing board.

MODERATE

Central ★ The Central is only a minute's walk away from all the facilities of the Branimir Centre (see **Arcotel Allegra** above). Although it has few specifically family-friendly amenities, the staff are pleasant and very willing to adapt, and there are apartments available that would be very suitable family accommodation. The noise of the trams can be a bit intrusive – ask for rooms at the back.

Branimirova 3, PP 97, 10000 Zagreb. ☎ 01-484-11-22. Fax: 01-484-13-04. www.hotel-central.hr. 76 rooms. From 720 Kuna (£ 68) double; from 1300 Kuna (£ 124) suite. AE, DC, MC, V. Rates stay the same all year and include breakfast. **Amenities:** Restaurant (breakfast only), adjacent casino. In room: A/C, TV, dataports and minibars in some rooms, hair dryer, Internet connection.

Dubrovnik ★★★ You can't get more central than the undulating glass tower of the Dubrovnik Hotel – it stands on the corner of Trg Bana Jelačića and Gajeva, opening onto both. If you've got teenagers they'll be delighted to be staying right at the heart of the city's social life, and even with very young children the staff are so friendly that you're guaranteed a pleasant stay. Renovated in 2003, it has a variety of room sizes and layouts, including suites and pairs of rooms with connecting doors (one of which has a great view across Trg Bana Jelačića). The double rooms have very big beds, so that families with younger children would be quite comfortable, extra beds can be installed, and cots are available on request. The restaurant has high chairs, and, though there's no children's menu, they are happy to offer smaller portions, or split meals between children. It can be noisy if there are functions on – ask for a room towards the top of the building.

Gajeva 1. P.P. 246, 10000 Zagreb. 01-487-35-55. *Fax: 01-486-35-06.* **www.hotel-dubrovnik.hr.** *280 rooms. For rooms appropriate for families 1000 Kuna (£ 95) double; from 1340 Kuna (£ 128) suite. Extra bed: 250 Kuna (£ 24). Rates include breakfast. AE, DC, MC, V. Parking 100 Kuna (£ 9.50) during the week, 85 Kuna (£ 8.30) at weekends.* **Amenities:** *Restaurant, cafe, bar; business centre, salon, room service, nonsmoking rooms, valet, rooms for those w/limited mobility. In room: A/C, TV, wireless/dataport, minibar, hair dryer, safe.*

Meridijan 16 ★★ FIND A newcomer to the Zagreb hotel scene (it opened in 2005), the Meridijan 16 offers a welcome addition to the stock of moderately priced hotels in the capital. Handily placed 200 metres south of the bus station, the hotel offers clean, attractive en-suite rooms (doubles, triples and one apartment), and has additional beds and cots available. Breakfasts, included in the price, are buffet-style, with any reasonable special requests being met. There is no restaurant, but the hotel is happy for you to order in, and will recommend takeaways. The hotel will drive you where you want to go in the city if the car is available (free!), but otherwise will call a cab.

Ulica grada Vukovara 241, 10000 Zagreb. 01-606-52-00. *Fax: 01-606-52-01.* **www.meridijan16.com.** *25 rooms. From 580 Kuna (£ 55) double, 725 Kuna (£ 70) triple (and a single apartment at 580 Kuna (£ 55).* **Amenities:** *breakfast room, car park with CCTV surveillance (70 Kuna, £ 6.50 per day), laptops with free Wi-Fi Internet access. In room: plasma Sat TV, Internet dial-up connection.*

Pansion Jaegerhorn ★ The Pansion Jaegerhorn has its disadvantages. Access isn't easy for one thing. You can either approach it from Ilica, Zagreb's main shopping street, through a small and colourful shopping mall (which incidentally includes an excellent toy shop), or from the leafy, stepped path, which is the alternative to the funicular railway (see p.208). Once you're in, though, the hotel is lovely. It is fitted out a bit like a hunting lodge, and has comfortable rooms. Outside, there is a cool and beautiful terrace built into the hillside. Cots and extra beds are available, and the restaurant is happy to provide child portions or divide adult portions between children. There are no high chairs, but bench seating in part of the restaurant makes seating younger children easy.

Ilica 14, 10000 Zagreb. 01-483-38-77. *Fax: 01-483-35-73.* **www. hotel-pansion-jaegerhorn.hr.** *11 rooms. 800 Kuna (£ 76) double; there are also two 'apartments' for 950 Kuna (£ 90) suite. Rates include* *breakfast. AE, DC, MC, V. Limited free parking. Amenities: Restaurant, terrace, bar. In room: mini-bar, A/C, TV.*

INEXPENSIVE

Youth Hostel Ravnice ★★

FIND Simply the best cheap accommodation in Zagreb. This is a privately owned youth hostel only a 15-minute tram ride east of Trg Bana Jelačića (take the No. 11 or 12 from Trg Bana Jelačića, get off at the Ravnice stop, just after Maksimir Park). Family run and recently extended, it is clean, friendly, and in a pleasant part of the city, with cafés, shops, a post office, cash machines and foreign exchange facilities nearby. There are now 64 beds in rooms of various sizes – find out what's available then fit to your needs. The essence of youth hostelling is cheerful and tolerant camaraderie, but if you don't want to share a room with strangers, and your family numbers don't exactly divide into the 2, 4, 6 and 12 bed rooms available, you may have to book more beds than you need. At a flat rate of £10 a night per person (whatever the room size) this will hardly break the bank. This is a youth hostel, so it can be noisy, but at that price who cares! For the quietest rooms, try to stay on the top floor.

Ravnice 38d, 10000 Zagreb. ☎ 01-233-2325. Fax: 01-234-56-07. www.ravnice-youth-hostel.hr. 13 rooms of 2 to 12 beds. Flat rate 15 € (110 Kuna, £10) per bed. Amenities: use of kitchen, towel hire, lockers, TV room, Internet, free linen, laundry service, car park, table-tennis.

FAMILY-FRIENDLY DINING

The centre of Zagreb is full of restaurants, and you'll be very unlucky indeed to stumble across a poor one – since they depend largely on locals for their trade, poor restaurants don't last long. There is no tradition of providing meals specifically for children, and you'll go a long time without seeing a children's menu. However, the vast majority of restaurants are happy to fall in with any reasonable requests regarding portions or off-menu items, and quite a few now also provide high chairs. There are many opportunities to buy 'street food', especially pizza by the slice, baguettes and the ubiquitous 'burek' (a savoury cheese or meat filled pastry), though this is something of an acquired taste. There are also lots of opportunities to put together picnic meals, and lots of places to eat them.

EXPENSIVE

Pod Gričkim Topom ★★★

CROATIAN Clinging to the side of the hill just below Strossmayerovo Šetalište, on the path and steps that take you down to Ilica if you don't want to use the funicular, Pod Gričkim Topom offers delicious food on a red-tiled terrace overlooking the rooftops of the city centre. Its menu has a variety of meat dishes, but its speciality is fish – the owner brings fresh fish almost every day from family contacts in Murtur on the coast. Although weekday customers are mainly business people, the restaurant is thronged with families at weekends, especially on Sunday, so they're used to children, and can provide high chairs.

Zakmardijeve stube 5. 📞 *01-483-36-07. AE, DC, MC, V. 65–125 Kuna (£ 6–12). Daily 11am–midnight*

Ristorante Sorriso ★★★
ITALIAN In an atmospheric brick basement on Boskovićeva, just east of the Croatian Academy of Arts and Sciences, Sorriso serves classy Italian food with a French twist. Good wine list (see Franz Ferdinand box, p.238).

Boškovićeva 11. 📞 *01-487-63-92. www.sorriso.hr. AE, DC, MC.V. 70–130 Kuna. Daily, 10am–midnight. Closed Sunday.*

Stari Vura **CROATIAN** Tucked
away in the basement of the Museum of Zagreb, which was once a monastery, the ambience of the Stari Vura is unrivalled. The atmospheric vaulting seems to give it an ecclesiastical air, and the food is traditional with a modern twist. There's plenty of room for children to move around, and a tolerant attitude towards them, though no high chairs or children's menu.

Opatička 20. 📞 *01-485-13-68. Entrees 65–180 Kuna (£ 6–17). AE, DC, MC, V. Mon–Sat noon–midnight. Closed Sun.*

MODERATE

Boban ★ **ITALIAN** Owned by the
father of famous footballer and national hero Zvonimir Boban (see p.53) (there's a shop selling his designer-wife's clothes and bags next door), Restoran Boban is a popular and lively Italian restaurant in the vaulted basement of Boban's kavana-bar, just down Gageva from Trg Bana Jelačića. In addition to all the usual Italian spaghetti, pastas, gnocchi and risottos, a small selection of Croatian meat, fish and vegetable dishes is on offer. They're happy to offer small portions, or divide meals between children, and high chairs are available. It can get very crowded, but that's usually at night, when the children should be in bed!

Gajeva 9. 📞 *01-481-15-49. www. boban.hr. 35–80 Kuna (£ 3.30–7.50). AE, DC, MC, V. Daily 10am–midnight.*

Capuciner ★ **ITALIAN** Just up
from Kaptolska Klet, Capuciner is one of those noisy, no-nonsense places that offers good-quality, authentic Italian food. You can eat outside or inside at tables with red-and-white check cloths. They also do a roaring takeaway delivery trade, so it gets a bit raucous, but it's ideal for families because the children can make as much noise as they like – who'd notice! They do every pizza you can imagine including a nutella one!

Capuciner Kaptol 6. 📞 *01-481-04-87. info@capuciner.hr. 25–80 Kuna (£ 2.40–7.50).*

Kaptolska Klet ★★ **CROATIAN**
One of a pair of good dining opportunities opposite the Cathedral (see p.205), Kaptoldka

22,000 Milja

Sometimes when you're on holiday you find just the place – just the right hotel, just the right restaurant, just the right park, beach or café. In Zagreb, the find of one of my visits was a café/bar. It was in a little square, down an alleyway off one of the main streets leading up to Ilica, Zagreb's main shopping street. But when I asked another customer the name of the square he laughed. 'This is not a square,' he said. 'It's just a space between the buildings'. So instead of an address, I'll tell you how to get there.

If you start from the Mimara Museum, walk in towards the city centre. After passing the National Theatre of Croatia and crossing Trg Maršala Tita, you'll find yourself walking along Frankopanska, with a modern church on your right. Just before getting to the main entrance to the church, look to your left – you'll see a short alley leading to a group of shops and café/bars. The first of the cafés is the 22,000 Milja.

Why did I particularly like it? Well, the inside décor is peculiar – it's nautical, as if you're inside a submarine. The theme seems to be '20,000 Leagues under the Sea' – why it's gone up to 22,000 I've no idea: inflation perhaps. The inside and outside seating is comfortable, the food and drink cheap (by capital city standards, very cheap). At weekends there's live music; when I was there it was excellent jazz.

There's a mixed crowd too – young couples with children, old men and women, and students from the Music Academy, which is also in the square. And that's something else that 22,000 Milja has – lots of other things around it in the square. Some of it isn't much use to families – the Stars Model Agency, or the Swedish Embassy, or the Eros shop ('Positive Vibrations'!). But there's also a mobile phone shop, which might be useful if you need to buy a charger, and a cigar shop (which seems to be associated with 22,000 Milja). And, best of all, the 'Land of Magic' game shop, thronged with youngsters of all ages.

So if you're in Central Zagreb, and you're looking for a place to have a drink or eat cheaply, or listen to live music, head for the 22,000 Milja in the square with no name (or the space between the buildings) just off Frankopanska. *22,000 Milja, B-2, Frankopansa 22;* 📞 *01-481-70-07*

Klet has a huge cool, shady courtyard, some of it under a colonnaded roof, with a more formal air-conditioned dining area inside. There are (a rarity in Croatia) options for vegetarians, and, for families with children, high chairs and (another rarity) a modest selection of toys. If you just want a drink and a snack, **Pivnica** ('Brewery') next door is run by the same management, and has the lovely rough tables, wooden benches and the low light of a village inn. If you're missing the pub, this is the way to go.

Kaptol 5. 01-481-48-38. *Fax 01-481-43-30.* **www.mediacaffe.net/kaptolskaklet.** *35–80 Kuna (£ 3.50–7.50). AE, DC, MC, V. Daily 11am–11pm.*

Opium ★ SOUTHEAST ASIAN In the depths of the Branimir Centre near the station, and next to the Arcotel Allegra hotel (see p.230), the Opium is highly regarded in Zagreb. The food is largely Thai (the chef is from Thailand), but there are Japanese, Indian and Chinese options on the menu as well. Though they do accept walk-in trade, it's better to book. This is a good place to eat before or after visiting the CineStar multiplex. Although there are no special arrangements for children, they seem to get on here very well.

Branimirova 29. 01-461-56-79. *Fax: 01-461-56-80.* **www.opium.hr.** *55–95 Kuna (£ 5–9). AE, DC, MC, V. Mon–Fri 8am–1am; Sat 8am–1:30am; Sun 11am–1am.*

Vinodal ★ ★ ★ CROATIAN Owned by the Boban family, and a couple of minutes walk from Restoran Boban, Vinodol has a firmly traditional Croatian menu, served in delightful surroundings. The beautiful vaulted interior and large shaded courtyard are set out for formal dining, and there's a deep archway furnished with coffee-tables and easy chairs. From the street the Vinodol's entrance is easy to miss – just that archway – but inside it's massive (a bit like the Tardis). Its flexibility and spaciousness make it ideal for families – you can choose to sit outside in the shade, or inside under cool, air-conditioned vaults, and there's plenty of room for pushchairs and for the children to move around. Their speciality is veal or lamb 'under the bell' ('Ispod peke'), that is, cooked under a metal or ceramic cover, which is available only at 1pm and 8pm.

Nikola Tesle 10. 01-481-13-41. *Fax: 01-481-13-43.* **www.vinodol-zg.hr.** *Main courses 50–95 Kuna (£ 5–9). AE, DC, MC, V. Daily 10am–11pm.*

INEXPENSIVE

Restoran Ivica I Marica ★ ★ CROATIAN It's the whimsical décor (based on the story of Hansel and Gretel) that is most likely to appeal to children: the whole place, inside and out, has the look of a fairy story. Starting as a family pastry and confectionery shop on fashionable (and pedestrianised) Tkalčićeva Street, Restoran Ivica I Marica recently expanded next door by adding a restaurant. It prides itself on eschewing what it calls 'industrial food' – all of its dishes are made from natural, whole and locally sourced ingredients, all its juices are freshly squeezed. The menu is traditional Croatian: 'Dishes from the Past' for example, or 'Delicacies from Grandmas Kitchen'. One meal is 'Beefsteak with egg "Noble Kid"' – not, we hope, Hansel or Gretel. You can end with sweets from the pastry shop, which are claimed to be healthy too, but, delightfully, don't look it! Although included in the 'inexpensive' section, it

Franz Ferdinand – The Group, Not The Emperor

Alex Kapranos, lead singer of highly-rated Scottish group *Franz Ferdinand*, is keen on Croatian food. And he should know – he writes a regular food column in the *Guardian* newspaper. While out in Zagreb's Sorriso restaurant with the people who run Dancing Bear, Franz Ferdinand's Croatian record label, he came across (and found delicious) ravioli made from poppy-seed flour stuffed with beetroot, scallops wrapped in prsut on truffle-infused polenta, Istrian wine and biska liqueur made from mistletoe. Prsut, he feels, is better than serrano or proscuitto – 'lean and salty ... not as exhausting on the tongue', owing its flavour partly to the 'Bura' wind that forces its way through gaps in the wooden walls of the smoke-houses where it is made. He took to Croatia's capital, too, speaking of this 'beautiful city's noticeable Austro-Hungarian flavour' and its 'careless grace and grandeur'.

can be quite pricy if you're having 'the works'.

Tkalčićeva 70, 10000 Zagreb. ☎ 01-481-73-21. Fax: 098-317-092. ivi-caimarica@adriazdravahrana.hr. 40–90 Kuna (£ 4–8.50). AE, DC, MC, V. Daily noon–11pm.

Vallis Aurea ★★ SLOVENIAN FIND

Just down towards Ilica from the lower station of the funicular (see p.208), Valles Aurea is a real find. Named after a vineyard in Kutjevo, Slovenia, the décor inside is inland Croatia, with heavy wooden carved tables and benches, and colourful table-cloths. But the secret of Vallis Aurea is in the little glass display case on the outside wall, next to the doorway – it's a list of daily specials. For 22–35 Kuna (£ 2–3.50) you get a choice from three or four good solid meals, with rice, beans or pasta. It's an absolute bargain, and a secret that locals have kept to themselves.

Tomićeva 4. ☎ 01-483-13-05. 22–35 Kuna (£ 2–3/50) Daily 9am–10pm.

8 History

In order to understand Croatia today, you really need to understand something of its history. Yet that's no easy matter – Croatian history is about as complicated and knotted as a creel of eels. But here's a quick trot through some aspects of Croatia's past.

30,000 years ago The earliest evidence of prehistoric settlement in Croatia came to light when the remains of several Neanderthals where discovered in Krapina in 1899 (see p.228). Neanderthals are not, however, considered to be human beings (i.e. they were not 'homo sapiens'), and so can't be thought of as the first people in Croatia.

9,000 years ago That honour goes to the Neolithic farmers who inhabited the coastal region, some of the islands and the Danube basin in eastern Slovenia around 9,000 years ago. The invention of farming had released them from the long darkness of the Old Stone Age, and freed up time for the production of better tools and weapons, which were in turn used for the development of shelter and for the adoption of a more reflective life.

3,000–2,000 years ago The people of the area now covered by Croatia, Bosnia, Serbia and Albania, although organised into different tribes, had enough in common (especially regarding their homes and building methods) to earn them a common name – the Illyrians. These Illyrian tribes give an inkling of where the names of some of Croatia's regions came from – the Histri lived in what we now call Istria, and the Dalmati in the south of what we now call Dalmatia.

4th century BC Greeks from Syracuse in what is today Italy started to push across the Adriatic into some of the Croatian islands.

229 BC This eventually brought them into conflict with Queen Teuta, who ruled the coastal area from Zadar all the way down to what is today Albania. The Greeks weren't making too good a fist of this, so in 229 BC they appealed to the Roman Empire for help.

229 BC–9 AD This event brought about the long process of conquest by the Romans. Their incursion into the region resulted in the annexation of the whole of the Eastern Adriatic by Tiberius (who later became Emperor). Roman road building facilitated trade, and Roman merchants poured into this new frontier region, followed by elderly Romans looking for a nice peaceful place to retire. Roman cities sprang up in what is today Pula, Zadar and Solin, near Split.

284–305 AD Local Split boy Diocletian became Roman Emperor, and in 293 made the momentous decision to partition Dalmatia into east and west – a division that was later extended to the whole Roman Empire (see below).

305 AD onwards In 305 AD the unheard of happened – the peaceful handing over of power by a Roman Emperor to his successors. Diocletian had had an enormous palace built as his retirement home in Split (see p.104), and he settled down for the last 11 years of his life, enjoying his wealth and persecuting Christians. Everybody needs a hobby when they retire!

From the 5th century AD The Roman Empire started its long period of decline, increasingly battered by invaders from the north and east. On the death of Theodosius in 395 AD, the Roman Empire was split into west and east. The western part was to be ruled from Rome, the eastern part from Byzantium (later called Constantinople, then Istanbul). Slovenia, Croatia and Bosnia-Herzegovina were assigned to the western half, Serbia, Kosovo and Macedonia to the east. The effects of the division are still in evidence today: west of the line is largely Roman Catholic, east is Orthodox; west uses the Latin script, east the Cyrillic. The western, Roman, Empire was briefly conquered by the Visigoths, but was then recaptured by the eastern Byzantine Empire. Nevertheless, the disintegration continued.

600–900 AD As the Roman Empire grew ever weaker, Croats, Slovenes and Serb tribes arrived from the north and east. The Croats who arrived at the Adriatic coast began to dominate the people who were already there and established a tribal state ruled by a Knez. Inland areas fell under a different group of independent Croat chieftains, allied to, but not subject to, the coastal Croats. The division between the two parts of Croatia, so noticeable today, was already beginning to be established. But pressure from Hungary to the north continued. It was around this time that Croatia embraced the Roman Catholic faith.

800 AD This period saw the conquest of Dalmatia by the Franks under Charlemagne, and the mass conversion of the Croats to Christianity.

910–928 AD Under Tomislav the continental and coastal Croats were united.

1102 AD Under the Pacta Conventa, Croatia accepted Hungarian overlordship, on the understanding that Croatian customs and traditions would be guaranteed. Croatia and Hungary continued as separate states, ruled by the same

(Hungarian) royal family (in much the same way as Scotland and England remained separate on the accession of the Stuarts, but both were ruled by James I). Croatian institutions were set up. The country was to be ruled by a 'Ban' or governor, appointed by the king, and advised by the Sabor (parliament) representing the nobility.

1091 AD Hungary invaded northern Croatia, but failed to wrest Dalmatia from Byzantine control. However, the Venetians were encroaching on the coastal regions at Byzantine expense.

1100–1400 AD During this period of what has been called the 'Hungaro-Croatian Empire', Croatian independence was slowly eroded. Although Hungary kept a tight grip on northern Croatia, there was continual friction with Venice over Istria and Dalmatia. There was a lot of fighting, especially during the reigns of Bela III and IV.

All of this started to look irrelevant as the Moslem Ottoman (Turkish) Empire began to expand at the expense of the (Orthodox) Byzantine Empire, and even started to threaten (Roman Catholic) Croatia, Hungary and Austria.

1400–1600 AD Western Europe went into shock when Constantinople fell to the Turks. Worse was to come. Bulgaria, Serbia and Bosnia followed suit. In 1493, the Turks defeated a Croatian army about 30 km south of the Plitvice Lakes. By 1500 the Turks were in Makarska; by 1510 they were on the River Sava, only 10 km south of Zagreb. Dubrovnik, which had managed to stay neutral throughout the bad times that affected inland Croatia, continued to stay out of trouble by negotiating a non-aggression pact with the Ottoman Empire. Venice did the same, so Croatia's coast was largely unaffected by the Turkish advances.

The Military Frontier By the 1540s, Croatia had largely disappeared – the coast and islands were ruled by the Venetian Republic (except for Dubrovnik, which continued to plough its own furrow), and inland Croatia was now under the control of the Turkish Ottoman Empire. Desperately trying to avoid what they saw as the Moslem hordes, Hungary created a fortified zone to act as a buffer between them and the Turks. This was called the 'Military Frontier', and was staffed largely by Vlachs who'd fled the Turkish advance into Bosnia (and who were therefore more motivated than most).

The Tide Turns As the 16th century became the 17th century, the Turks began for the first time to experience defeat, and were beaten at the battle of Sisak in 1593. Further setbacks culminated in failure and rout at the Siege of Vienna in 1683, and they sued for peace (and renounced any further claims to Croatia) in 1699. The border between Bosnia (which continued to be ruled by the Turks) and Slavonia were fixed – it's still the border today.

18th century The next century, far from being a time of peace and prosperity following the end of the Turkish threat, were dire for Croatia. The Hungarians tightened the screws on eastern Croatia, reducing its independence and strengthening Hungarian control, while western Croatia suffered fierce exploitation by the Venetian Republic. Coastal Croatia suffered painfully low prices for its raw materials, fixed by their Venetian overlords, who also insisted that these raw materials could be sold only to Venice. At the same time Croatia was allowed to import manufactured goods only *from* Venice, at – yes, you've guessed it – hugely inflated prices. For Venice, a win–win situation: for Croatia, lose–lose. To add to the damage, Venice stripped much of Western Croatia of timber for her enormous navy. The effect of this, in terms of bare, eroded rock, can be seen in many islands and part of the mainland to this day. Fishermen couldn't even salt their fish – salt was a Venetian state monopoly, and kept ridiculously expensive.

Napoleon The next Empire that Croatia had to deal with was that of the Corsican Napoleon Bonaparte. If Croatian nationalists were to ask, a la Monty Python, 'What has Napoleon ever done for us?' they'd have to admit that the answer must be 'a great deal'. Taking over Istria and Dalmatia (which he now called 'The Illyrian Provinces') he put in the very capable Marshal Marmont as governor. Marmont abolished feudalism, built roads and hospitals, made education compulsory, started to repair the damage done by Venice through a program of re-forestation, and even promoted the use of the Croatian language in schools and the media. He didn't get the credit that perhaps he deserved from a lot of Croats, who realised that there was more to his reforms than altruism. Napoleon's plan was to strengthen Croatia and the rest of the southern Slavs as a counter-weight to, and buffer against, the Habsburgs and Russia. At the same time devout Roman Catholics Croats objected to the fiercely secular approach of Revolutionary and Napoleonic France. Heavy taxation didn't help either.

Treaty of Vienna Napoleon's defeat in 1815, and the resulting Treaty of Vienna, saw Croatia unceremoniously dumped back into the Habsburg camp.

The Illyrian Movement Napoleon's reforms, and the increasing success of Serbia against the Ottoman Empire, were igniting powerful nationalist feelings among Croatians: the Illyrian Movement was born. Croats started to demand the reunification of eastern and western Croatia, of Dalmatia and Slavonia. Vienna, faced with the growth of nationalism in many parts of its empire, decided that discretion was the better part of valour, and fobbed Croatia off with encouraging noises. But this didn't last, and a crackdown soon followed.

The Year of Revolutions In 1848 nationalist movements in various parts of Europe led to an outbreak of revolutions that spread dramatically, each feeding on the other like some forest fire. This terrified the ruling classes across the continent. In Croatia, Austria bowed to public pressure for more autonomy and agreed to the appointment of Josip Jelačić, the commander of one of the Military Frontier's garrisons, as Ban, or governor, of Croatia. Jelačić immediately helped to put down rebellions in other parts of the Austrian Empire, hoping no doubt that this would lead to further concessions to Croatian nationalism from a grateful Emperor. These hopes were dashed when Ferdinand abdicated, and his son Franz Josef I succeeded. He was much more of a hard case, and the crackdown on Croatian nationalists proceeded again apace.

The Dual Monarchy In 1867 the so-called 'Dual Monarchy' of Austro-Hungary was established. The new Austro-Hungarian Empire split Croatia, with Austria getting Dalmatia, and Hungary getting the rest. As the

19th century came to a close and the 20th century saw the drift towards World War, Croatia and the rest of the 'South Slav' area became a hotbed of factions – Croats, Serbs, Roman Catholics, Orthodox Christians – all seeking position and advantage. Bishop Strossmayer, head of the Croatian National Party, drew up a plan for a united South Slav country to be called 'Yugoslavia'.

The Balkan Wars In 1912 and 1913, the Balkan Wars, in which Serbia made significant gains at the expense of the Turks, not only increased Serbia's power, but also increased her prestige among Croatians.

The Yugoslav Committee As Europe exploded into World War 1, Croatian politicians were coming to the conclusion that an independent Croatia was neither viable nor likely to come about, and that the creation of a united south Slav country – Yugoslavia – with Serbia was seen as the way to go. The Strossmayer Plan was dusted off, the 'Yugoslav Committee' was set up in Paris in 1915, and discussions with Serbia began in Corfu two years later.

The Kingdom of Serbs, Croats and Slovenes During the immediate aftermath of World War 1, a National Council of Slovenes, Croats and Serbs declared independence, and set up the Kingdom of Serbs, Croats and Slovenes. Italy, seeking rewards for its (eventual)

support for the victorious Allies, seized Zadar, Rijeka and Pula. Much to Croatian horror, the new, Serbian-dominated kingdom not only accepted the Italian incursions, but, at the Treaty of Rapallo in 1920, threw in the rest of Istria and several islands as well. The suspicion was that the Government wouldn't have been so cavalier with Serbian territory.

Yugoslavia Discussion over the nature and direction of Yugoslavia became heated. Whereas changing its rather cumbersome name to 'Yugoslavia' was pretty uncontentious, there was a clear division regarding how it should be organised: the Serbs, who were in the overall majority, wanted straightforward unitary government (well they would, wouldn't they?) while Croats, very much aware of their minority status within Yugoslavia, strongly favoured a federal organisation, where they would retain control of certain important functions of government. No surprises there either, then.

Left and Right Wing The interwar situation in Yugoslavia was further complicated by the addition of 'horizontal' political divisions to the long-standing 'vertical' national ones. The Communist Party looked to Stalin's Russia for inspiration, while the fascist Ustaše emulated Mussolini's Italy, Franco's Spain and Hitler's Germany. It was a confrontation being repeated in virtually every other country in Europe.

The Nazi Occupation No doubt about it, the early rounds went to the Right. In 1941 the Nazis marched into Yugoslavia, set up the Independent State of Croatia (the NDH), and installed a Ustaše puppet government. Yugoslavia was shared out between Germany and its ally Italy, Jews and Orthodox Serbs were massacred (estimates of how many vary from 60,000 to 10 times that number), and resistance took to the hills. And even in resistance, the left/right split persisted: the Communist Party (under its charismatic chief Tito) led the left-wing fight against the Nazis, and the Četniks led the right wing. In 1944 Winston Churchill decided that the Communists were the most effective in tying down German infantry and armour, and so threw British support behind Tito's men. Good decision – in October 1944 Tito rolled into Belgrade, and in May 1945 into Zagreb. Yugoslavia was the only country that didn't need the big divisions of the Russians, Americans or British to free themselves from Nazi control.

The Immediate Aftermath of the War As happened in many occupied countries, the end of the war brought a reckoning. Around 50,000 anti-communists fled northwards and were turned back at the Austrian border by a small force of British soldiers.

Many died, others were sent on forced marches to the south of the country.

The Republic of Yugoslavia

The triumphant Communist Party now oversaw the setting up of the Republic of Yugoslavia (29th November, 1945), consisting of Croatia, Serbia, Slovenia, Bosnia-Herzegovina, Montenegro and Macedonia. At first it based its approach very much on that of Stalin's Russia. Industries were nationalised, workers' co-operatives were established and other political parties were outlawed. Just another Iron-Curtain country in the making, it might be thought. But in 1948 any idea that Tito was just another Communist poodle was shattered when, fed up with Russia's interference in Yugoslavia's affairs, he renounced Stalin and started looking to the West for support. But he emphasised that he wasn't about to be a Western Block poodle either, becoming a mainstay of the Non-Aligned Movement. His approach to specifically Yugoslav problems, especially continued friction between the different national groups, was equally robust and any inter-ethnic friction was immediately jumped upon.

1950s and 1960s With the help of Western loans, Yugoslavia entered a period of increasing prosperity. The tourist industry boomed, and Yugoslav citizens were allowed more freedom than in any other communist country.

However, as has already been noted, the bulk of Yugoslavia's tourist areas – especially Istria and Dalmatia – were in Croatia. Croats complained that Belgrade got the money and Croatia got the traffic. This wasn't the only cause of resentment in Croatia. It was also felt that Serbs got all the best and most influential jobs: although Serbs made up only 12% of the population of Croatia, Serbs filled 40% of government posts, 70% of the police force and a massive 95% of the army.

The 1970s In 1971 a movement of intellectuals and students, the so-called 'Croatian Spring', began a series of protests at the treatment Croatia received within Yugoslavia. Tito, realising that nationalism was far more likely to destroy the new country than any external interference, took a hard line. The cauldron of resentment continued to bubble as Tito sat on the lid.

4th May 1980 When Tito died, three days before his 88th birthday, the cauldron's lid was off. Almost immediately, ethnic and nationalist rivalry and resentment began to come out into the open. The situation was made worse by the serious economic problems that Yugoslavia was beginning to face. Tito's 'economic miracle' had been largely financed by Western loans, which had to be serviced or repaid, a situation that was aggravated by world recession caused by the oil crisis.

1989 Demands for independence among the Albanian Moslem population of Kosovo led to a brutal reaction from Serbian leader Slobodan Milošević, not only in Kosovo itself, but at home where he instigated a purge of non-Serbs and liberals.

1990 Events in Serbia had persuaded many in Slovenia and Croatia that their only option was to press for independence. This would, of course, mean the break-up of Yugoslavia. Serbia was determined that, if Yugoslavian unity couldn't be preserved, then a 'Greater Serbia' should emerge from its disintegration, consisting not only of Serbia itself, but also the areas of Croatia and Bosnia where many ethnic Serbians lived. To pave the way, Serbia encouraged the Croatian Serbs' feelings of resentment towards Croatia, and promoted the belief that they would be under threat in an independent Croatia.

The Knin Referendum In June 1990, Croatian Serbs in the town of Knin, inland from Šibenik, held a referendum, despite the fact that the Croatian authorities had banned it. The result was a massive vote for autonomy. No surprise there, then.

Kninska Krajina The following month autonomy was declared under the name Kninska Krajina, and barricades were erected. The Croatian authorities sent police helicopters to end the rebellion, but they were turned back by Yugoslav Air Force MIGs. In February 1991 total independence from Croatia was declared, and unification with Serbia was sought. In March 1991 Knin paramilitaries took over the Plitvice Lakes, a manoeuvre that led to the first casualties of the conflict. In April, a nearby Croat village was 'ethnically cleansed' that is, its Croat population were evicted or killed.

Slovene and Croatian Independence On June 25th 1991, Slovenia and Croatia declared their independence. After token resistance, Slovene independence was accepted by Serbia – the EU wasn't about to accept Serbian tanks along Slovenia's border with Italy and Hungary, and Slovenia didn't contain a significant proportion of ethnic Serbs. With Croatia it was a different matter.

The War in Croatia Croat Serb villages in the Knin area responded to Croatia's declaration of independence with their own declaration of autonomy as the Republika Srpska Krajina (RSK). A six-month period now began in which the whole region (about a third of Croatia) was ethnically cleansed, with bombardments and air strikes from Yugoslav forces and Croatian Serb paramilitaries. Thousands of Croats were killed or forced to flee their homes. Industry was destroyed, and Croatia's vital tourist industry disappeared

The War

'Don't talk about the war'. That advice from Fawlty Towers is certainly spot on for the 1990s war between Croatia and Serbia (called either the 'Homeland War' or the 'Patriotic War' – most people I spoke to called it the latter, so that's what I've done in this book). It was an extremely bitter conflict – something between a civil and an international war. Really bad stuff went on, on both sides. And it was very recent. The international legal repercussions still echo around the corridors of Europe, and you'll come across quite young people who remember the war vividly. So, however tempting it might be to use a holiday in Croatia to introduce your teenagers to the realities of life, resist it. If Croatians bring the war up themselves, of course, it's a different matter.

World War 2 is more problematic. Again there were horrendous internecine battles between the quisling Ustaše government, the communist partisans and the right-wing Četniks. Yet Yugoslavia still rightly takes pride in the fact that it was the only country that freed *itself* from the Nazi yoke. And in the late 1940s, when it didn't like what Stalin was trying to make it do, it was the only communist country to tell Russia where to get off.

In the case of both wars, be guided by the person you're taking to.

virtually overnight. In January 1992 a UN-brokered ceasefire began, but Croatia was not at all happy with it – had it held, it would have confirmed huge Serbian gains over Croatian territory. To add to the confusion, war broke out in Bosnia during 1993, where the presence of a large Moslem minority complicated matters further. It is undoubtedly true that Croatia did things in Bosnia that did it no credit – Croatia was accused of doing in Bosnia what Serbia had done in Croatia. As regards Croatian territory held by Serbs, when diplomacy failed to get Croatia any joy, from June 1995 Croatian forces started a series of strikes to regain territory from Serbia and the RSK. Croatian

Serbs fled into Bosnia and Serbia, and there was a lot of looting and destruction of the property they left behind. Finally, in December 1995, the Dayton Accords, followed at the end of 1996 by a full peace treaty, finally brought the conflict to a close, though its repercussions have continued up to the present.

The Last 10 Years the governing party in Croatia, up to and after independence and throughout the war, had been the HDZ or Croatian Democratic Union under the leadership of Franjo Tuđman. An ex-army general and right-wing historian, Tuđman became President after the elections of 1990 and led the

Lavender fields

country throughout the difficult succeeding years. Although popular during the war, his autocratic tendencies and anti-democratic leanings in home affairs became more apparent after it. In external affairs he was seen as anti-Western and as an anti-Serb hardliner. This led to threats of UN sanctions over refusal to extradite Croatian war criminals, exclusion from the aid on offer to other ex-communist countries, and the fading of any hopes of EU membership. An increasing number of politicians, and a lot of the population as a whole, felt that Tuđman's continued presidency was costing the country dear. It was time, they felt, for a change. A coalition of ex-communists (the SDP) and rightish liberals (HSLS) formed to challenge the HDZ. Then in December 1999 Tuđman died of cancer. The SDP-HSLS alliance won the election in January 2000, though was itself replaced by a reformed HDZ-led coalition in 2003. Since then the return to more democratic methods and the succession of pro-Western governments has led to great advances in Croatia's diplomatic and economic position: her application for membership of the EU was accepted in 2004, and the tourist industry is advancing by leaps and bounds. The knotty problem of war criminals has continued though – all governments have had to try to reconcile external demands for punishment with the undoubted fact that many Croats see the men concerned as heroes who put their lives on the line in the struggle for independence.

9 Appendices

Language

Realistically, it's unlikely that you'll learn enough Croatian to converse comfortably with the locals when you're in Croatia – not unless you're spending several years preparing for the holiday, or you're a remarkably gifted linguist. However, the ability to say a few words always goes down well, so some of the most common expressions are included below. If you want to go beyond this, then surf the net, or better still buy a phrasebook, together with a pocket dictionary: they will take you a long way.

If you can't manage to learn a bit of Croatian, don't worry. The majority of people involved in the tourist industry speak at least passable English. Furthermore, if you're stuck, ask younger people to translate as they study English in school.

More important than learning useful words or phrases, though, is some familiarity with how the language is pronounced. If you get the pronunciation wrong, then not only will any efforts you make to learn some of the language be in vain (you may talk away like a good 'un, and they won't understand a word), but also you'll be totally unable to ask directions. And this really is important – whether you're walking around Dubrovnik or driving to Zagreb, looking for a particular hotel or asking for directions to a recommended restaurant, you'll get blank looks if you don't know your 'c' from your 'č' from your 'ć'.

At least one member of the party, then, needs to get to grips with Croatian pronunciation. It needn't, of course, be an adult – it's a task that can be delegated to one or all of the children! Luckily, Croatian pronunciation, although sometimes looking formidable when there are few or no vowels, is actually not that difficult. It's a lot easier, certainly, and a lot more logical than English. It's very regular. Each letter is pronounced in a certain way and is pronounced exactly that way each time it comes up. And most letters are pronounced in the most straightforward way you can think of in English.

Finally, a word on emphasis: Stress in Croatian is usually (though by no means always) put on the first syllable. So it's Zagreb not zagreb, Dubrovnik not dubrovnik. Stress is very rarely placed on the last syllable.

Enough introduction: Let's get down to the nitty-gritty.

Pronunciation

Most consonants are pronounced in the same way as in English: 't' as in 'turn', 'd' as in 'duck', 'g' as in 'got' and so on. Vowels are always pronounced the same, as follows:

'a' as in 'car'.
'e' as in 'wet'.
'i' as in 'seat'.
'o' as in 'cot'.
'u' as in 'book'.

The letters that will sort out the pronunciation men from the boys, sheep from the goats, are:

c/C: pronounced 'ts' as in 'bats'.

č/Č: pronounced 'ch' as in 'chick'.

ć/Ć: pronounced as a softer 'ch' as in 'future'. It is very difficult for the English ear to distinguish between 'č' and 'ć', but Croatian nationals insist that they're different sounds. Ask a Croat to teach you. And even then you'll probably get a situation where their face lights up and they say 'that's it!', and you don't like to explain that they still sound the same to you.

d: pronounced 'd' as in 'dog'.

đ/Đ: pronounced (and sometimes written) 'dj' as in 'judge'.

j: pronounced 'y' as in 'youth'.

s: pronounced 's' as in 'son'.

š/Š: pronounced 'sh' as in 'shower'.

z: pronounced 'z' as in 'zoo'.

ž/Ž: pronounced 's' as in 'measure' (or 'g' as in the French 'gites').

Remember – all letters are pronounced. So 'Ploče' is two-syllable, with the 'e' as the second syllable – 'Ploche'.

Some more examples:
Poreč   Poretch
Šibenik   Shibenik
Plitvice   Plitvitse
Kumrovec   Kumrovets
Čakovec   Chakovets

Glossary

English   Croatian

General

Yes   Da
No   Ne
good   dobro
bad   loše
I don't know   Ne znam
I don't understand   Ne razumijem
to   do
from   od
day   dan
week   tjedan
month   mjesec
year   godina
why   zašto
where   gdje
when   kada
how   kako
left   lijevo
right   desno
early   rano
late   kasno
behind   iza
in front of   ispred
far   daleko
close   blizu
Where is . . . ?   Gdje je . . . ?

Greetings and Pleasantries

Good day   Dobar dan
Hello/goodbye   Zdravo/Bok
Thank you   Hvala
Good morning   Dobro jutro
Good evening   Dobra večer
Good night   Laku noć
Goodbye   Doviđenja
See you later   Vidimo se poslije
How are you?   Kako sta?
Fine, thank you   Dobro, hvala
No, thank you   Ne hvala
Please   Molim
Please come in   Izvolite uđite
Excuse me/sorry   Oprostite
Let's go   Hajdemo
Please, sit down   Izvolite, sjednite
Can you help me, please?   Da li mi
    mžoete pomoći, molim?
Do you speak English?   Da li govorite
    engleski?
French   Francuski
German   Njemački
Italian   Italijanski

I understand   Razumijem
I don't understand   Ne razumijem
What's your name?   Kako se zovete?
My name is_____   Zovem se_____

Numbers

0	nula
1	jedan
2	dva
3	tri
4	četiri
5	pet
6	šest
7	sedam
8	osam
9	devet
10	deset
11	jedanaest
20	dvadeset
21	dvadeset jedan
22	dvadeset dva
30	trideset
40	četrdeset
50	pedeset
60	šezdeset
70	sedamdeset
80	osamdeset
90	devedeset
100	sto
1,000	tisuća
10,000	deset tisuća

Time

today   danas
tomorrow   sutra
yesterday   jučer
every day   svaki dan
week   tjedan
now   sad
soon   uskoro
later   kasnije/poslije
always   uvijek
What time is it?   Koliko je sati?

Days Of The Week & Months Of The Year

Monday   ponedjeljak
Tuesday   utorak
Wednesday   srijeda
Thursday   četvrtak
Friday   petak
Saturday   subota
Sunday   nedjelja

January   siječanj
February   veljača
March   ožujak
April   travanj
May   svibanj
June   lipanj
July   srpanj
August   kolovoz
September   rujan
October   listopad
November   studeni
December   prosinac

Getting Around

Excuse me, I am looking for . . .
   Oprostite, tražim . . .
I want to go to . . .   Želio(he)/ Željela(she)
   bih ići . . .
Is it far?   Da li je daleko?
How many kilometres from here?   Koliko
   kilometara odavde?
Turn back   Vratite se nazad
Turn/Go . . .   Vratite se/okrenite/idite . . .
left   lijevo
right   desno
straight ahead   ravno
street   ulica
square   trg
next to   pored
there   tamo
map   karta
I would like to buy a ticket   Želio/ Željela
   bih kupiti kartu?
ticket   (putna) karta
one-way ticket   jednosmjerna karta
round-trip ticket   povratna karta
ticket   ulaznica (for movies, museum)
Where is the . . . ?   Gdje se nalazi . . . ?
beach   plaža
bank   banka
church   crkva
drugstore   ljekarna
market   tržnica
museum   muzej
park   park
police station   policijska postaja
post office   poštanski ured, pošta
tourist office   turistički ured
railway station   vlak/željeznička stanica
bus station   autobusna
airport   zračna luka
taxi stand   taksi stajalište
Is the (post office) open?   Da li je potša
   otvorena?
I'd like to change some money   Želio/
   Željela bih promijeniti novac
exchange office   mjenjačnica

exchange rate   tčeajna lista
Where can I find a (good) . . . ?   Gdje
    mogu naći (dobrog) . . . ?
dentist   zubara
doctor   liječnika
hospital   bolnicu

Signs

entry   ulaz
exit   izlaz
toilets (men)   toilets/WC (muskarci)
toilets (women)   toilets/WC (žene)
hospital   bolnica
police   policija
prohibited   zabranjeno
not allowed   nije dopušteno

Health

I am sick   Bolestan sam/bolesna sam
I need a doctor   Potreban mi je liječnik
fever   groznica
headache   glavobolja
stomach ache   bol u trbuhu
dentist   zubar
I have a headache   Imam glavobolju
penicillin   penicillin
pill   tableta
aspirin   aspirin
I am on medications for . . .   Pijem
    lijekove protiv . . .
virus   virus

Baby Terms

baby   beba
baby food   dječja hrana
baby's bottle   bočica
Bandaids   flaster
Carry-cot   noscljka za bebu
Chemists   ljekarna
Child   dijete
Children's portion   dječja porcija
Cleansing lotion   tekućina za čišćenje
Constipation   tvrda stolica
Cotton wool   vata
Cough   kašalj
Cough medicine   sirup za kašalj
Crèche   jaslice
Diarrhoea   proljev
Disinfectant   dezinfekcijsko
First aid kit   komplet za prvu pomoć
Highchair   dječja stolica
Nappy   pelena
Pushchair   dječja kolica

Sun block   krema za sunčanje
Suntan lotion   losion za sunčanje

Attractions

bridge   most
cathedral   katedrala
church   crkva
island   otok
Old Town   Stari Grad
lake   jezero
ruins   ruše vine
sea   more

Shopping

How much/How many?   Koliko?
What is the time?   Koliko je sati?
a little   malo
a lot   puno
enough   dosta
(too) expensive   (pre)skupo

Food and Drink

Essentials:
Breakfast   doručak/zajutrak
Lunch   ručak
Dinner   večera
Knife   nož
Fork   viljuška
Spoon   žlica
Glass   čaša
Plate   tanjur
Menu   jelovnik
Bill   račun
Cheers!   živjeli!
Supermarket   samoposluga
Open air market   tržnica
Bakery   pekarnica
Bread   kruh
Butter   maslac
Pasta   tjestenine
Vegetables   povrće
Cheese   sir
Ham   šunka
Egg   jaje
Rice   riža
Salt   sol
Pepper   papar
Sugar   šećer
Coffee   kava
Tea   čaj
Juice   dzuz or Dus
Water   voda

Mineral water   mineralna voda
Milk   mlijeko
Fish   riba
Meat   meso
Potato   krumpir

Meat & Fish:
Cod   bakalar
Mullet   barbun
Sea-bass   brancin
Mussels   dagnje
John Dory   kovac
Sole   list
Hake   oslić
Trout   pastrva
Crab   rak
Mackerel   skuša
Beef   govedina
Goulash   gulaš
Goose   guska
Duck   patka
Chicken   piletina
Bacon   slanina
Venison   srnetina
Pork   svinjetina
Veal   teletina
Turkey   tuka

Cooking:
Grilled   na roštilju/ Na žaru
Baked   pečeno
Fried   prženo
Boiled   lešo

Deserts:
Cake   kolač
Strudel   savijača
Ice cream   sladoled
Gateau   torta

Other useful terms:
Restaurant   restora
Tavern   konoba
Inn   gostiona
White wine   bijelo vino
Red wine   crno vino
Sandwiches   sendviči

Getting a Room

room   soba
Excuse me, is there a hotel nearby?
  Oprostite, da li postoji hotel u blizini?
Do you have a free room?   Da li imate
  slobodnu sobu?
We would like a double room   Željeli bi
  smo jednu dvokrevetnu sobu
I would like a room with a: Želio/ ž eljela
  (she) bih sobu sa:
shower   tušem
bathtub   kadom
balcony   balkonom
air-conditioning   klimom
telephone   telefonom
How much is the room per night?   Koliko
  kšota soba za jednu noć?
per person   po osobi
per week   za tjedan dana
Okay, I will take the room   Uredu, uzet ću
  sobu
I'd like to make a reservation for a room
  Želio/ željela bih ezervirati sobu
I will stay for 2 nights   Ostat ću dvije noći
Can I look at the room?   Da li mogu
  pogledati sobu?
Do you have any other rooms?   Da li
  imate još koju sobu?

Family Travel

Travelling as a family can be fun, exciting and create memories to savour, but a bit of preparation will go a long way in forging a smooth journey and holiday. Although there isn't a glut of sites dealing with family travel in Croatia specifically, there are plenty of sites providing parents with essential holiday information and even sites popping up for youngsters, too. From what to pack and coping with flights to childcare and accessories, the sites below will help give you a headstart.

www.babygoes2.com: An innovative guide for parents travelling with babies and children with independent recommendations.

www.all4kidsuk.com: Links to tour companies offering family-friendly holidays, some of them in Croatia.

www.youngtravellersclub.co.uk: Currently in its early days, this is a site for children themselves, which deserves to succeed.

www.deabirkett.com: The website of *Guardian* journalist Dea Birkett, who specialises in travelling with children. It includes a very useful Travelling with Kids Forum.

www.babycentre.co.uk: The travel section throws up some interesting articles on family holidays.

www.mumsnet.com: Set up by a journalist, TV producer and radio producer. Product reviews, interviews and planning help.

www.travellingwithchildren.co.uk: Comprehensive site with lots of handy tips for travelling parents.

www.travelforkids.com: An American site that has some good information on different countries with 'what not to leave at home' type tips.

www.familytravelforum.com: Lots of useful stuff on family travel in general.

www.travelwithyourkids.com: Easy to navigate with advice you feel comes from real experience of things having gone wrong!

www.thefamilytravelfiles.com: Heavily American, but with a section on Europe.

www.family-travel.co.uk: Independent advice on travelling

with children: Lots of sound general advice.

Responsible Tourism

Although one could argue any holiday including a flight can't be truly 'green', tourism can contribute positively to the environment and communities UK visitors travel to if investment is used wisely. Firstly, by offsetting carbon emissions from your flight, you can lessen the negative environmental impact of your journey. Secondly, by embracing responsible tourism practises you can choose forward looking companies who care about the resorts and countries we visit, preserving them for the future by working alongside local people. Below are a number of sustainable tourism initiatives and associations to help you plan a family trip and leave as small a 'footprint' as possible on the places you visit.

www.responsibletravel.com: A great source of sustainable travel ideas run by a spokesperson for responsible tourism in the travel industry.

www.tourismconcern.org.uk: Working to reduce social and environmental problems connected to tourism and find ways of improving tourism so that local benefits are increased.

www.climatecare.org.uk: Helping UK holidaymakers offset their carbon emissions through flying by funding sustainable energy projects

www.thetravelfoundation.org.uk: Produces excellent material on how to care for the places we visit on holiday. It also produces a special guide for children aged 7–10 and parents incorporating 'Hatch the Hatchling Hawksbill' with a play and puzzle book. Highly recommended.

www.abta.co.uk: The Association of British Travel Agents (ABTA) acts as a focal point for the UK travel industry and is one of the leading groups spearheading responsible tourism.

www.aito.co.uk: The Association of Independent Tour Operators (AITO) is a group of interesting specialist operators leading the field in making holidays sustainable.

Useful Websites & Telephone Numbers

Below is a list of useful contacts to help your journey go more smoothly. In the first instance the thorough holiday information leaflet produced by the Croatian National Tourism Board (Croatia House, 162-164 Fulham Palace Road, Hammersmith, London W6 9ER, www.croatia.hr) is a great start to planning a trip. The different associations, operators and ground handlers below are by no means an exhaustive list, but an introduction to help available in Croatia.

Airlines:

Croatia Airlines: www.croatia airlines.hr

British Airways: www.british airways.com

easyJet: www.easyjet.com

Wizz Air: www.wizzair.com

Aer Lingus: www.flyaerlingus.com

Ryanair: www.ryanair.com

Airports:

Dubrovnik: www.airport-dubrovnik.hr

Split: www.split-airport.tel.hr

Zadar: www.zadar-airport.hr

Zagreb: www.zagreb-airport.hr

Tourist Boards:

Croatian National Tourist Office, 2 The Lanchesters, 162-164 Fulham Palace Road, London, W6 9ER. ☎ 0208-563-7979. Fax 0208-563-2616. www.croatia.hr

Ministry of Tourism (including statistics): www.mmtpr.hr

Regional Tourist Boards:
Zagreb: www.zagreb-touristinfo.hr

Istria: www.istra.hr

Kvarner: www.kvarner.hr

Zadar: www.zadar.hr

Sibenik: *www.summernet.hr*

Dalmatia: *www.dalmatia.hr*

Split: *www.visitsplit.com*

Dubrovnik: *www.tzdubrovnik.hr/*
www.visitdubrovnik.hr

Hvar Tourist Association:
www.hvar.hr

Trogir:
www.dalmacija.net/trogir.htm

Brela: *www.brela.hr*

Makarska: *www.makarska.com*

Croatia News/Information:
Visitor information: *www.visit-*
croatia.co.uk

Articles on Croatia: *www.hr/*
english

Holidays in Croatia: *www.*
find-croatia.com

Croatian News Agency:
www.hina.hr

Dalmatia Guide: *www.*
dalmacija.net

Dubrovnik Guide:
http://dubrovnik.laus.hr

Football: *www.hns-cff.hr*

Hotels:
Association of Croatian Hotels:
www.huh.hr

Family Run & Small Hotel
Association: *www.omh.hr*

Independent advice:
www.tripadvisor.com

www.virtualtourist.com

www.holidaysuncovered.com

www.holidaywatchdog.com

www.slowtrav.com

Tour operators and specialists:
Balkan Holidays: *www.balkan*
holidays.co.uk

Bond Tours: *www.bondtours.com*

Holiday Options: *www.holiday*
options.com

Thomson Lakes & Mountains:
www.thomsonlakesandmountains.
co.uk

www.crystalholidays.co.uk

Pole Travel:
www.traveholidays.co.uk

Inghams: *www.inghams.co.uk*

First Choice:
www.firstchoice.co.uk

Thomas Cook: *www.*
thomascook.com

Hidden Croatia: *www.hidden*
croatia.com

Cosmos Holidays: *www.cosmos.*
co.uk

Mytravel: *www.airtours.co.uk*

Page & Moy: *www.pagemoy.com*

British Airways Holidays:
www.ba.com

Perfect Places: *www.perfectplaces online.co.uk*

Small Family Holidays: *www.smallholidayfamilies.co.uk*

Villas, Apartments, Exclusive & Special Interest, Activity, Tailor-made
Croatian Affair: *www.croatian affair.com*

Villa Rentals: *www.villaretreats.com*

Andante Travels: *www.andante travels.co.uk*

Osprey Holidays: *www.osprey holidays.com*

Martin Randall Travel: *www.martinrandall.com*

Abercrombie & Kent: *www. abercrombiekent.co.uk*

Gold Medal Travel: *www.goldmedaltravel.co.uk*

Superbreak Holidays: *www.superbreak.com*

Great Escapes: *www.greatescapes.co.uk*

Adventure Company: *www.adventurecompany.co.uk*

Activities Abroad: *www.activities abroad.com*

Coach Holidays:
Travelsphere: *www.travelsphere.co.uk*

Wallace Arnold Tours: *www. wallacearnold.com*

Leger Holidays: *www.leger.co.uk*

Cosmos Tourama: *www.cosmos tourama.co.uk*

Sailing and Yacht Charter:
Cosmos Yachting: *www.cosmosy achting.com*

Nautilus Yachting: *www.nautilus-yachting.co.uk*

Setsail Holidays: *www.setsail.co.uk*

Sunsail: *www.sunsail.co.uk*

Templecraft Yacht Carriers: *www.templecraft.com*

Tenrag: *www.tenrag.com*

Top Yacht Charter: *www.top-yacht.com*

Neilson: *www.neilson.com*

Ferries:
Jadrolinija Ferry Company: *www.jadrolinija.hr*

SEM Meritime (Italy–Croatia Ferries): *www.sem-marina.hr*

Car Rental/Information:
Croatian Automobile Association: *www.hak.hr*

Avis: *www.avis.hr*

Budget: *www.budget.hr*

Hertz: *www.hertz.hr*

Adriatica: *www.adriatica.net*

E-Sixt: *www.e-sixt.co.uk*

Kompas No 1: *www.kompasno1.hr*

Mack Rent a Car: *www.mack-concord.hr*

National: *www.national.hr*

Rent a Car Matejuska: *www.matejuskarent.hr*

Holiday Rentals: *www.holidayrentals.co.uk*

Rail Travel:
Croatian Railways: *www.hznet.hr*

Seat 61: *www.seat61.com*

Camping:
Camping: *www.camping.hr*

Youth Hostels:
Croatian Youth Hostels Association: *www.hfhs.hr*

National Parks:
Plitvice National Park: *www.np-plitvicka-jezera.hr*

Krka National Park: *www.npkrka.hr*

Mljet National Park: *www.np-mljet.hr*

Kornati National Park: *www.kornati.hr*

Brijuni Islands National Park: *www.brijuni.hr*

Maps:
Croatian Maps can be bought from booksellers below:

Daunt Books: *www.dauntbooks.co.uk*

John Smith and Sons: *www.johnsmith.co.uk*

National Map Centre: *www.mapsworld.com*

Stanfords: *www.stanfords.co.uk*

The Travel Bookshop: *www.thetravelbookshop.co.uk*

Waterstone's: *www.waterstones.co.uk*

Maps online:
www.mapquest.com and *www.multimap.com*: punch in the address, and up comes the map

Safety abroad:
www.fco.gov.uk/travel : website of the Foreign and Commonwealth Office. It's huge, and contains everything you need to know about safety. It's also searchable.

Customs:
HM Revenue and Customs: *www.hmce.gov.uk*

Currency:
www.xe.com/ucc: a useful currency converter

Index

See also Accommodations and Restaurant indexes, below.

General

A

Accommodations. *See also*
  Accommodations Index; Camping
  best, 14–15
  Dubrovnik, 92–96
  Pula, 167–169
  Split, 114–116
  tips on, 40–41
  Zadar, 140–141
  Zagreb, 230–234
Adam and Eve (Šibenik), 143
Adriatic Sunshine, 128
Adventure Company, 152
Agri-tourism, 188–189
Air travel, 32–34, 39–40
American Express, 49
  Zagreb, 200
The Amphitheatre (Pula), 162
Antun Augustinčić Gallery (Klanjec),
  11, 224
Aquarium
  Poreč, 177
  Pula, 166
  Rovinj, 174
Aquarium and Maritime Museum,
  Dubrovnik, 74
Archaeological Museum
  Nin, 150
  Pula, 166
  Zadar, 136
  Zagreb, 214
Arch of the Sergians (Pula), 165, 166
Area codes, 52
Arts and Crafts Museum (Zagreb), 216
Ascension, Church of the (Šibenik), 143
ATMs (automated teller machines), 24

B

Babin kuk (Dubrovnik), 59, 76, 79
Balancing on the gargoyle
  (Dubrovnik), 70
Bale, 167
Baptistry/Temple of Jupiter (Split),
  109–110
Baredine Cave, 178
Basilica of Euphrasius (Poreč), 177
Baška Voda, 126
Batana, House of the (Rovinj), 173–174
Beaches, 48
  Dubrovnik, 79
  Klek, 84
  Makarska Riviera, 126

Benedictine Monastery (Lokrum), 87
Bijela Vila (Veli Brijun), 171
Biking and mountain biking, 46
  Dubrovnik area, 91
  Mljet, 89
  Split area, 128
Biokovo, Mount, 127
Blue Lake, 124–125
Boat trips and tours, 190
  Kornati National Park, 153
  Krka National Park, 148
Bogisić, Baltazar, Statue of (Cavtat), 85
Bol, 129
Bollé, Hermann, 205
Botanical Gardens (Zagreb), 215–216
Brač, 128, 129
Bratus, 126
Brela, 126
Brijuni Islands National Park, 170–171
Buje, 14, 167, 181
Bukovac, Vlaha, 85
Bunari Museum (Šibenik), 10, 144–145
Bundek (Zagreb), 7, 221, 223
Burglars' Tower (Kula lotršćak; Zagreb),
  208–209
Business hours, 49–50
Bus travel, 36, 40
Buzet, 8, 14, 185

C

Camping
  Autocamp Solitudo (Dubrovnik),
    95–96
  Autocamp Stoja (Pula), 168
  Split area, 128
Canoeing, 47
  Mljet, 89
  Split area, 128
Carnival, 26
Car rentals, 39
Car travel, 33, 35, 37–39
Cash machines, 24
Cathedral of St. Anastasia (Zadar),
  136–137
Cathedral of St. Domnius (Split), 109
Cathedral of St. Mary (Pula), 164–165
Cathedral of the Assumption of the Virgin
  Mary (Zagreb), 205
Cavtat, 16, 84
Central Dalmatia, 99–130
  top 10 family experiences, 100–101
Cetina Gorge, 124
Čilipi, 86
Cipiko Palace (Trogir), 119
The City Museum (Split), 110

Accommodations

Restaurants

Frommer's®

with your family
TRAVEL GUIDES

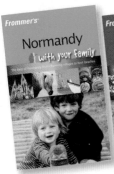

Frommer's Normandy With Your Family
ISBN 10: 0470319518
ISBN 13: 9780470319512
£12.99 ▪ $18.99

Frommer's Brittany With Your Family
ISBN 10: 0470055251
ISBN 13: 9780470055250
£12.99 ▪ $18.99

Frommer's The Algarve With Your Family
ISBN 10: 047005526X
ISBN 13: 9780470055267
£12.99 ▪ $18.99

Frommer's Croatia With Your Family
ISBN 10: 0470055308
ISBN 13: 9780470055304
£12.99 ▪ $18.99

Frommer's Mediterranean Spain With Your Family
ISBN 10: 0470055286
ISBN 13: 9780470055281
£12.99 ▪ $18.99

Frommer's Northern Italy With Your Family
ISBN 10: 0470055278
ISBN 13: 9780470055274
£12.99 ▪ $18.99

Frommer's The Balearics With Your Family
ISBN 10: 0470055294
ISBN 13: 9780470055298
£12.99 ▪ $18.99

Available from all good bookshops

Frommer's®
A Branded Imprint of ⊛**WILEY**